Steel City to Emerald City

Jan,

Warm Regards.

Virgil Tassio

Steel City to Emerald City

A Newspaperman's Life Journey

Virgil Fassio

All photos courtesy of the Fassio Family Collection unless otherwise credited.

Front cover photo: Virgil Fassio, *Seattle Post-Intelligencer* publisher, 1978-1993.

Publisher: That's Thirty Press, Seattle, Washington

Publication Management: Kent Sturgis Publishing Services, LLC

CreateSpace Independent Publishing Platform
North Charleston, South Carolina

Library of Congress Control Number 2017910625

ISBN-13: 9781548629649

ISBN: 1548629642

Printed in the United States of America

To my family—Sunni, Richard, David, and Michael

Thanks to Roger Oglesby, the last publisher of the *Seattle Post-Intelligencer*, and John Joly, my long-time colleague in Detroit and Seattle, for their input and early candid reviews of my first draft. I owe special thanks to Kent Sturgis, the experienced editor who used his skill to apply all the rules of editing and good writing to turn these memoirs into a finished manuscript.

"Were it left to me to decide whether we should have a government without newspapers, or newspapers without a government, I should not hesitate a moment to prefer the latter."
—Thomas Jefferson

Table of Contents

Introduction

The curiosity and probing questions from my sons in an oral history of my life videotaped for our grandchildren recalled experiences that had not crossed my mind for years and vivid memories of my family and the many people who influenced the course of my life before, during, and after a forty-six-year newspaper career that ended as the publisher of the *Seattle Post-Intelligencer*.

The transcribed tapes were the incentive to compile a more complete written account of my childhood and youth, schooling, the Navy and Naval Reserve, a biweekly newspaper and five dailies, foreign travel, and active civic involvement. My sons and many friends suggested that these reminiscences be published in a memoir.

My parents immigrated to America from Italy as adults and settled in Pittsburgh, the "Steel City." They had little formal education, but brought with them a strong work ethic and a desire to make a better life for themselves and their children. This was the familiar story of millions who left Europe and elsewhere to become Americans while still retaining some of their old-country customs.

When I was five, I remember my Dad promising me that someday, somehow, I would get a college education—no matter what it took. He impressed on me a strong belief that always doing more than what was expected in school or at work would serve me well.

A career as a newspaperman, however, was not what I originally planned. I never imagined that I would retire at age sixty-six after a long career that included three years on a biweekly newspaper and more than forty-three years in upper management on five daily newspapers, including fifteen years as publisher of the *Post-Intelligencer* in the "Emerald City," the best of all places, where we have lived and where our family has remained.

It was a time when newspapers were the primary source of news for most people.

Although most of my career was spent as an executive on the business side of daily newspapers, I always considered myself a journalist. I met presidents, kings, queens, and national heads of state around the world—men and women who shaped the destiny of their independent nations, particularly Nasser in Egypt, Nehru in India, Rahman in Malaysia, and Lee Yuan Kew in Singapore; military and government leaders in Europe and Asia; national, state, and local government, business, and civic leaders and well-known athletes as well, while taking an active role in the newspaper industry and in the affairs of Seattle and Washington state.

A Joint Operating Agreement with the *Seattle Times* in 1983 made it possible for me, then publisher of the *P-I*, to become deeply involved, publicly and behind the scenes, in progressive programs and organizations that helped make the Seattle area the special place that it is.

I got into the newspaper field in 1947 because I happened to be in the right place at the right time. As a twenty-year-old Navy veteran in my sophomore year at the University of Pittsburgh, I was with friends at a neighborhood bar when I started a casual conversation with a printer. My major was political science with a minor in economics. I had just started a reporting course as a journalism elective to fill out my schedule. The conversation led to a decision.

The printer and I would work together to start a paid-circulation biweekly newspaper, the *Beechview News*, in our community, one of the few in Pittsburgh that did not have its own paper. With his experience, the printer would be the publisher. With my interest in writing, I would be the editor. It sounded like a lot of fun and a good sideline until I graduated and pursued my real objective, a career in the Foreign Service. By the time I graduated, however, I had become the newspaper's sole owner, editor, and publisher.

On my way to Seattle, the "Emerald City," I worked several years each on the *Valley Daily News* in Tarentum, Pennsylvania; the Wilmington, Delaware *Morning News* and *Evening Journal*; the *Detroit Free Press;* and the *Chicago Tribune* and *Chicago Today*—all excellent newspapers. Two were part of major chains. I was hired by leaders in the industry, including three who later became the chief executive officer of their chains: Lee Hills with Knight-Ridder, Stanton Cook with The Chicago Tribune Co., and later by Frank A. Bennack Jr. with the Hearst Corp., my last employer.

I voluntarily left each job for a better opportunity and bigger challenge. I was enriched by my experiences at each newspaper. I started each new job with a clean slate, unhampered by personal attachments or tradition.

I took business and pleasure trips to more than eighty countries, including twenty-one trips to Europe with thirteen side trips to visit grandparents, uncles, aunts, and cousins in Italy, where most of my relatives still live.

I should have compiled these memoirs much sooner. Despite being a life-long newspaperman, and having worked early on as a reporter and editor, I never kept a personal journal. I did make occasional notes of interviews with news-makers, however, and kept meticulous records documenting my work.

This, then, is a humble account of "a newspaperman's life journey" as recorded, researched, and best remembered.

—Virgil Fassio, Seattle, 2017

Chapter 1

■ ■ ■

Family Roots

On January 26, 1979, I was chatting with President Jimmy Carter in the Cabinet Room, adjacent to the Oval Office. As publisher of the *Seattle Post-Intelligencer*, I had been invited to the White House with other newspaper publishers for an in-depth interview followed by briefings from cabinet officers and presidential aides. I thought of my parents, Domenico and Carolina Fassio, who came to America to pursue the American Dream. That day's unique experience, among many others, served as proof their son was fulfilling the dream.

Calvin Coolidge was president, the economy was robust, and Charles Lindberg was America's hero, having made the first solo flight across the Atlantic Ocean a few months earlier, when I was born on August 10, 1927. Although I have been called "Virgil" all my life, "Virgilio Fassio" appears on my birth certificate. I have two sisters—Christina, born in 1923, and Ida, born in 1925.

I was born at home in Pittsburgh's Mount Washington area, named after George Washington, who was a scout for the British during the French and Indian War in 1754. He had spied upon Fort Duquesne (later renamed Fort Pitt) from a high bluff offering a spectacular view of the Monongahela and Allegheny rivers at the point known as the Golden Triangle where they joined to form the Ohio River. In pre-World War II, Pittsburgh's population of about 650,000 was ranked ninth largest in the United States, which then had a total population of 135 million. Pittsburgh was known as the "steel capital" of the world. Locally, it was also known as the "Smokey City," indicating an air-pollution problem that was reduced in 1949 with enactment of anti-smoke laws.

BOTH MY PARENTS came from the Province of Asti in the Piedmont Region of northwestern Italy, famous for red wine and Asti Spumante. My father was born in Agliano Terme d'Asti in 1896, the second of five sons and two daughters of Giacomo and Angelina Fassio, sharecropper vineyard farmers. After his compulsory schooling ended at age twelve, Dad worked in the vineyards while his own father was away working in America from 1908-13.

In 1914, at age eighteen, Dad was drafted into the Italian Army. Italy entered World War I on the side of the Allies in May, 1915. Dad served until 1919 with the *Alpini* mountain troops in the Dolomites on the Austrian front. His mother died in 1918 in the worldwide flu epidemic. Dad's father died in 1948, just three months before his own death.

Italy did not exist as a nation until the process of *Risorgimento* (or Rebirth), a political and social movement that united seven independent states into the Kingdom of Italy in 1861. Other states were added in the next several years. The country had been the stage for clashes among European powers for many years. As a nation, Italy is eighty-five years younger than the United States.

Like many Italian soldiers, Dad hated the army. He felt he had risked his life for a king who did nothing for him or his family. Only with other Italians who served did I ever hear him talk about the war and I regretted not learning more about his experiences before he died. He did admit that he went home without leave a few times. I was told by a distant cousin in Italy that his own father and Dad served in the same unit. Once, they decided to go home for a weekend, but were stopped by a military policeman as they attempted to cross the Tanaro River near Asti. Lacking authorization, my dad picked up the policeman and threw him over the railing into the river. I don't know if this story is true, but I choose to believe it. At about five-foot-six or seven and weighing 180 pounds, Dad was the strongest man for his size that I ever met. He had a quick temper and was firm but fair with discipline. If he said "jump," my response was, "how high?" I never challenged his authority.

My mother, Carolina Pia, was born in 1902 in Isola, d'Asti, the second of four daughters and one son of Eugenio and Cristina Pia, who owned a small vineyard. Like Dad, she finished schooling at age twelve and worked in the vineyard. She, too, dreamed of coming to America. Her father, my grandfather, once spent five years working in the forests of Massachusetts and planned to return to the United States with his family. But World War I and then his parents' poor health prevented it.

Mom stood about five-foot-four, stout and strong. She could handle a garden spade as well as anyone. She was a good homemaker and a fair cook serving ample but simple dishes. She rarely raised her voice. Her quite discipline was just as firm and fair as Dad's, though he ruled the family.

DAD LEFT ITALY in 1920, never to return, with $20 in his pocket and not knowing a word of English. He joined a cousin, Henry Defer, in Akron, Ohio and worked as a laborer on a bridge project. Mom came in 1921, the only one in her family ever to emigrate. They married in Akron in 1921.

Dad's older brother, John, immigrated in 1913, served in the U.S. Army, and then settled in Baltimore. Dad hoped to bring over his three younger brothers, but Congress passed an anti-immigration law, the Immigration Act of 1924, setting quotas based on the national origin of the foreign-born population in the 1890 census, which showed a population that was predominately white, Anglo-Saxon, and Protestant. The flood of the more recent southern and eastern Europeans, mostly Catholics, and later Jews, Asians, and Arabs was reduced to a trickle. Italian immigration slipped 90 percent.

Uncle Cesare stayed in Torino (Turin), as did his sisters, Ninfa and Vittorina. Uncle Virgilio, my namesake, went to Argentina where he was killed in a hunting accident in 1940. Uncle Alessandro ("Henry") worked as a young waiter after coming to New York at age seventeen in 1927.

For many years, Uncle Henry was employed in prestigious restaurants in New York, Miami, and Hollywood before settling in San Francisco, where he went to work in Leone's Restaurant in North Beach. There he met and married Jeannette Leone. He entered the Army in 1943 and later returned to the restaurant business. Their daughter, Maria Fassio Pignati, a well-known opera singer in the Bay area, is my only first cousin in the United States. She is a national leader in the Sons of Italy organization and has been honored by the Italian government.

MY PARENTS MOVED to Chicago in 1922. They worked and studied English. During a recession in 1923, they moved to a small town near Pittsburgh. Dad worked in a coal mine but after a life outdoors, working in a mine was not for him. He moved to Pittsburgh as a pick-and-shovel laborer for Equitable Gas Co. In a short time, he became foreman of a crew of other recent Italian immigrants and was the company's lead foreman until his death. With an education, he could have been a fine engineer. He never earned much, but never missed a paycheck through the Great Depression. He always provided well for the family.

My parents never bought anything that they couldn't pay for with cash. Shortly before the October, 1929 stock-market crash that began the Great Depression, they paid $4,900 for a small five-room frame house at 1300 Lettie Hill Street at the intersection with Andic Way, both unpaved streets at the top of a hill on the northern tip of the Beechview community in Pittsburgh's South Hills area. Beechview was a diverse, blue-collar neighborhood. The house had a living room, dining room, and kitchen downstairs with two bedrooms and a bathroom upstairs. After the age of ten, I slept on the living-room couch.

My parents never wanted to live in a "Little Italy." This was America, not the old country. They became naturalized citizens, Dad in 1928 and Mom in 1940. Dad wanted open space away from crowded, built-up properties. This was that kind of place. There were no neighbors on one side and several hundred feet of wooded area on another. Across Andic Way (the "alley"), a wooded hillside occupied thirty-six acres. The two houses across the street sat atop a steeply wooded hillside that stretched several hundred feet down to Saw Mill Run, with a view of the south side of Mount Washington.

In addition to the house, the property had a garage, garden, and a chicken coop for twenty to thirty chickens. A Concord grape arbor shaded most of the sidewalk that led in from Lettie Hill Street, alongside a detached garage that was set back from the street. In a few years, Dad cleared more than an acre from the city-owned woods across Andic Way, making room for a much larger garden and two regulation courts for *bocce*, the popular Italian bowling game.

Our parents bought their first refrigerator and radio in about 1934, purchased from Sears-Roebuck. Dad learned to drive in 1939 at age forty-three and bought his first car, a used 1937 Plymouth, for $330.

When our family visited friends, we never had to be told to behave. Our modest home was a great place to live in and the neighborhood was ideal for a boy to spend his growing-up years.

Both of my sisters became life-long Beechview residents. Christina lived with Mom until our mother's death in 1964 and then remained in the Lettie Hill home after marrying John Piconi and raising a son, Paul. Christina died in 2014. Ida and her husband, Leonard Pulkowski, owned a home about a mile away where they raised four children—Carol, Nancy, Linda, and Leonard. The elder Leonard passed away in 1997. Ida still lives there.

■　■　■

Chapter 2

Growing up in Pittsburgh, the "Steel City"

Growing up in the 1930s and '40s was a much different experience than now. For one thing, parents, particularly immigrant parents, did not participate much in their children's' lives outside the home in those days.

My father never had a childhood. He was poor, worked hard, had an absent father in his teens, and then went to war. In Pittsburgh, he worked every day at the gas company and kept busy at home most weekends. He never tossed a ball or played with me, as dads do with their sons today. This was not unusual at that time. His idea of bonding was to have me work alongside him. I didn't enjoy being his helper when friends asked me to join them at play. Yet, with sons of my own, I understood later and appreciated that he was doing the best he could. He needed my companionship, probably more than my help.

Gathering eggs and feeding the chickens were regular chores. A green grocer came with his vegetable- and fruit-laden truck late Saturday afternoons in the summer and fall. He always saved his spoiled produce for our chicken yard and enjoyed a glass of Dad's wine, which Dad made himself, as did many Italian-Americans. Our Rhode Island Reds and Plymouth Rock chickens were well fed. The chicken yard needed to be scraped and cleaned regularly, especially after a rain. The manure was hauled to the garden area to age for a year.

Spading the garden every spring and keeping it free of weeds was another chore. We ate a lot of eggs, chicken, vegetables, and fruit. During World War II, we sold eggs for $1 a dozen when the common wage was $1 an hour. We also sold produce from the garden and traded produce and Dad's wine to Doctor LaRosa in exchange for dental care.

PROHIBITION WAS REPEALED IN 1933. Afterward, with a permit, an individual could make 100 gallons of wine for personal use. I accompanied Dad to the produce yards on Penn Avenue when the California wine grapes arrived in the fall. My parents grew up in one of Italy's most renowned wine regions, so Dad knew how to select the right grapes. Zinfandel was the preferred red grape. I was Dad's reluctant wine-making helper. I complained, telling him I would never drink the stuff—a vow made at age twelve that was broken many years ago.

I never made wine, but it is the only alcohol I drink today. (My wife Sunni and I formed Virsun Inc. in 1982 as a sideline and for several years were sole import agents for a line of Piedmontese wines, an enterprise that brought me closer to my family roots in the Asti area.)

When anyone visited, they were welcomed with a glass of wine. Every Christmas, I delivered gift bottles to several neighbors. Wine also provided income. The two *bocce* courts were busy on weekends.

Friends from all regions of Italy visited, often with wives and children. Men played *bocce*, with the losing team providing wine at fifty cents a bottle. I delivered the wine in a basket across the alley. In the evening, the men played cards or talked. I was allowed to listen and learned to understand several dialects in addition to the native Piedmontese spoken by my folks.

Sometimes I was allowed to take part in the discussions, but in English, and I occasionally voiced disagreements with the older men. Dad never objected. The men often played *morra*. Two men would shoot their hands out, yelling a number. Points were earned when a player called out the correct total of fingers displayed in both hands. They sang songs remembered from their youth in Italy.

Wine was provided more for social life than for profit. However, the wine-making was curtailed sharply in 1940 after government agents searched our small house one afternoon and found more than 100 gallons of wine. Dad was fined $100. Thereafter, he made less wine, but was still generous with it. Friends still visited. *Bocce* was still played and the wine was still enjoyed—on the house.

Although our parents never interacted with us outside the home, they did allow us to take part in any activity that was constructive and would not hurt ourselves or others. Honesty, in particular, was drummed into us at an early age. By their own example, they passed on to each of us a strong work ethic as well. As a boy, I had a little more leeway than my sisters. Sadly, both parents died suddenly of heart attacks, Dad at fifty-one in 1948 and Mom at sixty-two in 1964.

MY YOUTH WAS NOT ALL WORK and no play. We played outside in good weather. There were no television sets or computers to keep kids inside. We lived in a neighborhood where most families owned their homes and few ever moved. We knew all our neighbors for several blocks around. Boys and girls of all ages played together in the streets, empty lots, nearby woods, and the school playground. We played *bocce* and pitched horseshoes. On summer evenings, we played pick-up softball games in the street. At night, my sisters and I, with a few other neighbor kids, roasted potatoes in a fire mid-street and played hide and seek. The spuds got charred, but they were good.

We occasionally went to movies at the small Harris Theater in the Beechview business district. Tickets were ten cents. We never had an allowance. In winter, we rode snow sleds down the hilly streets until we almost froze and then went home to stand on top of the coal-fired, hot-air heat registers. We even tried skiing, using make-shift barrel staves for skis. On snow days, a buddy and I earned spending money by shoveling snow for the neighbors.

I loved baseball and followed the Pittsburgh Pirates on the radio and in the newspaper and wore a baseball cap from morning until bed-time, taking it off only for dinner. My childhood friend, "Bus" Lilliquist, had two baseball gloves. One was a catcher's mitt. He loved to pitch, so we played catch for hours. Dad never understood base-ball, but bought me my first glove, a first-baseman's mitt, for $1.19. In pick-up games, using a taped-up baseball, I was usually the small-est and youngest boy. If I wanted to play, I had to catch. I continued as a catcher on grade-school, sandlot, high-school, college, Navy, and semi-pro teams until age twenty-seven. A catcher never had a prob-lem making a team.

Our big excitement on October evenings was to ring doorbells and then run and hide. We never vandalized. It was good, clean fun. We dressed in simple costumes, nothing store-bought, with a face mask on Halloween and collected bags of goodies. Money was scarce and spent for the essentials. On birthdays and Christmas, my gifts were usually such things as a new pair of pants or shoes, a shirt, or a jacket, and so forth—as needed. I did get a wagon and a sled, but never a two-wheeled bicycle. I could count on one hand the toys received in those years. The gas company had a Christmas program with a prized gift for each kid. That's the way it was. We never felt deprived of anything.

Traveling in the Plymouth, we often visited Cousin Henry Defer's 164-acre farm in Streetsboro, Ohio, about 120 miles away. In early summer, 1940, we toured Washington, D.C. and then visited Uncle John at his farm near Baltimore and Mom's first cousin, Joe Pia, a mushroom grower, and his family in Kennett Square, Pennsylvania.

On many Saturday nights, we went as a family to the North Italian Independent League Club. Kids and moms talked or danced. Men played cards and told stories. Dad was a charter member. Membership was restricted to Italians who came from regions north of Rome, which were more industrialized than the poorer, mostly agricultural southern Italy and Sicily, from which most of an earlier generation of immigrants had come.

Many Italians identified themselves first by their region and then by their country. Before Italy became united in 1861-70, the regions were separated into several entities, each with its own identities, dialects, and customs. Italy was essentially two countries. Each speaking its distinctive dialects, the Piedmontese (far northwest) and Sicilians (southernmost) barely understood one another. The Tuscan dialect became the national language after unification.

My sisters and I understood Italian and our parents' Piedmontese dialect, which had many words similar to French, but like most children of immigrants, we were reluctant to speak it. I took two years of Latin and four years of Spanish in high school and college. Dad lamented that I was learning other languages while not taking advantage of my own family's language.

EVEN BEFORE FIRST GRADE, I developed a life-long love for horses. Horse-drawn wagons were still used. A junk man collecting rags and old iron made periodic visits. He would sit me atop his horse for a few blocks. A nearby farmer would put me on his horse while he plowed a field near the school. At the annual gas-company picnic in Kennywood Park, I used up almost all my tickets riding around the pony track.

I spent most of the summer of 1940 on the Defer farm in Ohio learning to milk dairy cows and help with farming chores while enjoying riding bareback on the two draft horses. Henry Defer Jr. always rode "Brownie," the docile one. "Red" was not so docile. On one ride, Red took me under a low-hanging branch. I didn't duck fast enough and was pushed right off his rump onto the ground. He kept going. I walked back.

Decades later, in the 1980s, I organized horseback rides during baseball spring-training trips in Arizona. These outings were enjoyed by the few guys who didn't golf but mostly by their wives. I regret that I never owned a horse of my own.

These were good years. I'm thankful for my parents and wouldn't trade my youth with anyone.

Chapter 3

■   ■   ■

School and Work

B eechwood Elementary School was a white, three-story brick building a ten-minute walk from home. I started kindergarten there in 1932. The teaching profession was highly regarded because teachers had college degrees at a time when most people did not attend college. We had good teachers, all women. I skipped a half-year in second grade. (Dad made a chart of multiplication tables and told me memorize them). In the upper grades, I played on the softball, basketball, and soccer teams. Shooting marbles was a pleasant diversion after lunch. Mom never missed parent-teacher nights. She and Dad closely reviewed my report cards.

I always went home for lunch except one day in seventh grade. After finally challenging a bully who frequently punched me, I agreed to a lunch-time bout in the boy's bathroom, complete with gloves, rounds, and seconds. We flailed away to a draw. But the harassment stopped and our teachers and parents never found out about the fight. It was a valuable lesson: never look for a fight, but never back down from one. You would never be physically challenged if you looked and acted as if you could handle yourself.

At home we had two books, a dictionary and a geography book, and we read the daily and Sunday *Pittsburgh Sun-Telegraph*, a Hearst paper. Beechwood had an excellent library so I read a lot, which helped me compete in class spelling contests. A traveling library provided books for summer reading. My favorites were histories and biographies of accomplished leaders.

In addition to learning the basics, we studied music and art and took gym and wood-working classes. I had no musical ability. Although I could draw, I was no artist either. For more than three years, I attended art classes at Carnegie Museum every Saturday morning. Recommended by their teachers, students from every school started with sketching, progressing to crayon and then water colors. I quit before we got to oil painting. Baseball was more fun on Saturday. At a baseball clinic sponsored by the city, I met Honus Wagner, legendary Hall of Fame shortstop. His autograph is extremely valuable today. I didn't get one!

In seventh grade, after occasionally substituting for a pal for a few years, I landed my first paying job and an introduction to the newspaper business—a *Pittsburgh Press* home-delivery route with forty-five to fifty customers. I collected twenty-eight cents every week for seven-day delivery. I deposited most of my $2.50 weekly profit into a savings account. Few tips were received, even for perfect service, but everyone paid promptly on collection day. There were no deadbeats.

I graduated from Beechwood in 1941. Three awards were given to each eighth-grade graduating class: a history award from the Daughters of the American Revolution; a citizenship award from the Sons of the American Revolution, and a certificate of honor from the American

Legion. My immigrant parents, who were citizens by then, never boasted to anyone about their children, but I knew they were quietly proud when their son received all three awards.

EUROPE WAS AT WAR and the United States soon would follow when I entered ninth grade in South Hills High School. Students came from schools in several surrounding communities. Most boys had entered the service before the end of the war in 1945. It was a serious time. Blue stars were placed in the windows of homes where a son or daughter served in the armed forces. Too many homes had gold stars indicating a family member had been killed in action.

I took academic courses with the expectation of attending college. I got A's in most subjects and B's in mathematics and some sciences. English and history were my best subjects. Knowing Italian helped with two years of Latin and two years of Spanish. My homeroom teacher, Miss Marie Messer, was a strong influence, encouraging me to excel.

I walked four miles each way to high school every day until becoming involved in extra-curricular activities, including the National Honor Society, and after that bought a streetcar pass that cost fifty cents a week. I played baseball as a junior and senior. In 1944, we won the Pittsburgh High School Baseball Championship. Our best pitcher was a left-hander, Bob Lucchino, who was my best friend for many years. We were saddened when Jack O'Day, whose no-hitter I had caught in 1943, was lost at sea with the Navy.

Dad reluctantly allowed me to play football as a senior. As a guard and place-kicker at five-foot-six and 162 pounds, I was not considered too small at that time. I tried cross-country one year. My only race was in wooded Schenly Park. After stopping with a buddy who felt sick, we got lost and finished a half-hour behind the rest of the team. The coach was quoted in the school newspaper as saying, "You can't make a race horse out of a draft horse." True. I was never a fast runner. Most catchers aren't.

The Stanley Theater in downtown Pittsburgh frequently featured the "big bands" of that era, playing live on stage after the movie. At one matinee, I heard a young, skinny singer with a big bow tie. The girls were shrieking. It was Frank Sinatra. I didn't think he was that swell. Some buddies worked as ushers for Broadway stage plays at the Nixon Theater and allowed their friends to sneak in without paying. We saw some entertaining plays.

In my senior year, I was elected president of the student council. We conducted a successful Red Cross blood drive during that term. I represented the school on a radio program with the superintendent of schools. Another highlight was my appearance before the student body of Westinghouse High School. Their student president visited our school, too. The purpose was to restore peace after fistfights broke out following a football game at Westinghouse. It was a tough neighborhood. I played in the game. We needed police protection leaving the locker room.

In 1945, I was offered the annual academic scholarship given to a member of each graduating class from the University of Pittsburgh, covering one-half of the tuition. I always knew that if I went to college, it would be Pitt.

MY HIGH-SCHOOL YEARS were also work years. I still had my chores to do at home and for a while delivered newspapers. It was wartime. There was full employment, and the Pittsburgh Coal Co. needed helpers.

When I told Dad a job was available every Saturday moving coal from sidewalks to coal-cellar windows after drivers dumped their load, he offered me $5 a week *not* to do this back-breaking work. I persisted. Dad relented, apparently convinced I would not last long.

For the next six months I went to the coal yard at 6 a.m. every Saturday and sat in a shack until a driver needed a helper. When coal buckets had to be carried up steps to a coal-cellar window, the pay was about $1 a ton. If a wheelbarrow was used, the pay was seventy-five cents. I worked every day during spring break in 1943. On the last day, there was more coal to deliver than a cellar could easily take, so I tossed in lumps of coal, one by one, to get the last ton into the cellar. This ended my coal-carrying career. The no-brainer experience built muscle and I deposited my earnings.

A neighbor got me a job with Pittsburgh Insul-Mastic Co., exterior building insulators, as the ground man helping two other men who worked on scaffolds spraying asphalt-asbestos compound on a building and covering it with blown-on slate granules. After a week, the driver of the crew failed to report for work. The boss asked if I could drive.

"Sure," I said. The boss knew I was fifteen and had no driver's license, but getting the work done was important. There was little traffic anyway.

Dad didn't know that for more than a year I had been practicing by quietly "borrowing" the Plymouth and driving it around at night in the dark. I picked up a few friends the third time I did this. Unfortunately, I was caught when Dad needed the car unexpectedly and it was nowhere to be found. He was too angry to apply a whipping. Instead, he grounded me for a year. That lasted one month.

(Although he never talked about his youth, relatives in Italy told me that he had his own escapades as a young man.)

I was the crew driver of various-sized trucks for the rest of that summer. I easily passed the driver's test in August. Every day went smoothly without incident except one. Rounding a bend on an uphill grade, the trailered air-compressor tilted over, spilling its gasoline, which was rationed then. The angry boss had to be reminded that he knew the driver was under-age and had little experience.

The wages started at sixty-five cents an hour, increased to eighty cents, and then $1 with a promotion to granule man. I continued to work weekends for the rest of the year and full-time the following summer. There was no overtime pay. We worked ten hours a day, seven days a week on occasion to take advantage of good weather.

The work was an education in life. Many co-workers were rough, with language to match, and had questionable backgrounds. But help was needed badly. The boss hired any worker he could find—no questions asked, no references needed. One new hire, a shifty man named "Bad Eye" Reese, turned out to be an escaped convict who was recaptured soon after abruptly quitting.

College would be a better education.

Chapter 4

■ ■ ■

Freshman at Pitt

In February, 1945, I enrolled at the University of Pittsburgh, a two street-car ride across the city. The centerpiece of the university was the forty-two-story Cathedral of Learning, the second-tallest college building in the world. The cathedral is a national landmark. There were thirty "nationality rooms" on the first and third floors, twenty-eight of them classrooms. The rooms were funded by nationality organizations represented in Pittsburgh's population. Each resembled a room in the sponsoring country. I had several classes in nationality rooms during my Pitt years. Pitt Stadium was a few blocks away. Also nearby were Forbes Field, home of the Pirates, Carnegie Museum, and Schenly Park.

At freshmen indoctrination, Chancellor John G. Bowman said he rejected an offer from Andrew Mellon, Pittsburgh banker and financier, to finance construction of the Cathedral of Learning because the offer was contingent on renaming the school Mellon University. Many years later, Carnegie Tech, funded by Andrew Carnegie, wealthy Pittsburgh steel magnate and founder of the Carnegie Libraries, was renamed Carnegie-Mellon University. It is a few blocks from Pitt. Both are highly rated universities.

I selected a major in political science and minor in international economics with the hope of becoming a diplomat after earning a Bachelor of Arts degree. I had never traveled more than 300 miles from Pittsburgh, but my goal was to join the U.S. Foreign Service and travel to other countries.

MY PAL BOB LUCCHINO also enrolled. The baseball coach, Ralph "Sarge" Mitterling, once a catcher for the Philadelphia Athletics, was happy to have the winning battery from South Hills. On the day of our first game at Penn State on April 5, 1945, the *Pittsburgh Sun-Telegraph* ran a two-column picture of each of us with the caption reporting that we "starred" for South Hills. Unfortunately, my first name was listed as "Vince," an easy mistake that was made occasionally.

Lucchino was our best pitcher. I caught every game and maintained a fair batting average. We had a lackluster season, though, losing most of our twelve games. Most games were played against nearby colleges in Pennsylvania, reached easily by bus or train.

We played the Naval Academy at Annapolis, Maryland, and the Army Academy at West Point, New York. Navy easily beat us as several hundred cadets, would-be admirals, cheered on their classmates and taunted us. Uncle John and Aunt Bertha came from Baltimore for the game.

The Annapolis trip was my second train ride. The first trip took place the year before when I went to Fort Knox, Kentucky, to spend a weekend with Uncle Henry, who was stationed there. The hot railroad car was crowded with servicemen. The windows were opened and smoke and dirt came in. It was not comfortable, to say the least. I spent most of the trip sitting on my suitcase.

The visit to West Point, 450 miles away, was even more memorable. Army had some well-known All-American football players on the team, including Glenn Davis, considered the country's best college player at that time. A cadet walked us all over the hallowed academy grounds and through historic buildings the morning of the game, probably hoping to wear us out. Our uniforms and gear failed to arrive by game time, so we used Army's sweat-suit outfits. We were losing when heavy rain stopped the game in the fifth inning.

The semester at Pitt had just ended. Lucchino and I were given our return train tickets and permission to stop over in New York City on the way home. Having little money, we couldn't afford to do much more than spend most of a day hanging around Times Square, taking in the sights and sounds. We were awed by the Big Apple.

SHORTLY AFTER ENROLLING at Pitt, I was rushed by several fraternities. After considering a few, I pledged to Phi Delta Theta, considered one of the best, and went through some so-called "screening" experiences to see if I fit in. Finally, after surviving the appropriately named "Hell Week," I was initiated. In retrospect, I realize that the events of Hell Week would be considered serious hazing by today's standards. But we put up with it. That's the way it was.

For the rest of the semester, I ate inexpensive lunches at the fraternity house and attended most of the social affairs. I was flattered by being accepted, but having more limited financial resources than my frat brothers, I probably should not have joined. Some members had cars and came from wealthy families whose fathers had been Phi Delts in their student days. My grades that semester were the lowest

I ever received. It took the rest of my college years to get up to a 3.5 grade-point average by the time I graduated.

After my initiation, I found that an uncomfortable amount of ethnic and racial prejudice existed at the fraternity. That summer, a friend from South Hills was rushed, but then black-balled because of his nationality. For these and a variety of other reasons, I decided never to set foot inside the fraternity house again. I was not a frat guy.

Chapter 5

■　■　■

U.S. Navy

Dad signed the permission form, my physical was passed, and I was sworn into the Navy on July 5, 1945 "for the duration of the war and six months." Active-duty orders were to come soon. The summer came and went. I batted cleanup for the Carrick Athletic Club, played in an all-star game at Forbes Field, and worked a few weeks behind the soda counter at John's Drug Store, which posted photos in its front window of all the Beechview men in the service.

Then we dropped atomic bombs on Hiroshima and Nagasaki. Japan surrendered. World War II was over. The official surrender signing took place September 2 aboard the USS *Missouri,* which was anchored in Tokyo Bay.

On October 2, I arrived at Camp Peary, (now a CIA training facility) near Williamsburg, Virginia, for ten weeks of boot camp as an apprentice seaman with other young men from the east and south. A semester of college and two years of drilling in high school as a member of Pennsylvania Military Corps, complete with khakis, earned me an assignment as master-at-arms in charge of sixty men in one of two barracks in Company 725. All went well, except for the trouble caused by a belligerent kid from Brooklyn who continually resisted getting up at 6 a.m., delaying the company from getting to the mess hall at six-thirty.

Delaying breakfast was a serious matter. After repeated warnings, one morning I doused the kid with water, and he jumped out of the sack with a knife in hand. With help, he was subdued. Everyone got up at six every day thereafter.

Half-way through boot camp, the assistant petty officer, a recruit who was in charge of the company when the commander was away (most of the time) had to leave for an emergency at home. I replaced him as APO with responsibility for the entire company of 120 men, making sure we went to our field-training classes and, of course, the mess hall, calling out cadence as we marched everywhere. The only training we missed was marksmanship at the shooting range, canceled because of a storm. I never fired a gun then or later on duty.

After a ten-day leave, I left Camp Peary as a seaman second class on a troop train to Camp Parks, near Oakland, California. I visited Uncle Henry at his restaurant in San Francisco a few times before shipping out on a troop ship for Pearl Harbor. At the staging area, when my name was called out at assignment muster, I had visions of sailing the Pacific to exotic places.

The bus that picked me up, however, traveled four blocks to my new barracks next to a mosquito-breeding sugar-cane field and shore duty in the communications office of Commander Service Force Pacific Fleet (ComServPac), adjacent to headquarters of Commander-in-Chief, Pacific Fleet (CinCPac), a ten-minute walk up to Makalapa Hill overlooking Pearl Harbor. I believe the barracks stood on the present site of Aloha Stadium.

On the first day, the officer in charge gave me a message to transmit. He was shocked that he had been sent a radioman "striker" who couldn't type. But I learned quickly. It was a valuable skill that served me well. Our mission was to communicate by teletype with all Navy ships in the Pacific. It was a choice assignment. Our watch section of two officers and ten enlisted men, mostly older radiomen, were great help for this eighteen-year-old, the youngest sailor in the section. Watches were eight hours on, eight hours off. On all-night watches, I drove a jeep to the mess hall to get steaks and ice cream for the section.

We had liberty every third day. I usually picked up Hal Dobbins, a boot-camp buddy from Atlanta who was stationed on a tugboat in the harbor. We would spend the day in Honolulu with an afternoon swim at Waikiki Beach. In a few months, I was promoted to seaman first class.

On occasion, a few of us toured Oahu Island in a jeep from the motor pool, located near a large crater left by Japanese bombers. We always stopped to snitch a few pineapples from the big Dole fields. Our section had several luaus at Wailea, an isolated beach on the northern shore of the island.

Our only co-ed social contact came at a dance at the all-girl Kamehameha High School, open only to girls who were at least part native Hawaiian. All the eighteen-year-old sailors invited to attend were screened. We each were given a dance card with different girls' names written on it and told we would be allowed to dance only once with each girl. Further contact was discouraged.

Pearl Harbor was full of ships. There were visible signs of the USS *Arizona* and other sunken ships destroyed in the Japanese attack on December 7, 1941—"a day that will live in infamy," as FDR put it in declaring war. In Honolulu, I frequently ran across friends from South Hills High, Beechview, and even a close neighbor, Jerry Kiralfy. All were on ships heading back to the mainland. Among them were several smaller vessels on their way to Nationalist China as a gifts from the United States. I saw some of the same ships in Shanghai forty years later, this time as part of Communist China's navy.

John Lang, a section buddy, and I played baseball for ComServPac. Our opponents were Army, Air Force, and Marine teams stationed at bases on the island. Many big-league stars had played on these teams, including Joe DiMaggio, but almost all had gone home by then to be discharged in time for the 1946 season. I shot about 150 playing my first round of golf at Schofield Army Base, not an encouraging introduction to the game.

HAWAII WAS A MEMORABLE experience. I was eighteen, stationed on a tropical island, and earning $60 a month with few expenses. Still, I wished the duty had been aboard a ship stopping at ports in Australia, Japan, and the Pacific.

In late July, 1946, I was in line for promotion to radioman third class when my Hawaii duty came to an end with shipment aboard a troop ship to San Francisco, where I visited Uncle Henry again and enjoyed some good Italian cooking. At my suggestion, several Navy friends had stopped at Leone's on their way home. I thought I was sending my uncle some paying customers, but learned he gave my friends a free meal.

I crossed the country on a slow-moving troop train to Bainbridge, Maryland, where I was discharged from active duty in early August, a few days before my nineteenth birthday. My enlistment in July, 1945 qualified me as a veteran of World War II. After my discharge from active service, I re-enlisted in the Naval Reserve.

Following a quick stop to see Uncle John in nearby Baltimore, I boarded a train for Pittsburgh and a joyous family welcome.

Chapter 6

■   ■   ■

Pitt and the *Beechview News*

With the G.I. Bill providing all tuition, books, and $65 a month, I picked up the second half of my freshman year at the University of Pittsburgh in September, 1946. Government service was still my goal. Political science, international economics, and Spanish were my favorite subjects. Knowing that my benefits based on service time would not cover the cost of the remaining three and a half years of college, I took sixteen or seventeen credits every semester, instead of the normal fifteen.

I lived at home, commuted by streetcar, and brought my lunch most days. The first year went well. My grades in all subjects were 3.0 or better. I decided to work hard and skip baseball in the spring. Pitt's enrollment had increased by thousands as veterans took advantage of the G.I. Bill, one of the best programs the federal government has ever provided for our veterans. Many of my classmates were in their late twenties or thirties and had little chance of ever getting a college education without this assistance.

Dad contracted to build concrete-block garages and retaining walls on weekends that year with some of his gas-company crew and me as helpers. That summer, we tore down the two corrugated-tin garages next to our home and built a two-car, concrete-block garage. Dad did the skilled work. I mixed the mortar and provided unskilled labor. We still raised chickens and I did my family chores. I played baseball a few games a week for Carrick A.C. in the Greater Pittsburgh League.

I WAS TWENTY with a "ruptured duck" lapel pin signifying that I was a veteran and therefore had a waiver from the legal drinking age of twenty-one. In October, 1947, while enjoying a beer with friends at Rizzo's Café in Beechview, a life-changing meeting took place. I struck up a conversation with Tom Miller, a forty-year-old printer. I enjoyed writing and was taking an elective course in reporting. Before the evening was over, Miller and I decided to start a biweekly tabloid newspaper together, the *Beechview News*. Tom would be the publisher and handle advertising. I would be the editor and writer.

With its rivers, hills, and valleys, Pittsburgh was divided into distinct communities. Beechview was one of the few that did not have its own newspaper. Dad was not enthused with this "opportunity," but as usual, he didn't interfere. I invested $300, a lot of money then. Miller and I were partners. He provided his printing "expertise," which I later learned did not include any actual experience with a press. This was the first of many surprises, but I was learning fast.

Tom Miller's friend, a fellow church member, found us a printer. I later learned the friend had received a kickback for steering our business to him. Meanwhile, Miller lined up some advertisers among the merchants in the small Beechview business district while I found enough news to fill four pages initially. We published our first biweekly edition in November, 1947 and distributed copies to many homes and every retail store. The cost was five cents a copy or $1 a year for twenty-six issues. We signed up everyone we knew. I solicited home subscribers in my spare time and started a campaign for a much-needed community swimming pool. Meanwhile, Miller sold the ads. Local merchants were supportive. Most people subscribed when asked. We paid our first printing bills. It looked like the joint venture might be a success.

FOR THE FEBRUARY-JUNE semester, I took another reporting course without changing my objective of joining the Foreign Service. I was busy with classes, studying, and gathering news, but enjoyed the challenges as editor. With a love for baseball and an invite from Coach Mitterling, I made the 1948 Pitt varsity baseball team and caught half the games. Competition for the catcher position was stiff with all the servicemen home.

We were playing Penn State at Pitt Stadium on a warm Saturday in early May. Mom and Dad came to see their son play. It was their first baseball game. Though I had been playing baseball since I was twelve, my parents thought the catcher's gear was part of everyone's uniform. We were ahead by a run in the ninth with two outs and the tying run on second. The next batter hit a single to left. The left-fielder scooped up the baseball and threw hard to home plate. The ball came in chest high. The runner, a 225-pounder, rolled me over, but I held onto the ball. Game over. We won.

"You're crazy," Dad said. "You could get killed. Is this what you have been doing? You and the guy throwing the ball are the only ones working. Everyone else is standing around"—a simple but accurate description.

Two weeks later, on May 24, 1948, Dad had a sudden heart attack. He died in my arms. He was fifty-one. What a shock. Dad was the picture of health. He never missed a day of work for illness and until that morning never complained. In the many years since, I have thought of all the questions I could have asked about his earlier life and experiences, but didn't.

Dad's siblings in Italy were all younger so I didn't get much from them either.

MEANWHILE, THE BEECHVIEW NEWS was not doing well. Tom Miller had lost his day job and was experiencing personal financial problems. We owed more than $1,000 for printing, rent, and other expenses. As a partner, I shared responsibility for the debts. A lawyer offered two options: sue Miller for embezzling from a minor or assume sole ownership. I chose to acquire the paper and work out of the debt.

In my eighth-grade English class, I had written and typed a four-page "newspaper," the "Beechview News," listing myself as editor and publisher. It was prophetic. Seven years later, at age twenty, I was editor, publisher, and owner of the real *Beechview News*. The 1937 Plymouth, my only inheritance, was necessary for commuting to Pitt and calling on advertisers.

A new printer was engaged at a much lower cost ($80 to print an eight-page tabloid), the office was closed, and I moved into space in a merchant's store. A telephone-answering service was set up. It took a lot of door-knocking to sell $1 subscriptions that summer and a renewed campaign to sell new advertisers. But the bills were paid. The merchants and printer helped this young publisher to succeed. The family got involved, too. Ida typed the advertisers' invoices and prepared mailing labels. Mom and Christina attached the labels to the papers and brother-in-law Leonard Pulkowski distributed to stores.

A few local citizens became contributing reporters for a byline but no pay. My column, "Viewing the News," appeared in every issue. Our circulation, a combination of mail subscriptions and single-copy sales, grew to 2,000. The paper made a small profit. I didn't realize at the time that this unplanned experience would set the stage for my life's work.

A routine was established: selling ads and writing stories every weekend and a few evenings, getting the eight-page paper out on time every other Friday, and studying between classes and at home. The 1948 fall semester went well. I took editing as an elective my senior year. Christmas ads were a financial bonanza. The *Pitt Evening News* ran a three-column, front-page headline: "Two semesters of Journalism are Enough for Newspaper Success" above a complimentary feature story and a picture captioned "Virgil Fassio, editor, news reporter, layout editor, advertising manager, and circulation manager, sits behind the copy desk awaiting inspiration for the next issue of the Beechview News."

PLAYING FOR SOUTH SIDE in the Greater Pittsburgh League that summer, when possible, I was thrilled to go up against a boyhood hero, Paul Waner, a Pittsburgh Pirate legend and Hall of Famer. Years before, he had been in right field when I went to a Boy's Day game (free admission) at Forbes Field. Waner retired from professional baseball, but owned a batting range and played in North Side's home games. Hit by a pitch, I went to first base, where he was playing. He called time to rub my back. Waner was well known for his drinking habit, although it never seemed to affect his play. That day I could tell that he'd had a few. Another memorable game was in

Western Penitentiary. The inmates cheered for us instead of their fellow inmates.

The G.I. Bill benefits ran out in February, 1949. Time had erased the academic scholarship of 1945. Extra credits taken each semester and summer-school classes made it possible, with extra help, to graduate in three years and eight months.

Frank Carver, Pitt's athletic-information officer, and retired Admiral Tom Hamilton, the athletic director, knew my situation: father deceased, G.I. Bill benefits used up, extra credits carried each semester, good grades, a baseball player, and a struggling newspaper publisher. They provided me with a baseball scholarship—full tuition and books—to complete my education when the government benefits ran out. It was the only baseball scholarship given at that time. These two men also influenced my life in later years.

Because automobiles had not been produced during the war, new and used cars were hard to get. In March, 1948, Dad made a $100 deposit on a new Plymouth. More than a year later, I paid $1,727 for a new dark-green 1948 Plymouth and sold my 1937 Plymouth for $300. Advertisers were impressed. They figured that business must be good. I learned that looking successful helps in life.

After graduating with a Bachelor of Arts degree with honors, I made plans for a family vacation that summer and fall. I turned operation of the newspaper over to two friends in August, September, and October. Alfred Vennare became acting editor and Bob Lucchino would handle advertising. They made every deadline and kept the profits while I was away.

Chapter 7

■ ■ ■

First Visit to Italy

M om, Christina, and I sailed from New York aboard the M/N *Saturnia* bound for Genoa in early August, 1949. Mom had left Italy in 1921 and had not seen her parents, three sisters, and a brother in twenty-eight years. We were booked in third class. Most passengers were Italian-Americans or Canadians returning with their families to the homeland after long absences. Few tourists were aboard. The ship had an all-Italian crew.

Although we were traveling on a tight budget, it was a comfortable and relaxing eleven-day voyage with a brief stop in Naples. Travel was relatively inexpensive in the early post-war years. I celebrated my twenty-second birthday at sea with new friends—another young American and two Canadian girls our age. We sneaked onto the first-class deck with the help of a few friendly crewmen and swam in the pool every day.

Mom's parents and sisters were easy to spot in front of hundreds of greeters when we docked in Genoa. The welcome was heart-warming. We headed for Asti.

Asti, an ancient city with remaining vestiges of ancient Roman history and culture, had a population of about 75,000. It is the capital of Asti Province in the Piedmont Region of northwest Italy, bounded by Switzerland and France. The Asti area and much of the rest of Piedmont is a vast vineyard, producing some of Italy's finest red wines, much of which are exported to the United States.

Asti was recognized as a Roman colony in 89 B.C. By the thirteenth century, it had become one of the richest and most powerful cities in Italy. Destroyed by fires and sieges several times, it still has many of its medieval buildings and some of the 120 towers erected during its heyday.

In Asti, we rented a room in an apartment within walking distance of a fifteenth-century cathedral across the courtyard from my grandparent's living quarters and their small grocery store. A grandson, Vittorino, ran the store. Not having refrigeration, people shopped daily for staples.

LIKE MOST OF EUROPE, Italy was recovering and rebuilding slowly from the devastation of the war. Much of northern Italy had been bombed, but had not seen local combat. The Germans, however, occupied the north after Italy surrendered to the Allies in September, 1943 and treated their former Axis partners as enemies. A seventeen-year-old cousin, for example, went to the town square on an errand and was picked up by the Germans in retaliation for a partisan attack. After the war, he walked home from Germany, where he had been forced to work in a factory.

By the end of the war, communism had a strong following in many western European countries, particularly so in the industrial cities of Italy. Under Italy's parliamentary system, many parties

with differing ideologies were represented to form coalition govern-
ments. There was a fear that communists might take over, but they
never gained control in Italy or elsewhere in the western European
democracies. The U.S. Marshall Plan was the key to the rebuilding of
Europe's infrastructure and in curtailing the spread of communism.

Dad received a letter in 1943 from a boyhood friend who also
had served in WWI. The letter was from Camp Miles Standish,
Massachusetts, where he was a prisoner of war. At age forty-six, the
friend had been conscripted with other older veterans to fight for
the Italian army again in North Africa in WWII. "We sweltered
all day and froze at night in the desert, and surrendered as soon as
the American soldiers came," he wrote. While a POW in the United
States, his eighteen-year-old son, a resistance fighter blowing up
German trains and installations in northern Italy, was killed in an
ambush.

MY GRANDPARENTS were in their mid-seventies and delightful. Grandma Christina Pia was short, with auburn hair. Grandpa
Eugenio was about five-foot-nine, straight-standing, and possessed
a keen sense of humor. The only English he remembered from his
time working in the United States many years before was "Big Nose,"
an appellation given to him. His hobby was weaving reeds around
wine jugs. (I have one). He bicycled everywhere, as most people did.

One memorable bike ride was an eight- to ten-mile trip to Aunt
Maria Pia's in Repergo. We stopped at an old friend's house so
Grandpa could introduce his grandson from America—a novelty.
The old gent got out his oldest and best *barbera*, a red wine saved for
special occasions, and dusted off the bottle to celebrate. This hap-
pened at three stops visiting old friends on the way. The bikes were

wobbly by the time we reached Repergo. Aunt Maria, Mom's sister, and Enrico had eight children. They worked the vineyards, shared with the *professore* who owned the vineyard and lived above it in the large house. Farm work was labor-intensive. The stable with oxen and other livestock was attached to the house, as it was on almost every farm.

Everywhere we went, hard-to-find veal, chicken, and pasta were served. Otherwise, everyone ate rabbit, raised as a staple food. All were quietly pleased when they learned rabbit was my favorite meat. Word got around. We ate a lot of rabbit on that trip.

Aunts Amalia Berzano and Albina Manini, Mom's other sisters, lived in Casabianca, a small village on the outskirts of Asti. The sisters owned their own small vineyards. Albina had four children. Amalia had a little boy, Giuseppe, who became like a brother to me. He was named after Mom's only brother, Giuseppe, who lived in Asti and worked in a factory. They had a daughter, Annamaria.

Several cousins in the Asti area were close in age to Christina and me, but none knew any English. I got on fairly well with my Spanish and fractured Piedmontese. While visiting my father's side of the family in Torino, where they had moved from Asti many years earlier, Aunt Carla, the wife of Dad's brother Cesare, insisted that I learn the true Italian. I learned enough to converse and no longer speak Piedmontese. Cesare's son, Gian Franco, also became like a brother. Dad's two sisters also lived in Torino. Ninfa Pia had no children, but Vittorina Morando, the youngest, had a young daughter, Renata.

My relatives lived in different environments. Those in Asti were rural and small town, while the Torino relatives were urban and big city, but the hospitality was first class everywhere we went.

TORINO (TURIN), ABOUT THIRTY-FIVE MILES west of
Asti, has a population of about 800,000. It is a big, industrial city
and the home of FIAT (*Fabrica Italiano Automobile Torino*), the large
automobile company. Torino became a Roman colony in the first
century. It was the capital of Italy during unification of the Italian
peninsula, Sicily, and Sardinia into a single government in 1865 before the capital was moved to Rome. The leaders of unification and
the royal family, the House of Savoy, were Piedmontese.

Torino retains much of its Roman layout and medieval appearance, but a large part of the city dates to the seventeenth century
when it was enlarged and enriched in baroque-style architecture. It
is a beautiful city, but not well known to tourists, despite its palaces,
castles, distinctive covered sidewalks, and the best Egyptian museum
outside of Cairo. In the Cathedral Chapel of the Holy Shroud is
an urn containing a shroud in which, according to legend, Christ
was wrapped for burial. (In 2009, Torino was the site of the Winter
Olympics.)

Our Torino stays were filled with exciting experiences. Uncle
Cesare and I rowed on the Po River. We bicycled with Gian Franco,
then twelve, about twenty-five miles into the countryside and
climbed to an ancient monastery. We toured all parts of the city and
watched Juventus play other pro soccer teams in a packed stadium.
Mom had written Uncle Cesare that I played baseball in college and
published my own newspaper. Citing these credentials, he arranged
three memorable visits.

We met with a banker who had become an enthusiastic baseball
fan while a U.S. prisoner of war and was trying to bring baseball to
Italy. He provided the Juventus Club, famous internationally as a soccer team, with baseball equipment. A team begun practicing. He was

delighted that an American player was willing to help coach. Team members ranged in age from sixteen to twenty-five, all of them from well-to-do families, including a future chairman of FIAT.

I bicycled to the field that afternoon. When I picked up a baseball in the outfield and tossed it back to the players, they yelled *"Il Americano!"* I practiced with the team every time I was in Torino and wrote about my experience later for a newspaper column. I have a signed card identifying me as an honorary member of the Juventus Baseball Club. It took many years for an inter-city baseball league to be organized. In a small way, I may have encouraged them. (In 2010, Alex Liddi joined the Seattle Mariners, becoming the first Italian-born, raised, and developed player to play in the major leagues.)

Uncle Cesare took me to FIAT's Mirafiore plant. While waiting in the lobby for our guide, the doors of the factory burst open and several hundred workers soon filled a big, empty showroom. A leader appeared on the balcony to tell the workers that "we have to show a demonstration of force," among other extortions. With each statement, excited workers held up copies of the communist newspaper, *Unita*, and chanted its name. We were advised to leave and return the next day. These strikes occurred often, usually for no reason. Outside, two jeeps with *Carabiniere*, officers of the national police agency, were ready for action.

The next day was quiet. We toured the plant in a large, open vehicle and rode on the oval testing track. In the large parking lot were few cars, but hundreds of bicycles. Civilian auto production had stalled during the war years. But demand for FIAT's cars was growing and many were exported.

Uncle Cesare also arranged a tour of *Gazetta Del Popolo*, a Torino newspaper with national distribution. The staff welcomed this

American journalist from Pittsburgh as if I represented a major U.S. newspaper.

I HAD THE PLEASURE of escorting Mom, Christina, and the two Canadian girls and their mothers on a trip to Florence, Rome, and Venice. Tourists were scarce in Europe so soon after the war. Our group of seven travelers had bargaining power wherever we went. It was easy to negotiate discounted rates in the *albergos* and *pensiones*. We toured all the art museums in Florence, numerous ruins, St. Peters, the Vatican Museum, and the Sistine Chapel, among other sights in Rome.

We made a side trip to Paris, too. Christina, the two Canadian girls, and I toured the Louvre, Eiffel Tower, Notre Dame, and other attractions.

I had to get home after more than two months away. Mom and Christina stayed a few more weeks. In mid-October, I sailed from Genoa aboard the M/N *Vulcania*, sister ship of M/N *Saturnia*. Ida and Leonard picked me up in New York for the drive to Pittsburgh. It was time to get back to work. The *Beechview News* was part-time work. Now I hoped for a full-time job with a daily newspaper.

Chapter 8

■ ■ ■

The *Valley Daily News*

Before traveling to Italy, I contacted the State Department to pursue my interest in the Foreign Service. The response was not encouraging. Even if I passed all the exams, administered in Washington, D.C., likely there would be no openings for several years. War-time staffs were being reduced by attrition, effectively closing the door on my goal of becoming a diplomat.

I was too busy to look for a job after returning from Italy. The Christmas season, the most profitable time of the year, kept me busy at the newspaper. While abroad I did not give much thought to the *Beechview News*, except to submit a column, "Through the Gates of the Old World," for each edition. Vennare and Lucchino had done a good job getting the paper out in my absence with the help of my family.

Meanwhile, one of my Pitt benefactors, Frank Carver, shared my name and background with a few daily newspaper contacts. One of them wanted to talk to me. I was too occupied selling ads to follow through immediately and then thought it was too late. In late

December, however, George Stuart called. Stuart, in his sixties, was a rolled-up-sleeves kind of editor at the *Valley Daily News* in Tarentum, Pennsylvania. Was I still available? I was. That's when I discovered the best jobs often come when you are not looking for them.

THE ALLEGHENY VALLEY and the Kiski Valley were industrial areas that were home to the major plants of Pittsburgh Plate Glass Co. in Creighton, Allegheny Ludlum Steel in Brackenridge, Aluminum Company of America in New Kensington, and several small plants. Farmlands surrounded the rural areas outside several communities.

The *Valley Daily News* was a highly regarded small-city paper with complete local news coverage that eventually served more than thirty cities, boroughs, and townships by aggressively expanding its reach beyond Allegheny County. The paper took strong editorial positions intended to improve each community. The Borough of Tarentum, population 10,000, on the Allegheny River about twenty-five miles northeast of Pittsburgh, was contiguous with the Borough of Brackenridge and Harrison Township. The total population of all three communities was 38,000. The newspaper had a six-day evening circulation of about 14,000.

I started as a reporter on the *Valley Daily News* in January, 1950 at $35 a week, plus car expenses. My assignment: open up a new beat in the cities of New Kensington and Arnold and Lower Burrell Township, all directly across the Allegheny in a more heavily populated area dominated by the competing *New Kensington Dispatch*. Some of the *VDN*'s major advertisers in New Kensington were unhappy with the *Dispatch*.

The *VDN* publisher, Eugene Simon, knew of my *Beechview News* ownership. It was okay to go home every weekend and commute daily every other week to work on the *Beechview News* in the evenings. In the spring, while staying over in Tarentum, I played baseball for Freeport in the Tri-County League. The schedule worked well.

Reporters on small newspapers typically cover all the news in their area—crime, government, fender-benders, features, and weddings, and they took pictures, too. One of my first stories was about a woman's African violet greenhouse. It was interesting work. Most reporters covered high-school football games on Friday evenings. Every school had a rabid following. The region was known for producing some of the country's top college players.

My morning beat included Citizens General Hospital, the police headquarters and mayor's office in New Kensington, and the police and mayor in Arnold. Back in the office, I turned my stories over to Lem Schwartz, city editor, or to George Stuart in time for the afternoon deadline. After lunch, I drove over to Valley Heights, a section of Lower Burrell that we were committed to cover, and picked up copy from our correspondent, a homemaker who was paid by the inch.

Back in the office, I supervised placement of the stories as a printer made up the Valley Heights page for the next day's paper. I was familiar with type and frequently helped the printer of the *Beechview News* fill the pages. But I made a mistake at the *VDN*. One day, seeing a "hole" on the page that a short story would fill, I picked up type to fill the empty space. That's when I got a taste of the jurisdictional power of the International Typographical Union, one of the nation's first unions. Suddenly, the chapel chairman whistled loudly for all work to halt. The composing room shut down for fifteen minutes. The silence was deafening. It was a "crime" for non-union members to touch the type—a lesson I learned the hard way.

A reporter on the New Kensington paper and I covered some of the same stories. He mentioned the low morale on his paper, which had absentee owners, and said some reporters were trying to organize as members of the American Newspaper Guild. He suggested I do the same at the *Valley Daily News*. But I had no interest. Morale was good at the *VDN*. Everyone seemed to enjoy their work. The organizing effort did not succeed in New Kensington.

COMMUNIST NORTH KOREA attacked South Korea in June, 1950. The United Nations Security Council voted to take military action. On June 25, President Harry S. Truman announced that the United States would send troops to defend South Korea and activate some reserves. I re-enlisted in the Naval Reserve that spring and expected to be called up.

Not wishing to return to active duty as an enlisted man, I phoned the Office of Naval Officer Procurement (ONOP) in Pittsburgh to apply for a commission and was instructed to come in the following Tuesday. Seeking advice, I met with my other Pitt benefactor, Tom Hamilton, the retired admiral who was well known in Navy circles. He phoned the ONOP and was told that a directive the previous day ordered that no new applications be accepted. Hamilton was irate.

"This man was told to come down Tuesday," Hamilton said. "This is Tuesday, and I'm sending him down. Do you understand, commander?"

That day, I was the only applicant taking the exams for a naval commission. Recommendation letters were submitted.

In the meantime, I was ordered to join a reserve unit in Pittsburgh as an enlisted man and began attending drills every Wednesday evening. In October, however, orders came to report for active duty in

Philadelphia within seven days. I got a thirty-day extension to give me time to try to sell the *Beechview News*. I called the owners of the nearby *Dormont News* and the *Mt. Washington News*, but neither was interested. With a letter advising that a commission was on its way, I was scratched from the enlisted roster.

The commission dated October 2, 1950 offered two choices: immediate active duty or assignment to a reserve unit. Choosing the latter, I went back to Division 4-42 as an ensign and personnel officer, expecting to get orders for active duty any day. The orders never came. The Korean War ended in early 1953. I went to sea for two weeks of training in 1951 and each year for many years thereafter. I served as commanding officer of Surface Division 4-1 in Wilmington, Delaware and retired as a commander, Naval Reserve, with more than twenty-one years of service as an enlisted man and as an officer, without any active duty as an officer except for the annual training cruises.

In March, 1951, Gene Simon called me into his office. He told me that if his company ever bought the competing *New Kensington Dispatch*, I could be its publisher. To gain experience on the business side, he wanted me to become the *VDN*'s circulation manager with an immediate raise from $60 to $80 a week; a seat on the News Printing Co. board of directors; membership in the International Circulation Managers Association (ICMA) and attendance at its June convention in Washington, D.C.; and membership in the Inter-State Circulation Managers Association (ISCMA) with members in Pennsylvania, Delaware, Maryland, New Jersey, West Virginia, and Washington, D.C., which met twice a year.

I decided to try the job six months.

Gene's offer was unprecedented. The prevailing view among his fellow publishers in the Pennsylvania Newspaper Publishers

Association (PNPA) was that it was a mistake promoting a reporter with no experience to circulation manager. But Gene took a chance with me. I was twenty-three. It turned out to be a life-changing move. I realized that I never would win a Pulitzer Prize for reporting. Likely I would have gone into another field had this opportunity not presented itself.

I have Gene to thank for so much of my newspaper career. I left the *VDN* in 1958, but he and I remained close friends. I always remembered to thank him when I moved to a better newspaper job.

My promotion wasn't completely a gamble for Gene. After serving as a Navy officer in WWII, he was teaching at Penn State University when he married Elisabeth Howe, daughter of Charles Howe, who founded the *Valley Daily News* in Tarentum in 1909. Howe was an effective leader in the community and his newspaper was widely respected. The paper did not accept liquor or tobacco advertising.

Gene joined the *VDN* as circulation manager after a brief period of unpaid training on the Harrisburg, Pennsylvania *Patriot-News*, whose publisher was a friend of Howe. By changing from an office-collect employee system to an independent carrier-salesman system, while expanding into nearby towns and introducing other innovations, he raised circulation to about 14,000. When Howe died in 1949, Gene became publisher.

Gene made his mark in many ways. He sold the newspaper, renamed the *Valley News-Dispatch* after buying the *New Kensington Dispatch,* to Gannett in 1974. Then he bought a large cattle ranch near Faywood, New Mexico, and wrote an insightful weekly column on national and local issues for several New Mexico newspapers for many years. He was born to be a rancher. He worked hard and became recognized as one of the most capable and successful ranchers in the region. After I retired in 1993, I visited Gene and Libby several times. In 2006, I was asked by the publisher of his memoir, *Cows and Columns,* to write a back-cover note.

I wrote: "Before Gene Simon's 'second' career as a New Mexico rancher and provocative 'must-read' weekly columnist for twenty-seven years, he was a daily newspaper publisher in Pennsylvania for more than twenty-five years and highly regarded as one of best small-city publishers in the country. Gene was my first boss and role model as a newspaperman and as a publisher–fair, fearless, dedicated to good journalism, and committed to making his newspaper a leader in improving the community and the lives of its citizens. I am proud to call him mentor and friend."

THE ICMA CONVENTION in June convinced me that my career change had potential. As the ICMA's youngest member, I was accepted as a peer, one who asked a lot of questions while meeting and rubbing shoulders with titans of the industry—circulation directors from the major papers in New York, Chicago, Detroit, Philadelphia, Los Angeles, Boston, Pittsburgh, and Washington, D.C. There were many more newspapers in those cities in the 1950s than there were thirty years later, and there are even fewer metropolitan papers today.

Most circulation directors lacked a college education, having come up through the ranks. Circulation was a rough, competitive business, particularly in the big cities. I had a college education, an editorial background, and could speak before a crowd.

Circulation is the lifeblood of a newspaper. It is the most important and valuable asset. It establishes the range of a newspaper's influence with its readers, advertisers, and ultimately its profitability. Circulation typically provides 25 percent of a daily newspaper's revenue and determines the value of the 75 percent revenue that came from advertising. In addition to publisher's circulation statements submitted every six months, the newspaper's paid circulation is audited annually by the Audit Bureau of Circulation (ABC), which issues detailed reports that are evaluated by advertisers making space buys.

At its peak in the 1960s, U.S. newspaper circulation exceeded 65 million daily and was delivered by more than 1 million carriers, mostly boys. This was the business I was learning that would be the foundation of my career until 1976. I started with two clerks in the office, one assistant in the field to help manage more than 150 carrier-salesman, and a mailroom staff of five.

IN JULY, 1951, I took my first two-week training cruise as a Naval Reserve officer aboard a patrol craft escort from Philadelphia to St. Petersburg, Florida. A green officer in more ways than one, I became seasick many times over the years on our first day at sea. Early on, I learned that being honest about my lack of knowledge and experience engendered support from more experienced sailors, especially chief petty officers accustomed to training new officers. I stood watches as junior officer of the deck on the bridge. At port in St. Petersburg, I was the officer of the deck for a four-hour watch with a .45 revolver strapped to my waist. I never fired a shot!

Back home, the geographical problem of two jobs with new responsibilities at the *VDN* was taking a toll on me. In early September, 1951, after a hectic weekend and days of commuting home with work at night, I was signed up to donate blood at a Red Cross mobile station in Beechview—a drive I promoted in my newspaper. With a resting pulse rate of 110, the doctor refused to take my blood until I was sufficiently rested.

If I didn't give up my job or my paper, he said, I would not live to see forty. That did it. Immediately I renewed my effort to find a buyer for the *Beechview News.*

Fortune was smiling on me. A local businessman wanted to buy the paper. I sold the name, files, subscription list, and a used desk for $2,500 to James K. Linkhart, a newcomer to Beechview who rented space for a print shop on Broadway, the main street. The newspaper fit nicely into his business operation. Linkhart had no prior newspaper experience, but his wife enjoyed writing. I helped them put out the first few issues. What a relief it was to sell the paper. It was time to concentrate on my job at the *Valley Daily News.*

My last issue, and the last of nearly 100 columns of "Viewing the News" written over four years, appeared on Sept. 21, 1951. I would not be listed as a publisher again for twenty-seven years.

I look back on my role as owner and publisher of Beechview's first newspaper with some pride of accomplishment. With the backing of several community activists, we waged a vigorous campaign for a community swimming pool from the earliest days. Eventually it was built by the City of Pittsburgh across from Beechwood Elementary School.

We organized the first-ever Beechview Business Council, which met regularly. Above all, we gave the community a sense of identity and brought its citizens together. Unfortunately, the newspaper ceased publication in 1955.

The *Beechview News* was a rich experience. My involvement started as a hobby, an opportunity to report, write, and sell advertising as a college student while hoping for a career in the Foreign Service. I never expected to spend my entire working life in the newspaper industry.

Chapter 9

■ ■ ■

Record Gains

It was late afternoon. The *VDN* circulation manager was tired. Earlier, I had done a hard, physically demanding job for the first time—using hand-operated, wire-strapping equipment to tie more than 200 newspaper bundles for the carrier-salesmen and several stores. Sixteen thousand papers had to get out. The regular operator, a strong seventeen-year-old student, had failed to report on schedule at 2 p.m. The *VDN* had a deal with Har-Brack High School in which a few students could be excused early to work in the paper's mailroom. One of them was the missing student, who was paying off an unpaid balance he owed as a carrier-salesman.

At 5:30 p.m. the student came in dressed in dirty work clothes. He had taken a laborer's job on the Tarentum-New Kensington Bridge project. He was not going back to school, despite his star-quality as a football player. He was sure he would never get a scholarship. He was poor and black. So what was the use? The coach at Har-Brack, a football powerhouse in Western Pennsylvania, and I persuaded him to return to school.

The rest is football history. Chester "Cookie" Gilchrist was an all-state fullback for two years. He was big and could run, pass, kick, and play defense. After graduating in 1956, he played in the Canadian Football League for several years and was a well-known all-star. When the new American Football Conference started in 1962, he joined the Buffalo Bills, whose star quarterback was Jack Kemp, and led the league in rushing with more than 1,000 yards that year. He starred in the National Football League for several more years. *Sports Illustrated* magazine ran his picture and obituary in 2012.

Cookie was just one of several hundred boys, twelve and older, who delivered the *VDN* during my seven years as circulation manager. I got to know many of these fine young men and their parents. Several grew up to become prominent in the region. Three retired as heads of departments on the newspaper. Richard Welsh was an outstanding carrier-salesman when I joined the paper. After he graduated from high school, I hired him as a district manager before I left in 1958. He later became circulation manager and then headed circulation for the two Pittsburgh newspapers. He was recognized as a leader in the industry.

Although I always referred to these young businessmen as carrier–salesmen, others called them "junior merchants" or "little merchants." We were just "paperboys" when I had a route as a kid. Whatever the name, they were independent contractors who bought newspapers from the publisher at wholesale and resold them to customers at retail, earning a profit on each sale. A subscription to the *VDN* cost thirty cents a week.

When he was circulation manager, Gene initiated a few novel programs for carrier-salesmen. I instituted several more. Some promotions were imitated by other newspapers. They included:

* Bonuses of $1, $2, or $3 a month, depending on location, for perfect delivery service and prompt payment of their bills.
* Free membership in the Allegheny Valley YMCA.
* A $1 incentive for opening a checking account at one of fifteen participating banks. The carriers deposited their collections and paid their bills by check.
* A $10 bonus for a 100 percent route on which every home subscribed. (We had a few.)

Circulation managers on small-city dailies have small staffs. Initially, I had one assistant to handle 150 carrier-salesmen. As circulation increased and carriers were added, we hired Mario "Marty" Corso, as my assistant, and "Bud" Cooper from another department. Corso, a former school teacher, succeeded me when I left the *VDN* in 1958.

We never had a problem finding carriers. They recruited their own substitutes. Coveted routes were passed on to younger brothers. The unique benefits of a *VDN* route were well known. Carriers had standing with their peers. Before a youngster took over a route, we visited his home, explained the responsibilities—reliable delivery, weekly collections, prompt bill payments—and benefits to the new carrier and at least one parent. The carrier then signed the independent contractor agreement.

Most parents wanted teenagers to have a job that would not only earn them money but, more important, teach them valuable life lessons.

"Busy boys are better boys," as the saying goes.

The most popular benefit was the opportunity to earn trips, prizes, and cash in periodic sales contests. The *VDN* annually promoted a weekend getaway for readers on the Pennsylvania Railroad, which ran through town. Several hundred readers bought tickets. I had covered the 1950 trip to Detroit as a reporter with Danny Angeloni. As circulation manager, I helped plan the trips and used them as incentives for carriers who could earn a free trip by signing up new subscribers. We promoted weekend packages to New York, Chicago, Washington, D.C., and even to Disneyland. The excursions were important to our sales promotion strategy and added to our paid circulation.

Carrier-salesmen earned overnight trips to Cedar Point in Ohio and day trips to Pittsburgh Pirate games, too. Winners of sales contests could get their pictures taken with a member of the team, usually a rookie. Two baseball excursions stand out. In 1953, the Pirates signed twin brothers Johnny and Eddie O'Brien, future baseball stars who had been All-American basketball players at Seattle University. They were signed as "bonus baby" infielders by Branch Rickey. Both became good friends twenty-three years later in Seattle.

In 1955, the rookie pictured with the carriers was a Puerto Rican outfielder, Roberto Clemente, who spoke little English, so we conversed in Spanish. Clemente later was enshrined in the Baseball Hall of Fame.

Prizes of merchandise and cash were the incentives for carrier-salesmen to knock on doors seeking new subscribers to earn bicycles, baseball gloves, and other things their parents might not be able to afford. Sales meetings created enthusiasm. Regular flyers promoting the contests were sent in the carriers' bundles. The results were record-breaking circulation gains, mostly home delivery, which led other newspapers in Pennsylvania.

We also expanded circulation into several more small communities, while solidifying circulation in the core area. We had a 4,000 circulation gain in New Kensington, Arnold, and Lower Burrell in 1955 following six months of delivering free samples to 10,000 homes, a highly unusual investment in the industry. The move was been requested by the New Kensington-area merchants unhappy with the local *New Kensington Dispatch*, which had out-of-town owners. Five years later, the *VDN* purchased the *Dispatch* and renamed the merged papers the *Valley News-Dispatch*. In 1956, the *VDN* purchased the weekly *Butler County News Record* in Zelienople, and an almost-weekly visit to the paper was added to my schedule.

As we were showing the largest-percentage circulation gains in the state almost every year, we instituted another innovative program: hiring local high-school teachers as part-time district managers after school. As an afternoon daily, the program had mutual benefits. We had no problem recruiting teachers and had five at one time.

FOR THE YEARS 1952-53 and again for 1955-57, the International Circulation Managers Association presented me with the ICMA's top award for carrier promotion in the under-25,000 circulation category, "in recognition of a well-conceived and executed newspaperboy program designed to draw public attention to the many opportunities for personal advancement and wholesome character development offered to boys through newspaper route management."

In 1953, I spoke on circulation promotion at the annual meeting of Pennsylvania Newspaper Publishers Association. It was the first of dozens of speeches I gave over the next four decades to trade groups—the American Newspaper Publishers Association, ICMA, ISCMA, and conferences of advertising, promotion, financial, production, and editorial executives around the country.

Chapter 10

■ ■ ■

Important Events

I n 1953, the 200-member Inter-State Circulation Managers Association tapped me to be its sergeant-at-arms for its two conventions a year that rotated among cities in Pennsylvania, Delaware,
Maryland, New Jersey, West Virginia, and Washington, D.C. The
same year, at age twenty-five, I was elected ISCMA's secretary-treasurer, a position I held for twelve years.

The secretary-treasurer ran the association. The position required
a lot of hours and the pay of $500 was miniscule, but the work paid
long-term dividends.

In 1955, I attended a two-week circulation managers' seminar at
the American Press Institute on the campus of Columbia University
in New York City. Founded in 1946, API conducted seminars year-
round for experienced professionals from different departments of
newspapers. Industry leaders led all-day discussions of various topics
in all-day sessions.

My participation at that seminar, my work as secretary-treasurer
of ISCMA, and the *VDN*'s circulation gains earned me an invitation

to lead a discussion of circulation promotion at the circulation managers' seminar in 1958. After canvassing attendees, I summarized everything I could about circulation promotion, drawing from my experience and research, in a booklet for each attendee. From then until 1976 I led the discussions of circulation issues at every API seminar for publishers and editors; for advertising, promotion, circulation, and production managers; and for foreign editors and publishers. By the API's twenty-fifth anniversary I had appeared at forty-nine seminars.

IT WAS MARCH, 1952. The USS *PCE856* was sailing from Philadelphia to Havana, Cuba. I had signed up for this two-week training cruise, my second as a Naval Reserve officer. One day before reaching Havana, Fulgencio Batista seized the government in a revolution. With Cuba unsettled, we were diverted to Miami, not too bad a substitute port of call but still disappointing.

The following March I made it to Havana aboard the *PCE853*. My knowledge of Spanish was the key to becoming the leader of several officers on our movements in Havana with a hired driver. It was a wide-open city with all kinds of vice. Big-time racketeers from the States owned gambling casinos and nightclubs there. We visited a first-class nightclub, the Sans Souci, which was owned by the rackets "chief" of New Kensington. The Pittsburgh Pirates were training at a beach resort.

On the last night, Joe Undercoffler, who was also from Pittsburgh, and I stopped in a local café for a nightcap. The locals were so friendly that we didn't leave until about 4 a.m. with a gift of a bottle of rum. It was a rough departure as we sailed by the Morro Castle—not the sea, but our stomachs and our heads!

In March, 1954, Port-au-Prince, Haiti was the cruise port, this time aboard a destroyer escort. We had to anchor in the bay. The ship was surrounded by small craft with locals hawking all sorts of native goods. A few of us took a motel, toured the city, and ventured into the nearby mountains on a tip that we might find a voodoo ceremony. But it was a false lead. In the early morning, we could hear people trudging by our motel on the way to market. Haiti was very poor.

On the return cruise to Philadelphia, the ship stopped for a day at the U.S. Naval Base on Guantanamo Bay at the southern tip of Cuba. At the time, it was the chief U.S. base for the West Indies. The land on which the base sits had been leased in an agreement with Cuba in 1903 and reaffirmed in 1934. After September 11, 2001, the base became a detention center for accused foreign terrorists and supporters of terrorism.

Training duty in years that followed took us to U.S. ports only—Norfolk, Virginia and Newport, Rhode Island. I was learning little by little. Promotions came on schedule. Weekly drills continued.

INVOLVEMENT IN THE COMMUNITY came easy. I represented the *VDN* in the Tarentum-Brackenridge Rotary Club, the area's leading service club. One project was to organize with the Allegheny Valley Lions and Kiwanis clubs to erect a billboard on Route 28 welcoming travelers as they entered Tarentum. The billboard was still there last time I visited.

Several of us, all in our twenties, organized the Allegheny Valley Junior Chamber of Commerce. The Jaycee members came from a variety of occupations. Several later became heads of local businesses and industrial plants. We organized many social activities, but our major purpose was to serve the community. We sold Christmas trees, staged amateur shows, and raised money for other good works. We painted the homes of elderly people, but on one occasion found ourselves disillusioned. We had been giving up our evenings and a weekend to paint a house when the elderly couple's able-bodied son showed up and proceeded to supervise our work, not realizing we were volunteers.

Meanwhile, baseball remained dear to me. In 1952, I played again for Freeport in the Tri-County League. The next year, the Allegheny Valley Merchants team was organized and I became its player-manager. This entailed signing players, making sure everyone played, using meager gate receipts to buy hamburgers and refreshments after games, and lugging around all the gear in my car. I gave it up at the end of 1954, at age twenty-seven, and never played baseball again.

IN 1956, I TOOK ON additional duties as the *VDN*'s promotion manager and helped promote a two-week trip to six countries in Europe. We became the first U.S. newspaper to sponsor a trip to Europe for its readers and made the trip available to the readers of a suburban Philadelphia weekly as well. More than 200 people flew to London, took a ferry to Holland, then traveled by train along the Rhine River to Lucerne, Switzerland and then on to Milan and Rome before ending in Paris.

Instead of going home immediately, I flew to Asti and Torino to visit all my relatives. It was a joyous reunion with my grandparents in Asti. They both passed away a few years later. Italy had significantly recovered since my visit in 1949.

I had an embarrassing experience at the Rome apartment of Stan Swinton, Associated Press bureau chief for the Mediterranean. While gesturing with my hands, an Italian trait, I knocked over my drink, shattering the glass and spilling brandy onto the varnished floor. A maid was summoned. I apologized. Swinton understood. He even took Gene and me to a swanky restaurant afterward. Many years later, I reminded Swinton of the incident and apologized again. He remembered.

Several newspapers, including a few metropolitan dailies, were interested in knowing more about the trip, especially given the response from so many readers in a small market. Our foreign excursion was a major success, we believed, because it was a logical extension of the domestic trips. Readers of the *Valley Daily News* knew it would be another good experience.

Marcel Duriaux, who organized the European trip, picked up several other newspaper accounts after word got around. Duriaux owned Hemisphere Travel Service in New York. I had worked closely with him on promotions and logistics. He was also the founder of the Society of Editors and Commentators, which conducted trips to foreign countries for publishers, editors, and radio and television station owners for fact-finding and interviews with heads of state and U.S. officials. Gene Simon traveled with him and was among the first American journalists allowed inside Russia after Stalin's death in 1953.

Chapter 11

■ ■ ■

Round-the-World Adventure

A trip around the world in 1958, at age thirty, was the fulfillment of a youthful dream, but in a style far exceeding my wildest expectations. Twenty years earlier, a neighborhood pal and I vowed that someday we would travel the globe. We had in mind working our way aboard a tramp steamer and in other adventurous ways. The boyhood friend drifted away and the realities of earning a living delayed the dream.

Beginning on January 20, 1958, the dream became a reality. I was invited by Marcel Duriaux to be his assistant on a fact-finding trip for newspaper and broadcast executives, mostly from small- and medium-sized markets. For thirty-seven days, we circled the globe meeting and interviewing heads of state in several countries in Europe, the Middle East, and the Far East, mostly newly emerging independent nations and recipients of U.S. aid. Because of my active Naval Reserve status, I had to submit complete details of the cities and contacts on our itinerary to the Fourth Naval District prior to departure.

Duriaux had conducted similar trips to many countries. He was an "unofficial diplomat," having met more world leaders than anyone not in public life. A native of Switzerland, he spoke several languages and had worked for the International Red Cross during World War II, visiting prisoner-of-war camps on both sides of the conflict.

This trip was a unique experience. How lucky could a young guy be? I was a small-city newspaperman. My excitement was intense. My fellow travelers, including Gene, paid upwards of $10,000 each for the trip. I went along without cost, but was expected to earn my way. I did.

Before departing we convened the group in Washington, D.C. for an all-day briefing at the State Department about each country we would visit—the government, the economic and social structure, and relations with the United States as well as an assessment of the communist threat.

This was followed by an overnight flight to Paris, where we met at an afternoon reception with Felix Gaulliard, at thirty-eight the youngest prime minister in France's history. That evening, we met with W. Randolph Burgess, U.S. Ambassador to the North Atlantic Treaty Organization (NATO). Sputnik, the small sphere recently launched by the Soviet Union a few months earlier and the first satellite to orbit the earth, came up as a subject of concern in Paris and elsewhere. Was the United States losing the race to explore outer space?

Pausing in Paris gave us time to shake off "jet lag," although none of the many airlines on which we flew operated jet planes. Most were old DC-3s purchased from U.S. or European carriers.

The trip began in earnest from Paris. After brief stops in Rome and Athens, we arrived at Cairo, Egypt, in the wee morning hours.

A camera bag didn't make it to Shepheard's Hotel. I got no sleep that day. The airline finally found it on the plane. I was learning fast— never again!

My inseparable companions for more than fifteen flights covering 25,000 miles were a hand-operated sound recorder, three cameras and accessories, a brief case filled with passports, and airline tickets.

In addition, Duriaux carried a special satchel with instructions to me, "Never take your eyes off that case, no matter where we are." It contained several thousand U.S. dollars. Guarding it was one of many responsibilities I picked up along the way, but the most important. In each city, I arranged for ground transportation, made sure everyone got a wake-up call, confirmed airline schedules, recorded expenses, and relieved my boss of as many details as possible.

AS WE DISEMBARKED at each airport, our group usually was greeted by a representative of the U.S. Embassy, a staffer from the U.S. Information Service (USIS), a liaison from the host country's foreign ministry, and the inevitable photographer from the local press. Formalities completed, everyone piled into limousines for a ride to the hotel—everyone but me. I had to get all passports stamped, move sixty-four pieces of luggage through customs without being opened, accompany the luggage aboard a truck to the hotel, and then mark room numbers for bellboys to deliver the bags.

For a few anxious hours in Karachi, a publisher's bag disappeared, creating a serious problem for me. The bag did not show up in his room. Turned out the missing bag was delivered to the room of another publisher, who was unaware of the error because after checking in he had stopped in the bar for a couple of hours, as he usually did, on his way to his room.

Cairo was a good introduction to the Middle East and to the Muslim world. A camel ride and tour around the Sphinx and Great Pyramids, ex-King Farouk's palace, the call to prayer several times a day and the sights, smells and sounds of a bustling Arab city were unlike any other place I had ever seen. We had in-depth briefings at the U.S Embassy and enjoyed a reception hosted by Ambassador Raymond Hare.

We met El Hassuna, secretary-general of the Arab League, who emphasized that the "creation of Israel, which displaced a million Arabs in order to solve the Jewish refugee problem, was the biggest obstacle to peace in the Middle East." All these years later, it still is.

The highlight of our visit to Cairo was our meeting with President Gamal Abdel Nasser on a pleasant Sunday afternoon. Nasser, an army officer, led a secret revolutionary group that ousted King Farouk in a bloodless revolution in 1952. Nasser became president in 1954 and negotiated a treaty that got Great Britain out of Egypt after seventy-five years under British rule. He nationalized the Suez Canal in 1956. Britain and France tried to intervene but withdrew under pressure from the United States. Nasser became the most dominant and influential leader in the Arab world, restoring Arab dignity after long humiliation by foreign powers.

That morning started like a cloak-and-dagger drama. President Nasser had not seen a foreign correspondent for several months, but, as grass-roots newspaper executives, we were granted an interview at the Barrage, his country home on the Nile fifteen miles away.

News of the scheduled interview leaked out. The phone in our suite buzzed constantly all morning. Wire services and radio-television reporters were anxious to join us. I had to deny that a meeting was scheduled and say that our boat ride was merely an afternoon outing. No one else had been able to interview Nasser in the days leading up to the Egypt and Syria's formation of the United Arab Republic, a union of the two countries that was announced a few days later. But Duriaux, who met Nasser the year before, managed it. (The UAR dissolved in 1961 after a *coup d'état* in Syria.)

Our group gathered in the garden. I operated the recorder. Nasser was very candid. Key points centered on the U.S. friendship with Israel and the Arab position on Palestinian refugees: "We will push them (Israel) into the sea"; regarding the Arab philosophy: "A friend of our enemy is not our friend," and the U.S. offer of aid to build the Aswan Dam on the Nile, an offer withdrawn when the two countries failed to sign a treaty, forcing Egypt to accept aid from the Soviet Union despite the fact that the Communist Party was outlawed in Egypt.

To emphasize his non-alignment, Nasser surprised us by referring to President George Washington's farewell address warning America not to enter "any entangling alliances." Nasser said that his major challenge was to raise his nation's standard of living and to get better control of the large landowners.

Nasser was one of the most impressive men I ever met. After the interview, he invited us into his home for a delicious lamb dinner. Unfortunately, a photographer I hired for the occasion failed to produce pictures of that dinner. (My duties included hiring a local photographer to supply participants with pictures of themselves with the host dignitary, or to take pictures myself.) On our return to the hotel, correspondents from all the wire services, the *New York Times*, and other major newspapers were on hand for our own press conference. Nasser lamented the lack of favorable U.S. press coverage, claiming that our newspapers were controlled by Jewish owners.

"There are no Arab owners of American newspapers," Nasser told us.

Before leaving Cairo, we toured the famous Egyptian Museum that housed mummies of ancient pharaohs and the famous mask of King Tutankhamun (seen again in Seattle forty years later), visited a steel mill, and dined aboard a Nile riverboat entertained by belly dancers.

WE LANDED IN BAGDAD, Iraq's capital, after a short layover in Beirut, Lebanon, the latter a beautiful city described as the "Paris of the Middle East." Iraq was another recipient of U.S. aid. The country, like most of the Middle East, had been part of the Turkish Ottoman Empire until WWI when it was pieced together by France and Britain to include Kurds in the north, Sunni Muslims in Bagdad and the surrounding area in the middle of the country, and Shiite Muslims in the south. This set the stage for serious ethnic and religious problems later.

Iraq gained its independence in 1932 as a constitutional monarchy, but retained a strong British influence. We met several Iraqi officials, including acting Prime Minister Sayed Amin Al-Mumaiyiz and Nuri as-Said, soon to become the prime minister.

Iraq had its problems, but was stable then and was a U.S. friend, according to the embassy staff. The country was arming itself due to the existence of Israel. In Iraq, as elsewhere in the Arab world, Palestinian refugees were considered the region's most serious problem.

(Iraq's stability was short-lived. In July, 1958, King Faisal, the crown prince, and Nuri as-Said were assassinated in a *coup d'état*. The new leaders were overthrown a few years later by the Baa'th Party, mostly Sunni Muslim, later led by Saddam Hussein. It was not until after U.S. troops invaded Iraq in 2003 that we came to understand the deep, centuries-old divisions among Sunnis, Shiites, and Kurds in the Muslim world, divisions that have led to armed conflicts.)

A side trip to Babylon was something of a surprise. Passing through the dry, barren countryside we came upon a store made from dried mud featuring signs advertising Coca Cola and Pepsi Cola. The ruins of the fabled Gardens of Babylon were a disappointment. The site was not protected. Goats were grazing and children were playing among the ruins. An interesting cultural experience took place at the home of my Iraqi liaison where I filled out some required paperwork. I heard him speaking to his wife in another room, but never saw her. He served the tea himself.

Over cocktails at the embassy party, Bob Atwood, owner of the *Anchorage Times*, made an attractive job offer, which I turned down. Twenty years later, Bob Danzig and I visited Atwood in Anchorage with a Hearst offer to purchase the *Times*. Atwood was not interested. Much later, I consulted for the paper. Atwood was an influential leader in the campaign for Alaska statehood, which was achieved in 1959.

TEHRAN, IRAN—Persian, Shi'ia Muslim, and non-Arab—was different from most of its Arab neighbors. We were greeted with a lunch and tour of *Etelaat*, a leading newspaper that had a daily circulation of 65,000. We received briefings from Ambassador Selden Chapin and representatives of the USIS and U.S. International Aid (USIA) at the Embassy and from several Iranian government officials. Oil production was the driving economic force with the government taking 50 percent of the profits. At that time, the country had nothing to do with the Arab-Israeli conflict.

In Saad Abad Palace, we viewed the crown jewels and met the Shah of Iran, Muhammad Reza Pahlavi. He was an impressive figure, attired in a highly decorated military uniform when he entered the Peacock Throne Room. He stood for a short discussion and greeted each of us with a handshake. In power since 1941, the Shah was ousted briefly and fled the country. He was restored to power in 1953 with the help of the United States and other western powers after dismissing the democratically elected prime minister, Muhammad Mossadegh, who was not friendly with the West and favored nationalizing the western-controlled Anglo-Iranian Oil Co.

(The Shah signed a defense agreement with the United States in 1959. He became more autocratic, increasing his control of the government. The secret police, Savak, suppressed religious activities. Corruption was rampant. Discontent grew. His foreign policy was dependent on the United States. Our ties remained close and our support strong. In 1979, however, he was overthrown and fled to Rome. Ayatollah Khomeini returned from exile to form an Islamic-based government. When the United States admitted the Shah for medical treatment, the U.S. Embassy in Tehran was stormed. Fifty-two Americans were taken hostage and held for 444 days. The hatred by Iran's Islamic regime dates back to 1953 when a U.S.-backed *coup d'état* removed the country's democratically elected prime minister. Tensions were eased slightly in 2016 when the United States and several other nations lifted economic sanctions after Iran agreed to stop its development of its nuclear-arms capability.)

THE FLIGHT TO KARACHI, Pakistan passed over mostly barren, dry, mountainous terrain with a short layover in Kandahar, Afghanistan. I have a vivid memory of a *mujahedeen* with a rifle and

a bandolier of bullets across his shoulder and a small airport termi-
nal with a men's room. No women were permitted. (The isolated,
land-locked country was rarely visited by Americans until September
11, 2001, followed by a U.S. invasion in 2002 and more than fifteen
years of continued conflict—the longest war in U.S. history.)

The ride from the Karachi airport passed through an area that revealed part of the immense refugee problem created by the partition
of India into two countries when Great Britain granted independence
to the region ten years earlier. The Muslims left India. The Hindus
fled the new nation of Pakistan. Both sides of the road were full of
tents and make-shift shelters with goats and cows mingling among
the people, all Muslim refugees.

The bustling port city of Karachi was then the capital of West
Pakistan and East Pakistan. In the partition, Pakistan was split into
two regions with India in the middle. Each side had its own ethnic-
ity, language, and customs. Islam was the only bonding force. The
separation created other serious problems. East Pakistan was the most
densely populated country in the world. It was the size of Florida, but
was home to 45 million people, compared to Florida's population of
4 million. West Pakistan was sparsely populated. (East Pakistan later
split off to become the independent country of Bangladesh).

Most countries we visited in 1958 had stable currency exchanges.
Not true in Pakistan. On a sunny afternoon, Duriaux and I strolled
down Karachi's main street, feeling safe but looking out of place
among many thousands of Pakistanis. Several approached us to buy
a few U.S. dollars at an inflated price paid in rupees. When Duriaux
said he had a few thousand dollars, the big players moved in. A sale
of dollars was made at two to three times the official exchange rate

with the deal to be consummated that evening in our hotel lobby. The hotel bill was paid in cash at the official rate.

In Karachi, as in all other capitals, we started with U.S. Embassy briefings on the political, social, and economic situation, mostly as it related to our aid. We were told that Pakistan, as a new country, was unstable and was being held together by President Iskander Mirza. The country's main problems had to do with education, agriculture, and irrigation. Ambassador James M. Langley hosted a reception to which prominent local leaders had been invited. One of the many small details assigned to me at this and all other receptions was to pinch everyone's elbow as a sign when it was time to leave.

President Mirza met us at his residence. Dressed in formal attire and accompanied by Pakistan's chief justice, the president was on his way to the airport to greet the King of Afghanistan. Pakistan had come dangerously close to war with Afghanistan a few years earlier, but relations were better by 1958. Afghanistan was considered to be pro-Soviet, while Pakistan was an American ally. We witnessed the formalities at the airport. The visiting king was dressed in a fully decorated military uniform.

The next day, we were guests at an air show featuring precision flying by Pakistani Air Force pilots flying U.S.-made jets. This event may have been intended to impress the visiting king and the assembled diplomatic corps, including the ambassador from India—Pakistan's neighbor that was viewed then, as now, with suspicion.

We had a pleasant afternoon discussion with Prime Minister Feroz Khan Noon in the garden of his residence. It was apparent the Pakistanis wanted to impress us. Later, our group participated in a round-table discussion with members of the National Association of

Journalists. Pakistan had a free press and many newspapers, but the high rate of illiteracy kept the circulation very low.

Kashmir came up at briefings and interviews, as it did later in India. Kashmir, a region shared by Pakistan and India divided by religion, was in dispute then and remained an unsettled problem in 2017. Both Pakistan and India wanted U.S. support of its position in the dispute, but our government wisely remained neutral. Our publishers were scheduled to visit Kashmir, but the side trip was canceled due to security concerns. It was the only disappointment of the trip.

THE FIRST SIGHTS OF NEW DELHI, India were an elaborate parade with uniformed horsemen in formation and decorated elephants; the orange-flower decorated slab where Mohandas K. Gandhi was assassinated in 1948, and the historic Red Fort, followed by embassy briefings and a reception hosted by Ambassador Ellsworth Bunker, one of America's top diplomats.

For me, the highlight of the trip was our meeting with Jawaharial Nehru, first prime minister of independent India, a large country where as many as sixteen native languages were spoken. Served tea by six uniformed servants, we were seated in a semi-circle, with Nehru at the head, Duriaux to his right and me to the Duriaux's right holding an earpiece while hand-cranking the sound-recording machine. Nehru wore a long, tan ("Nehru") jacket with a handkerchief tucked into his sleeve and tight, white leggings. He quietly, candidly, and eloquently responded to questions.

It was easy to visualize the leadership qualities and quiet strength of this man whose advocacy for independence as early as 1921 led to his imprisonment by British administrators nine times before independence was achieved in 1947. As prime minister, he established a secular, socialistic democracy, successfully carrying out five-year plans with a policy of peaceful non-aligned co-existence with all nations. The caste system was abolished in the constitution, but it was so deeply a part of India's history and culture that subtle elements remained. We saw a lot of cows, sacred to Hindus, moving freely on the streets.

A bonus was a side trip to Agra and the famous Taj Majal, one of the wonders of the world, on our way to the Punjab region to visit the very high Bhakra Dam, being built under supervision by a leading American engineer. At the construction site, an army of laborers carried buckets of cement up ladders. It was not sophisticated, but it was efficient and provided employment for hundreds of workers. We toured a community training program in Nilokeri, a village where representatives from the hundreds of other villages learned basics of sanitation, mid-wifery, and other services to take back to their villages. A majority of India's 400 million people at that time lived in villages without electricity. (India's population had grown to more than one billion by 2017.)

In India, as in other former British colonies, the high quality of civil-service employees was evident, an inheritance from the British. I was responsible for handling and clearing passports and luggage through customs. As advised, I had to be firm and demanding with customs officials on a few occasions to prevent agents from opening the publishers' bags, for which I had no keys, anyway. The officials responded to an authoritative voice.

WE ARRIVED IN RANGOON, capital of Burma, after a quick stop in Calcutta. At the U.S. Embassy we received briefings from more officials, including Ambassador Walter McConaughy, than in any other country. Burma (now called Myanmar) is 80 percent Buddhist. Under British control for almost a century before gaining independence in 1948, Burma maintained its neutrality, a wise policy given its 1,000-mile border with China. It also shared borders with India, Bangladesh, and Thailand.

At that time, the government was anti-communist. But it did join a program with the Soviet Union in which construction of a hotel, stadium, and hospital were to be repaid with rice, the source of 80 percent of Burma's foreign exchange. Burma was the world's leading rice producer.

The United States loaned Burma $25 million to be repaid in forty years. Our relationship was said to be "harmonious." I had to be careful on the steps leading up to the largest Buddhist temple, the ancient gold-leaf-covered Schwedagon Pagoda, to avoid red betel-juice spit stains. Betel leaves with a nut are the favorite chew in the region. On a memorable side trip north we witnessed the last action of the British Empire in Burma, a turnover of a large memorial and cemetery for British, Burmese, Indian, Australian, and New Zealand soldiers killed in WWII. It was a moving ceremony. We met U Nu, soon to become the prime minister, and several high-ranking British officers. (The city of Rangoon was later renamed Yangon.)

THAILAND, WHERE BUDDHISTS comprise 96 percent of the population, has been a kingdom since 1150. (The *King and I* and *Anna and the King of Siam* were popular American movies.) Unlike most Southeast Asia countries, Thailand was never colonized. Thais were considered the best politicians in Asia. Some unrest and a brief period of martial law ended in 1957. Since then, the country has been stable.

Bangkok, the capital, is the headquarters of South East Asia Treaty Organization (SEATO), which brought together Australia, France, New Zealand, Pakistan, Philippines, Thailand, Britain, and the United States. The organization is pro-western and provided a buffer against a large Soviet presence in the region and heavy barrage of propaganda from China. We met with Pote Sarasin, secretary-general, and were hosted at a reception including representatives of all SEATO partners. We interviewed Prince Wan, acting prime minister and minister of foreign affairs, who reaffirmed his government's friendship with our country. He said the trend in Asia toward democracy was increasing. We met with several embassy staffers but did not meet the ambassador.

The principal Buddhist *wat* (temple) among Bangkok's 400 richly decorated *wats* is the Chapel of the Emerald Buddha within the walls of the Royal Palace. We toured the nearby area with the floating markets, vendors on small boats peddling produce on canals, houses on stilts, and the distinctive architecture of the temples and shrines.

In an unusual switch, our group of interviewers was in turn interviewed by Thai journalists. They were surprised to learn that our newspapers are privately owned and not controlled by political parties. They told us that no newspaper in Thailand could survive without a political subsidy and that some reporters were paid by the parties, too. When we asked a reporter a tough question, he demurred, saying he was not an editor. An editor said he was not a reporter, so we did not get an answer.

WE GOT A SURPRISE on arrival at the famous Raffles Hotel in Singapore. Neighboring Indonesia, across the Malacca Straits, was threatened with revolution. Many of the Dutch, erstwhile colonists, were getting out as quickly as possible, filling Singapore hotels, barricading their rooms, and refusing to leave. We dealt with the shortage of rooms as best we could, but not to everyone's satisfaction.

Singapore, then a British Crown Colony, is at the southern tip of the Malay Peninsula. The population is 80 percent ethnic Chinese. We enjoyed a tea party and briefing at the residence of Governor-General Sir William Goode. U.S. Consul General Avery Peterson provided a good overall description of Singapore. Well planned, well built, and well managed by Britain, Singapore long has been a trading center.

One of the most charismatic men we met on the trip was Lee Kuan Yew, then chief minister. Lee became prime minister when Singapore became independent the year after our visit. In or out of office, Yew was a recognized leader for the next fifty years. He turned his country into an economic powerhouse and a model state. He died in 2015, the last survivor of the leaders we met.

THE FEDERATION OF MALAYA (later renamed Malaysia) gained independence from Britain in 1957 and comprised Malaya, Sarawak, and North Borneo. An Islamic country with religious freedom, its population was 50 percent Malay, 30 percent Chinese, and 10 percent Indian, plus mixed races. It had the lowest illiteracy rate in Southeast Asia. At the time, considerable guerilla activity was being contained in the north. U.S. Ambassador William Byington was a genial host. We met Tegku Abdul Rahman, the first prime minister, at his residence overlooking a manicured multi-colored flower garden. He confirmed his nation's firm friendship with the United States. We enjoyed some free time at the race track. The horses looked the same as those at home. The crowd looked different, but bet and cheered just like Americans do.

UPON ARRIVAL IN SAIGON, South Vietnam, we learned that erratic and unpredictable flights to Hong Kong, our next stop, made it necessary to split our group. After a brief look at Saigon, I escorted eight members to Hong Kong and missed the briefings from U.S. Embassy experts and Vietnamese leaders. During a one-day layover in Manila, Philippines, I hired a small bus for a tour of the city, including stops to see the U.S. Navy ships in Subic Bay and the camp where the Japanese kept American prisoners in WWII.

In Hong Kong, while awaiting the arrival of the other publishers, I couldn't resist ordering a tailor-made suit at the Peninsula Hotel. And then we waited. I had to stall the Miramar Hotel to avoid cancellation of our rooms. The rest of the group was delayed two days and then arrived in a WWII vintage C-47 cargo plane with bucket seats. The U.S. Consulate handled Hong Kong, a British Crown Colony, and Macau, a Portuguese colony, both attached to the mainland and having a majority ethnic Chinese population.

The consulate offered a window into Communist China, with a staff of 150 Americans and a few hundred locals. The consul-general, Everett Drumwright, and his staff experts gave us a full report on China. It was obvious the consulate was monitoring the communist nation closely. The United States did not recognize Communist China and, although Hong Kong offered plenty of products made in China, U.S. citizens were not allowed to bring them home.

No visit to a British Crown Colony is complete without having tea with the British governor-general. Our Hong Kong stay was enlivened by celebrations for the Chinese New Year with lots of fireworks and the constant popping sound of small cherry bombs dropped from apartment windows.

THE REPUBLIC OF CHINA, on the island of Taiwan, was the China that the United States recognized as opposed to the communist "Peoples Republic of China" on the mainland. In our rooms we found several books containing propaganda promising that the Nationalist Chinese would return to the mainland one day. The government was led by Nationalist Chinese who fled the mainland after the communist takeover in 1949. The famous Nationalist Generalissimo, President Chiang Kai-shek, gave us brief handshakes. We interviewed Vice President Chen Cheng and Premier D. K. Yui and lunched with Foreign Minister Sampson Shen.

At the time, ten U.S. agencies operated in Taiwan and 9,000 Americans lived there, according to embassy experts led by Ambassador K.L. Rankin. We had signed a mutual-defense pact and the U.S. Seventh Fleet was ready if needed to protect Taiwan from an invasion by Communist China.

Before departing, the mayor of Taipei, the capital, hosted an elaborate thirteen-course dinner complete with speeches, a dragon dance, and toasts to our respective countries and leaders following a reception hosted by a Taiwanese general and admiral.

WE STOPPED IN OKINAWA to refuel enroute to Japan. The first morning in Tokyo started with an off-the-record briefing by Ambassador Douglas MacArthur II, who resembled his famous uncle, General Douglas MacArthur. He told us the U.S. occupation was in its third phase. First, the war ended in 1945 and the country was occupied with a goal of installing democracy. Second, the occupation ended and sovereignty was re-established. And third, MacArthur told us, was the task of dealing with a sovereign Japan and the economic factors affecting 91 million people. It was the most thorough briefing given to us by any American ambassador.

This was followed by an interview with Air Force Gen. Frederic N. Smith Jr. at the headquarters of U.S. Forces, Japan. He cited military threats facing Japan from several thousand troops in Russia, China, and North Korea, plus the three communist nations' formidable naval power. We now had a stake in the security of Japan, having set up a Japanese constitution that allowed a defensive military only and outlawed Japan from ever going to war again.

After a tour of the Diet (legislature) building we met across the street with Prime Minister Nobusuke Kishi and Foreign Minister Fujiyama. We were given a rare look into the war room where Japan's military leaders plotted the surprise raid on Pearl Harbor. Japan was still rebuilding. The few cars on the streets were all small and designed with the steering wheel on the right. It was a market to be had, but U.S. automakers failed to meet the challenge.

My transportation liaison in Tokyo was Hisashi Ito, a young public-relations officer with Japan Airlines, who escorted Marcel and me on a night-club tour of the famous Ginza District and worked with me to arrange our flight to Honolulu and on to San Francisco on the first flight of a new Douglas plane. (Thirty years later, I had a drink with Ito at the JAL-owned Essex Hotel in New York. Ito was then senior vice president of JAL in charge of all North American operations. Small world!)

HONOLULU WAS THE LAST major stop on our fabulous world tour. Acting Gov. Farrant l. Turner brought us up to date on the movement supporting statehood (achieved in 1960). We toured Pearl Harbor and revisited the eerie underwater graves of U.S. warships. As best I could determine, Aloha Stadium stood on the site of the military barracks where I bunked during my Navy service in 1946. Our final interview was with

Admiral Felix B. Stump, commander-in-chief, Pacific, on Makalapa Hill next to the building where I had worked.

While several of us were relaxing prior to our departure for home, we were joined by the executive officer of CinCPac, Captain William J. Lederer. He asked for our opinions of the U.S. diplomatic personnel in the embassies we visited. Having had many contacts with lower-level embassy staffers, I answered as honestly as possible. I observed that most employees appeared not to have ventured far from the enclaves where they lived with staffers from their own and other embassies. They were mostly Ivy League graduates.

We didn't realize he was conducting research to confirm what he already knew. To my surprise, a best-selling novel, *The Ugly American*, about the failures of fictional U.S. diplomats in a fictional Southeast Asia country, created a stir when it was published a few months later. The authors were Eugene Burdick and William J. Lederer. Lederer had published two other books, *All the Ships at Sea* and *Ensign O'Toole and Me*.

Our entire group was together for the last time on the flight to San Francisco. After goodbyes, everyone headed home. I stayed over for few days to visit Uncle Henry and Aunt Jeannette.

THE TRIP OF A LIFETIME was over. I was so busy during the trip that I didn't come to realize the enormity of my experience until some days later as I returned to everyday life.

The global journey was enriching and deeply satisfying. It opened my eyes to a few realities, too. I observed the diplomatic service at all levels. Although my college years were spent studying for the Foreign Service, I came to understood that Pitt was not a "preferred" college that produced our nation's future diplomats. The preferred colleges were Georgetown, Yale, Harvard, Princeton, and other Ivy League schools. That's where the career foreign-service staffers all seemed to have matriculated.

It was sobering, too, to observe that none had "foreign"-sounding names, with an "i" or "o" ending, like mine. Yet, I was convinced that my humble background and upbringing as a first-generation American gave me an understanding of other peoples that would have been an asset to my country.

At any rate, the lack of openings in the diplomatic service in 1950 turned out to be a blessing in disguise. I never regretted my decision to become a newspaperman.

Domenico and Carolina Fassio hold their son Virgil
and daughters Christina and Ida, 1928.

The author entered Pittsburgh's South Hills High School at a ninth-grader
1941, not long before the United States entered World War II. In 1945,
after a semester at the University of Pittsburgh, he joined the U.S. Navy and
was assigned to a communications unit near Pearl Harbor, Hawaii.

The author was a catcher for the University of Pittsburgh Panthers in 1945, 1948, and 1949. He caught for grade-school, sandlot, high-school, college, Navy, and semi-pro teams until age twenty-seven.

Virgil Fassio served twenty-one years in the U.S. Navy and
Naval Reserve, retiring with the rank of commander.

Virgil Fassio, center, with Indiana newspaper publisher Joseph Nixon
and the Shah of Iran, Muhammed Reza Pahlavi, in Tehran in 1958.
The author accompanied a delegation of U.S. publishers who toured the
world visiting U.S. allies and countries receiving American aid.

The author records Marcel Duriaux's interview of Jawaharlal Nehru, first prime minster of India in New Delhi in 1958.

Chapter 12

■ ■ ■

Wilmington News & Journal

By 1958, the *Valley Daily News* circulation reached 25,000, a gain of more than 10,000 in seven years. Several other newspapers noted the *VDN* growth and started to show interest in what we were doing. That year, I accepted a position as circulation manager of the *Morning News* and *Evening Journal* in Wilmington, Delaware.

I thoroughly enjoyed my eight years with the *VDN*. It was difficult to leave. With about 100 employees, everyone knew everyone else. No politics. It was a big, happy family, with no social barriers among bosses, underlings, and departments. Many of my fellow employees retired after a life-long career there. I can remember their names and faces, more so than on any other paper except the *Seattle Post-Intelligencer*.

My successor, Marty Corso, remained a close friend until his passing. Danny Angeloni and I got together when I was in Pittsburgh. I attended a few *VDN* retiree luncheons after many years and still recognized most of the former employees. Gene Simon became my closest friend of all through the years.

THE *WILMINGTON MORNING NEWS* and *Evening Journal* were owned by Christiana Securities, the holding company of the Du Pont family. A representative of Whitlock & Company, which promoted magazines in combination with home-delivered newspapers, had been asked by Fred Walter, general manager of the News-Journal Co., to inquire about my availability. The two newspapers had conducted their first tie-in sales campaign and did not achieve the expected results. Several similar promotions at the *Valley Daily News* yielded solid circulation gains.

I had returned from the around-the-world trip at the end of February and settled back into my job as *VDN* circulation and promotion manager. The Wilmington offer came in July. I was torn between my high regard for Gene, my boss, and the opportunity to advance to a much larger operation with a higher salary. Gene didn't want me to go, but admitted years later that he knew it would happen eventually. Years later, after retiring, I visited his ranch in New Mexico several times.

Wilmington, population 80,000, was a manufacturing and commercial center on the Delaware River with an important seaport. E.I. Du Pont de Nemours Co., the chemical giant, was the major employer. For most of the twentieth century, the Du Pont family owned two Delaware newspapers. The *Morning News* and *Evening Journal* had been consolidated in 1919 when feuding factions of the family reconciled, forming the News-Journal Co. and Christiana Securities.

Delaware was the least-populated state in the union, with fewer than 550,000 residents, and the second smallest—only ninety-six miles long and thirty-six miles wide with southern beaches on the Atlantic Ocean. The "First State" (its motto) to ratify the Constitution, Delaware joined the Union in the Civil War, but was considered to be part of the South. It had many Confederate sympathizers and was a slave state until 1865.

THE EXECUTIVE EDITOR of the *N-J* papers when I joined as circulation manager in August, 1958 was Fendall Yerxa. Department heads met weekly in the office of Publisher Charles Lee Reese Jr. to report on their operations and discuss ways to improve and better serve the market. Yerxa was an excellent editor and managed a fine news staff on both papers. He left about a year later to become executive editor of the *New York Herald-Tribune*. (We were to meet again in 1976 in Seattle where Yerxa was a journalism professor at the University of Washington and a television news commentator.)

People in the newspaper business tended to move around. It was not unusual to encounter former associates off and on during your career. (Yerxa's son, Rufus, was a young boy when he and his father and I worked together in Wilmington. By 1991, Rufus Yerxa had become the deputy U.S. trade representative in the George H. W. Bush Administration. He spoke to the annual meeting of Washington Council on International Trade in Seattle when I was the council's vice president.)

Fendall Yerxa's successor in Wilmington was Creed Black, an experienced editor. Except for attending annual executive dinners hosted by the owners, I had no contact with any of the Du Ponts. The family is said to have regularly applied pressure on the editor to slant news stories in favor of the family or Republican politics (or, conversely, to ignore bad news about them) and complained about favorable coverage of Democrats. Creed, a pugnacious and persistent editor, adamantly refused to slant the news. He resigned in 1964 when the Du Ponts sent a public-relations executive from the DuPont Co. to become his new boss in charge of the news operation.

The *N-J* papers did not print Creed's resignation letter, but the Philadelphia papers and trade publications did. I was sorry to see him go. We shared many ideas for improving the papers. Creed later became publisher of the Lexington, Kentucky *Times-Leader*, a Knight-Ridder newspaper. He had a distinguished career and was recognized by his peers with leadership roles in the industry.

None of this interfered with my job: to build circulation of the *Morning News*, at 29,500, and *Evening Journal*, at 69,000. Both had been stagnant for several years. Until the *Delaware State News* was launched in the capital at Dover in 1959, the *MN* and *EJ* were the only dailies published in Delaware.

A MAJOR HANDICAP was the American Newspaper Guild. Ours was the only newspaper in the country in which the guild represented only the circulation department, a situation created by poor management. Also unique was a thirty-five-hour work week, which was covered by three supervisors, nine *Morning News* and fifteen *Evening Journal* district managers, and the six country roadmen. All had to be convinced that motivating young carriers to become salesmen as well as delivery boys was a key part of their job. A few never should have been hired but, with union protection, they were not easy to dismiss. Over time, some were fired, however, more for dishonesty than for incompetence.

I always had the facts and was never reversed in several grievance meetings where the employees were represented by a guild representative from Philadelphia.

Personnel Director Carl Slabach was instrumental in testing applicants and finding better replacements who, once hired, received special, individualized training from me. Born and raised in Pennsylvania Dutch country, Slabach became a close friend and was the only colleague I kept in touch with after leaving Wilmington. We enjoyed the race tracks, Brandywine Raceway (harness racing) and Delaware Park (thoroughbreds), never betting, winning, or losing much. We golfed occasionally, but I never broke 100 in my life. We were on the same team in the *N-J* Bowling League. My *bocce* experience as a boy was only slightly helpful at the bowling alley. But bowling was a good way to become better acquainted with employees in other departments.

Under my management, costs were reduced in most areas, including the two unionized mail rooms and in transportation, which was handled by independent truckers.

The seven-hour-a-day schedule limited carrier contact. I frequently rode with a *MN* district manager before 6 a.m. and with an *EJ* district manager after school to meet and talk with their carriers. The most popular carrier incentives were trips to the New York World's Fair (1964-65), outings to see the Philadelphia Phillies and Eagles and Baltimore Orioles play, and field trips to Washington, D. C. District sales standings were posted for all to see and special incentives were created for district managers, especially a major crab feast. A monthly newspaper, the *Carrier Express*, featured news about carriers and offered sales tips. The entire staff was invited to Christmas parties each year.

We built motor-route delivery routes by sampling every home on roads with at least five houses to the mile. I sometimes did this myself with a boy helper. By the time I left in 1965, we delivered *N-J* papers everywhere in the state's three counties—Newcastle, Kent, and Sussex. We had begun to show substantial year-over-year gains. The

99,000 total circulation of both papers in 1958 increased steadily. In the meantime, we conducted a readership survey, which helped identify readers' interests. One result was the addition of a new community-spotlight feature that profiled a different Delaware city or town each week.

We made a major decision to take back the responsibility for sales of our papers from independent distributors in suburban areas and in cities and towns south of Wilmington. The distributors had been handling all newspapers coming into their areas, not just ours. Because revenue from sale of the *N-J* papers covered most of the distributor's overhead, we were making it possible for the *Philadelphia Inquirer* and *Philadelphia Bulletin* to ride on our coattails, so to speak, building considerable daily and Sunday circulation in Delaware at relatively low cost. After we installed our own carrier-salesmen, we promoted to these areas directly and soon increased circulation.

One unusual role for the circulation department was to assist the news department in covering elections when the *News-Journal* conference room became the Delaware headquarters for tabulating unofficial state and national results on election night. Having built a carrier organization covering every town in the state, circulation became involved in the vote-counting effort in 1960. We paid our most reliable carrier-salesmen to copy results posted on the doors of polling stations and to phone the numbers to our office. It was a good system. A news department intern who worked with us was John Craig, who later became editor of the *Pittsburgh Post-Gazette.*

IN 1960, I WAS APPOINTED one of several delegates from Delaware to the 1960 White House Conference on Children and Youth. Among the 7,000 delegates were many advocates of more stringent regulation of youth employment, particularly work as newspaper carriers. Minimum carrier age in most states was twelve for boys and sixteen for girls, though few girls delivered papers at that time. Most carriers were independent contractors. As a recognized spokesman for newspaper-route management and a strong believer in the benefits of the work experience for young people, I was determined to make every effort to forestall further regulations.

Representing the Inter-State Circulation Managers Association (ISCMA), I contacted several other regional associations to ask for their help in two ways: first, to try to get at least one circulation manager in each state appointed to serve on his state's appropriate children and youth organization, if any, and, second, to ask every newspaper in the country to report the number of young people delivering its papers. We established that more than 1 million youngsters delivered newspapers every day in the United States. I was appointed to the board of the National Council of Organizations for Children and Youth representing International Circulation Managers Association (ICMA). The association met several times during the 1960s.

This work earned me the ICMA President's Award at the association's convention In Miami in June, 1964. This led to a meeting with Cresap, McCormick, and Paget, a head-hunting firm in New York City, regarding an opening for circulation director of the *New York Daily News*, the largest newspaper in the country with 2 million daily and 3 million Sunday circulation. I spent an interesting day with several principals of the consulting firm, but the job went to the circulation director of the *Los Angeles Times*. Frankly, this was no disappointment. The *News* had problems with the drivers' union, which was reputed to be controlled by organized crime.

In Wilmington, I usually worked six days a week. My work as secretary-treasurer of ISCMA involved preparing a program with advertising for two conventions a year, a followup report of the convention proceedings, and a bimonthly newsletter; collecting dues, maintaining minutes and financial records, and later selecting the members who went through the chairs to the presidency, particularly recognizing men from small as well as metropolitan papers. Large or small, each operation was different and I always learned something in these contacts with other circulation executives.

I CONTINUED IN THE NAVAL RESERVE with weekend drills, two weeks of annual training duty, cruises at sea, and correspondence courses. All this time, I had a mobilization assignment in case of a call-up to active duty: security officer at the Naval Amphibious Base in Little Creek, Virginia. I never got the call.

In 1963, I drove my 1960 Rambler (a lemon) to Norfolk for two weeks of duty aboard a large supply ship. On arrival, I learned the ship was not sailing into and out of Norfolk, as anticipated, but instead was going to Newport, Rhode Island. Further, as an unneeded reserve lieutenant commander, I was being detailed to the USS *Sheldrake*, a geodetic survey vessel, which was also going to Newport. The *Sheldrake* needed an outside observer for annual competitive drills and exercises. But my car was in the wrong place. The problem was solved when the supply ship hoisted my Rambler onto the top deck for transport to Newport. I gave satisfactory marks to the *Sheldrake* for damage control, abandon-ship drills, and fire-fighting exercises, but needed the expertise of chief petty officers every step of the way.

A reserve cruise in January, 1964 was spent at sea for the entire two weeks aboard a destroyer, the USS *Hood*, out of the Brooklyn

Navy Yard. I understood that the regular pinging we heard had to do with our training mission to track our own submarines. I later learned that the underwater noises we heard were from Soviet submarines. The Soviets tracked our subs, too.

The same cruise cured me of smoking, a habit acquired when I was fifteen. I quit on January 1, barely beating the first Surgeon General's warning that linked smoking with lung cancer, and went to sea ten days later. I was assigned as junior officer of the deck. The watch OD was a chain-smoker. Every time he lit up, I got nauseous and headed out of the pilot house to the wings of the bridge. It was freezing. The destroyer was pitching and rolling in high seas. I never smoked again!

In late 1963, I was promoted from executive officer to commanding officer in charge of ten officers and 150 enlisted men in NR Division 4-1, an unusual assignment for someone who never served a day of active duty as an officer, except for annual training duty.

On November 22, 1964, my mother, sixty-two, collapsed and died of a heart attack while watching television at home in Pittsburgh with my sister, Christina. There were no warning signs that we knew about. It was a painful loss.

Everything was running smoothly at the *N-J*. I had learned to deal and negotiate with two unions while managing sixty employees, including many hired after a careful screening. We became aggressively sales-oriented. Combined circulation of 99,000 in 1958 increased to almost 130,000 by mid-1965, despite a price increase from seven to ten cents per copy. Almost everyone in Delaware had easy access to the *Wilmington Morning News*, as did residents of nearby counties in Pennsylvania, New Jersey, and Maryland. The *Evening Journal*, meanwhile, covered the city and close-in suburbs like a blanket.

I had handled many challenges in Tarentum and Wilmington and was ready to face bigger challenges. I was not looking for another job, but one found me.

Chapter 13

■ ■ ■

Detroit and the *Free Press*

Detroit was a frontier town in 1703 with a population of 2,500, one of few settlements in Michigan Territory. By 1965, Detroit had become one of America's largest cities with a population of more than 1 million. It called itself the Automotive Capital of the World. The car was king in Detroit and much of Michigan. The industry was booming. The Big Three—Ford, General Motors, and Chrysler— firmly believed that Americans still wanted big, luxurious cars. They did not take seriously the new threat posed by the smaller, well-built cars imported from Japan and Korea.

Detroit was the headquarters of the United Auto Workers, which played one auto-maker against the others in negotiations and was prone to strike to achieve its objectives. The UAW did not recognize the Asian imports as a threat, either.

Detroit was also headquarters of the International Brotherhood of Teamsters. Teamster Local 372, an autonomous newspaper union, had separate contracts with the morning *Detroit Free Press* and the *Detroit News*, a larger evening paper. There were some separate craft-union contracts, but several had joint contracts with both newspapers.

The *Detroit Free Press* was founded in 1831 as the weekly *Democratic Free Press* and *Michigan Intelligencer*. It became a daily two years later. During the Civil War, the *Free Press* established itself as the primary source of battlefield news and was one of the founders of the Western Associated Press, which later became the Associated Press, the world's largest news-gathering agency.

JOHN S. KNIGHT AND ASSOCIATES, including his younger brother, James L. Knight, bought the *Free Press* for $3.2 million on April 30,` 1940 and immediately set out to transform the *Press* from a paper once described by a critic as a "tired institution in its coverage and presentation of news" with "editorials that were out of step with the times" into an aggressive, politically independent paper that has been recognized as one of the country's best newspapers ever since. John Knight had been editor when he inherited the *Akron Beacon-Journal* from his father in 1933. He bought the *Miami Herald* in 1937.

At three Knight Newspapers and several other papers acquired over the years, Knight gave local editors considerable freedom from central authority. He wrote his "Editor's Notebook" column every Sunday and won a Pulitzer Prize in 1968 for his columns about the Vietnam War. Knight was careful to keep the news and business departments separate. He believed a newspaper should be profitable. A profitable newspaper is a good newspaper, he believed, and a good newspaper will be profitable.

Detroit had three daily newspapers: the Hearst-owned *Detroit Times*, the locally owned *Detroit News*, and the *Free Press*, which was third in circulation when Knight stepped in. By 1945, the *Free Press* circulation had gained 79,000 daily and 108,000 Sunday to take the lead. Advertising also showed steady gains. Knight had made it a point to visit key business leaders in town.

LEE HILLS BECAME executive editor of the *Free Press* in 1951. The paper was in second place at that time, trailing the *Detroit News* circulation by 12,000. The period from 1951 until December, 1960, when the *Detroit Times* closed, was the most exciting time in *Free Press* history and saw creation of a "new" newspaper. The paper embraced technological changes and waged an aggressive circulation battle. In *On Guard: A History of the Detroit Free Press*, by Frank Angelo, Hills was described as an "intensely single-minded man, one who is committed to reaching journalism's highest peak."

Hills joined the *Miami Herald* in 1946 as managing editor and won two Pulitzer Prizes. He and John Knight developed a close relationship. Hills was an outstanding journalist with a good business sense. He became publisher of the *Free Press* several years later. In 1967, he became the first person outside of the Knight family to serve as president of Knight Newspapers Inc. and in 1971 became its chairman and chief executive officer. In 1974, he became the first chairman and CEO of the newly merged Knight-Ridder Newspapers Inc., with the largest daily circulation of any newspaper group in America.

The fierce Detroit circulation war took a major turn in 1960. Rumors had been rampant that Hearst was planning to close the unprofitable *Detroit Times*. Tade Walsh had succeeded Roy Hatton, *Free Press* circulation director from 1905 to 1959. Walsh and his staff had been working with circulation people at the *Times* on a joint project. They knew each other. Both papers viewed the *News* as their competitor, rather than each other. Several key circulation supervisors and district managers were assured the *Free Press* would hire them if the *Times* folded. It was expected the *News* would buy assets, including the circulation lists, without hiring the people.

All departments of the *Free Press* had long planned for battle and were ready to respond quickly when Frank Angelo, managing editor, got a call at 3:15 a.m. on Monday, December 7, 1960 reporting that all *Detroit Times* employees had received telegrams informing them that they no longer had jobs.

The *Free Press* immediately hired a number of newly unemployed *Times* staffers, including some writing stars as well as circulation people. A key figure in bringing over *Times* circulation people was Bob Cullinan. Many *Times* district managers brought their carriers and subscriber lists with them. The *News* thought it had purchased all the assets. As the only afternoon paper, the *News* picked up most of the *Times'* afternoon readers and took over a substantial circulation lead.

The *Detroit News* was founded in 1873 by James Scripps. The *News* later bought other competing newspapers in 1919 and 1921 before buying the *Times*. The *News* was owned by the Booth family, descendants of Scripps. Other Booth Newspapers in Michigan were in Ann Arbor, Battle Creek, and Grand Rapids. The *Free Press* had circulation in all three cities.

THE FREE PRESS WAS RANKED eighth largest among 1,750 U.S. newspapers in 1965. It was the only morning paper among thirty-nine dailies in Michigan, a statewide paper with home delivery in all forty-seven counties in the Lower Peninsula, several in the Upper Peninsula, and Windsor and other towns in nearby Canada. Its primary market were the counties of Wayne, Oakland, Macomb,

Livingston, Washtenaw, and Monroe. This was the big leagues. Like all morning papers, it was strong in the outlying areas and did not have to deal with the unique transportation problems that challenged evening papers. The evening *Detroit News* was stronger in the more populated areas of the city and suburbs, which gave it the lead in advertising, common then in cities with both a morning and evening paper.

Chapter 14

■   ■   ■

An Exciting New Job

I was intrigued when Mike Tynan, circulation director of the *Miami Herald*, called me in Wilmington to confirm my attendance at the upcoming June, 1965 ICMA convention in St. Louis. John B. "Jack" Olson, general manager of the *Detroit Free Press*, wanted to meet me there. I met Jack and liked him immediately. We were on the same page.

The next step was to meet in Detroit with Lee Hills, publisher of the *Free Press*. That went well. Hills was impressed with my ability to converse with his wife, Tina, who was fluent in Italian and Spanish. I was impressed with them and liked everything I heard and saw.

By this time, my long-range career goal was to be a general manager. I liked my job at the *News-Journal*, but knew that my goal would never be reached in Wilmington.

I joined the *Detroit Free Press* as circulation director on August 1, 1965. I succeeded Al Korach, who decided to retire in his mid-50s after only a few years as circulation director. A good supervisory organization was in place, led by Bob Cullinan, the best assistant circulation director I could possibly have. Bob was a few years older and a veteran of the Detroit newspaper wars. Together we made a good team. He came to the *Free Press* with several men who were some of my best supervisors when the afternoon Hearst-owned *Detroit Times* folded. Tade Walsh, who died in a car accident a few years later, recruited them and several district managers when the *Times'* closure was imminent. He had outfoxed the *Detroit News*.

The *Free Press* contract with Teamsters Local 372 covered more than 460 district managers, drivers, and helpers to work with 7,000 carriers. State roadmen were not covered. The forty clerks in the circulation office all were members of the American Newspaper Guild, which also covered the news, advertising, and business departments. The Detroit papers had fourteen separate local unions negotiating twenty-three contracts. A strike in 1964 lasted 134 days. Detroit was a tough union town.

The first big hurdle I faced at the *Free Press* was to overcome the skepticism of many of the veterans. They didn't see how a young guy from a much smaller operation could possibly handle the tough competitive battle in Detroit. I welcomed the challenge.

In my first two months, I visited every division office in the city and suburban departments and met every one of the more than 300 district managers, relief men, and promotion men in the six-county primary market area. I outlined some of my objectives and sought their feedback.

Then Jack Olson and I visited with each of our nine out-state roadmen and with independent and combination agencies in the Lower Peninsula and north to the Upper Peninsula. In Sault Ste. Marie, on the Canadian border, our agent sold to sailors on ships passing through the river locks. We crossed the Detroit River to

Windsor, Ontario, where we had good circulation. Everyone welcomed my visit. The "boss" was communicating directly with them. My predecessors had been desk-bound.

FOR THE SIX MONTHS ending September 30, 1965, *Free Press* circulation averaged 509,000 daily and 555,000 Sunday, trailing the evening *Detroit News* by 189,000 daily and 374,000 Sunday. In my first year, the Free Press gained more than 29,000 daily and 25,000 Sunday while the *Detroit News* gained fewer than 1,899 subscribers daily and 19,000 Sunday. The battle was on. It was great fun. The gap narrowed thereafter.

The Audit Bureau of Circulation's publisher's statements for the year ending September 30, 1967 showed the *Free Press* with the best year-over-year gains in the United States. (Numbers are rounded.) We gained more than 53,000 daily and 51,000 Sunday, reducing the *News* lead to 110,000 daily and 320,000 Sunday. By November 17, when a strike started, *Free Press* circulation passed 600,000. The *Detroit News* fired its long-time circulation director. He was hired as an assistant at the *Boston Globe* and was known to tell people that the guy at the *Free Press* had cost him his job.

A NEWSPAPER'S CIRCULATION success requires three things: first, a good newspaper that meets the needs and wants of its community and attracts and holds readers; second, a competent circulation sales and service staff; and third, the cooperation and coordination of all departments working together as a team.

The *Free Press* was a good newspaper that got even better. In January, 1966, while Frank Angelo was managing editor, the assistant managing editor in charge of news, Derrick Daniels, developed a new front-page feature called "Action Line." The interactive column was a place where readers could voice complaints about city hall or just about anything else, with the newspaper promising to "solve problems, get answers, cut red tape, and stand up for your rights." The column was an overnight success. The paper was deluged with phone calls and an Action Line staff was quickly assembled. It became a model for the industry and remained on the front page of the *Free Press* until 1980 when it was moved inside.

Other factors contributed to our spectacular growth. Most big-city circulation chiefs grew up on their papers, frequently in only one part of the operation. They accepted the status quo and the role of "experts." I had fourteen years on small- and medium-sized papers where I learned the entire operation and, figuratively speaking, frequently had to look in the mirror to see who was going to perform a task. I didn't have to be quite so hands-on at the *Free Press*. The paper had a capable, experienced organization.

The dock dispatchers were the experts, handling more than 110 drivers and the truck runs, which had grown over the years. The names assigned to each run were confusing, so we mounted a wall-sized map of our six main counties and assigned an intern to trace every run, inserting pins to indicate each stop. As suspected, it was a mess. Truck runs often overlapped and traveled the same routes. The changes we made saved money and improved efficiency and speed. So much for "experts."

MONEY WAS THE BEST INCENTIVE of all. The Teamster contract provided for commissions to district managers for each paper sold in his district above a base salary and car expenses. Except for single-copy managers in downtown Detroit, all city and suburban district managers were responsible for their own distribution to carriers, honor boxes, and stores. When a district position vacated due to retirement or resignation, the job was open for bid on a seniority basis, as were positions in any new district created because an older district grew too large and needed to be split. Managers affected by the split were guaranteed their previous commission for a short time while heavy promotion was dedicated to regaining their previous circulation.

Hours worked were no problem because the incentive was more money. Relief men covered the two days off each week and shared in the commission. These were all well-paid jobs. We organized more carrier sales contests than ever before, similar to those in Tarentum and Wilmington, but on a bigger scale.

Any major changes in working conditions had to be discussed with the union. I believed that district managers should have more time to work with carriers. We took street sales (stores and racks) and bundle distribution from most city districts, creating home-delivery-only districts and adding truck runs, all at no added cost. Because most factories had three shifts, the *Free Press* had many unique City Edition districts delivering to homes between 8-9 p.m. Conversion to morning, one district at a time, had begun. We converted the last 31,000 homes after retaining 80 percent for morning delivery. Many became single-copy buyers. In many city and all suburban districts, it was practical to keep the existing system of single-copy distribution.

We changed nine state combination distributors to *Free Press* only. An apartment-manager incentive program was started. We stepped up the Metropolitan Club program in which we partnered with local service clubs, firefighters, and social agencies, using our own solicitors and paying the organization a commission for each new customer. An independent telephone solicitor covered areas at the district manager's request, offering two weeks of free samples of the paper with a call to subscribe. A supervisor was in charge of boy crews.

These were among special sales programs that produced new readers, but the most important of all were our incentive programs directed at the carriers—trips, prizes, and cash. All these programs were ongoing, adding circulation.

The daily and Sunday *Free Press* were excellent, well-promoted editorial products. Editor Frank Angelo was a native Detroiter. If anyone could be called "Mr. Detroit," it was Angelo. He knew the market better than anyone. Dave Henes was one of the industry's best-known promotion directors and served as a president of the International Promotion Managers Association. (Dave later retired to the Phoenix area. We got together on my visits to Arizona for Seattle Mariners' spring training. Angelo and Henes both remained close friends.).

Like most industrial centers, Detroit was considered a lunch-bucket city where an afternoon paper was preferred because many blue-collar workers found it convenient to read their home-delivered newspaper late in the day after work. Retail and office workers, on the other hand, had reading time at home in the morning or bought a copy on their way to their work where a paper was often read by several people.

However, the trend was shifting in Detroit. The morning *Free Press* was gaining steadily against the afternoon *News*.

Chapter 15

■ ■ ■

Riot, Strike, and Recovery

On Sunday, July 23, 1967, all hell broke loose in Detroit's densely populated black neighborhoods. I had been away from the office all day and was heading downtown at six-thirty for dinner when I learned of the riot on the radio. The unrest started when police raided a "blind pig," an illegal liquor speakeasy, and made eighty arrests. Snipers were reported to be firing at cars from bridges over the freeways. Looting was reported. Hundreds of stores were set on fire. The rioting spread five miles from the speakeasy and 800 people were arrested the first day.

I immediately drove to the Free Press. Drivers had loaded several trucks with the State Edition for transfer to long-range contract haulers for deliveries as far as 400 miles north. The presses were running, but the trucks were not moving out. Elton Schade, secretary-treasurer of Teamster Local 372, was telling the drivers not to leave the plant, citing the danger from snipers and rioters.

I picked out a driver who was respected by the others and told him I personally would lead convoys out of the city on three major freeways. If snipers were waiting, my Cadillac would be the first target. The driver encouraged the others to follow me. I led convoys of trucks out the three major freeways looking out for snipers and rock-throwers, but not seeing any. This may have seemed like grand-standing, but the papers had to get out. In any event, my action earned the employees' respect and paid dividends in future labor relations.

Minority leaders were unable to stop the riot. Martial law was declared and a curfew enforced. Gov. George Romney (Mitt Romney's father) sent in the Michigan Army National Guard and President Lyndon Johnson responded to calls for help by dispatching 4,700 paratroopers of the 82nd and 101st Airborne Divisions from Fort Campbell, Kentucky. We were unable to distribute papers in the riot areas. City Editor Neal Shine borrowed an armored vehicle from the Chrysler Corp., making it possible for *Free Press* reporters to roam the streets in relative safety as looting and gun battles continued for a week.

The final accounting was grim: 43 deaths, mostly innocent victims; more than 1,100 injuries, 7,200 arrests, 2,000 buildings destroyed, and damages totaling between $45-50 million. The *Free Press* published profiles of each victims. The paper won a Pulitzer Prize in 1968 for its excellent coverage.

The rioters looted and burned several chain stores, which they believed had been charging higher prices in the black neighborhoods than they did elsewhere in the city. *Free Press* district offices were not damaged and few of our news racks were. The *Detroit News*, on the other hand, sustained damages at some offices, and many of its news racks vandalized. The *Free Press* was viewed as a liberal newspaper. The *News* was conservative. It appeared the rioters had shown their preferences.

Detroit became a different city. Not integrated, the black and white sections became more polarized. Once safe for everyone, many neighborhoods were no longer safe. Some district managers and carriers were robbed. Home delivery of either newspaper could not be sustained in some areas, even with adult carriers. The white flight to the suburbs accelerated. The *Free Press* reached an all-time high of more than 600,000 daily subscribers by November 1, overcoming the minor losses in the riot area.

IN EARLY NOVEMBER, 1967, a *Detroit News* district manager was murdered in a district office. Morale was already low and sank even lower when some of the *News* brass did not attend the manager's funeral. On November 15, the *News'* contract with Teamster Local 372 expired. Secretary-treasurer Elton Schade, just twenty-seven years old and having ambitions to be another Jimmy Hoffa, called a strike against the *News* for midnight, alienating the other newspaper unions and drawing a sharp reprimand from leaders of the International Teamsters.

When the craft unions, which had joint contracts with both papers, failed to cross the picket lines, the *Free Press* closed down and laid off all union employees. We retained more than forty managers, supervisors, and other key employees in the circulation department. We stayed busy. We did not want to lose anyone.

While the Teamsters voted to strike at the *News*, Teamsters at the *Free Press* did not. Working under a separate contract with Local 372 that also expired November 15, *Free Press* teamsters rejected a motion to strike. This was a vote of confidence in our leadership. As department heads, Bob Cullinan and I considered it important to visit employees at funeral homes to offer condolences when family members died. We remembered what this had meant to us in the past. The employee did not forget, either. This was a practice I followed on both previous papers.

The strike lasted for 267 days. All unions settled at the same time. It was the longest U.S. newspaper strike on record. Both newspapers resumed publication on August 9, 1968. Bob and I were on the *Free Press* team negotiating the Teamsters contracts. The *News* representative was Leo Kelly, the paper's assistant circulation director. Leo was passed over for the top job, which he deserved to have. We became friends. A year later, I recommended him for circulation director at Knight's *Akron Beacon-Journal*. We stayed in regular contact and always got together at ICMA meetings.

DURING THE SHUTDOWN, division supervisors in city and suburban areas repaired, painted, and spruced up sixty-four district offices, painted the *Free Press* presses, and reached out to their people. Most district managers kept in contact with their carriers, too, even though the managers were not being paid and the carriers were idle. Letters also went to carriers. State roadmen established additional sales outlets, solicited subscribers, set up tubes for new motor routes, and split several agencies. Reader insurance stayed in effect and bills for premiums went sent as usual—a big help in keeping track of readers who moved during the strike. I also wrote a new manual for district managers.

The biggest project, completed with the expert cooperation of the Data Processing Department, was to computerize the distribution system. Soon ours was the most sophisticated system in the industry.

While we moved ahead in all areas as best we could during the shutdown, we learned that the *News* had done virtually nothing, apparently just waiting out the strike. *News* losses were heavy. Morale was low. Management and the union distrusted one another. On the other hand, morale at the *Free Press* was good.

A few days before startup, we invited all field personnel to a breakfast. About 80 percent of the 300 invitees attended. There was no ill feeling about the nine-month layoff. The employees knew it had been caused by their counterparts at the *Detroit News*. Their enthusiasm to get back was encouraging. They wanted to beat the *News*. They were happy with their newly spiffed-up district offices. We hit the ground running, offering many incentives that helped get us back to pre-strike circulation in five months. Meanwhile, the home-delivery price was increased from fifty to sixty cents a week. Sunday was increased to thirty cents. We were ready for the circulation battle we knew was coming.

THE ABC CIRCULATION FIGURES for the strike-shortened period ending September 30, 1968, compared to September 30, 1967, showed *Free Press* daily circulation at 530,000, a 60,000 loss, and at 578,000 on Sunday, a decline of 53,000. Reader-insurance participation dropped 33,000, to 142,000. The *News* lost 108,000 daily and 120,000 Sundays. The circulation gap between the two papers shrank to 62,000 daily and 249,000 on Sunday.

Free Press losses would have been much greater if the Detroit Tigers had not had a winning season. Typically, in most years, the beginning of baseball season brought about a 10,000 daily and Sunday increase. Due to the strike, it was difficult to measure accurately the increase in 1968. The Tigers were on their way to winning the American League pennant, their first since 1940, and went on to beat the St. Louis Cardinals in a thrilling seven-game World Series.

The pent-up emotions of a city that revered its sports teams burst out. Detroit went wild. It needed the win after the riots and months without coverage of area sports. Some feeble attempts were made by others to publish papers during the strike and out-of-town papers increased their penetration into our market, but none satisfied readers.

The *Free Press*, like all morning newspapers in cities with major-league sports, had an advantage. Afternoon and evening games hit the morning publishing cycle. Detroit had the Pistons in the National Basketball Association, the Redwings in the National Hockey League, and the Lions in the National Football League, in addition to the Tigers and college teams.

Bob Cullinan, with many inside contacts at the *News*, suspected as I did that *News* circulation losses were greater than reported. We hired an outside consultant who visited scattered *News* district offices under the pretext of seeking information about the neighborhoods. He learned that massive sampling was taking place and that the free papers were being counted as net paid circulation, a violation of ABC rules.

When the *News* released its circulation statement for the six months ending March 31, 1969, I went to the ABC headquarters in Chicago to request a special audit. The *News*, as the audit disclosed, was "unable to locate lost records" to support its circulation statements and was temporarily suspended from the ABC. The first suspension of a metro daily in many years was an embarrassment in Detroit and elsewhere in the industry.

Recovery was slow but steady. The six months ending September 30, 1969 showed *Free Press* daily circulation at 562,000, a gain of 32,000, and 611,000 on Sunday, a gain of 24,000. The *News* lost 28,000 daily and 26,000 Sunday from the discredited figures reported two years before. The circulation gap had closed to 47,000 daily and 214,000 Sunday. Both papers increased for the September 30 1970 report with the gap almost the same.

DISTRICT MANAGERS WERE BILLED for papers at whole-sale and resold them to carriers and stores. They handled single copies through some stores, but mostly through honor boxes provided by the company. Unsold newspapers were returned for credit. Unfortunately, pilferage from the honor boxes was increasing, as were the district managers' losses. Coin-operated racks returned the full single-copy price and a meaningful profit, but were expensive.

With an innovative plan, we offered to rent the new racks for $5 a month, the highest fee charged by any paper, to any manager requesting them. Most managers resisted. However, a few tried them and passed the word that they were paying for themselves by cutting down on losses. We recovered the investment in a year and then went on to make a profit on rack rentals. We ordered fifty at a time, purposely keeping the supply low as the demand increased. The few hundred racks in use before the strike increased to more than 2,100, which we understood was the most sold by the manufacturer, Sho-Rack Co., to any one newspaper. In time, every district manager installed the racks, which yielded sales of more than 60,000 daily and 10,000 on Sunday.

Elton Schade of Teamsters Local 372 argued that racks should be provided at no cost. He filed for arbitration. We won the hearing. He always put on a show by contesting every change we proposed, although I always took care not to violate our union contract. Schade lost almost every challenge. Confrontations almost became fun, especially when we won.

The only arbitration I lost in Detroit was over the discharge of a long-time sales employee who we caught cheating on his collections and falsifying returns. Even though we had ample evidence, the arbitrator ruled in his favor because "he had a long career without a problem." We had to reinstate him. Bob later caught the man stealing. This time, the same arbitrator upheld the discharge. Justice was served. The ruling served notice that we were vigilant and likely motivated a few borderline employees to stay on the side of honesty.

The International Brotherhood of Teamsters Union headquarters was in Detroit where union leaders often lunched at Carl's Chop House. With hopes of becoming a power in the international union, Schade could be seen there almost every day. To let everyone know how important he was, he would arrange for someone to phone the restaurant and have him paged. Schade drove a Cadillac. He was like all the other officers of Teamster locals in Detroit who drove Cadillacs, Lincolns, or Chryslers. When they visited the office of a company employing Teamsters, they wanted to be seen as "equal" to management. Despite his efforts, Schade's Teamster career never made it beyond the newspaper local.

The news continued to conduct massive sampling, reduced some rates for home delivery, and initiated other measures to protect its lead, but it was a losing battle.

Chapter 16

■ ■ ■

Community Activities

My only civic involvement in Detroit was not one that I ever would have envisioned. Following my own advice to "always do more than is expected of you," I had indicated a willingness to represent the newspaper in the community.

Lee Hills had just the place for a guy who worked with boys locally and was involved nationally. Lee needed a *Free Press* representative to replace him on the board of directors of the Detroit Area Council of the Boy Scouts of America. This wasn't what I had in mind. I had never been a Boy Scout. As a twelve-year-old, I wanted to join, but Dad nixed the idea. He said the same skills could be learned playing in the nearby woods, raising chickens, and doing other chores. Joining the scouts was an unnecessary expense during the Depression. Hills said that not having been a scout wasn't a problem.

In late 1967, the board was comprised of forty-nine movers and shakers in Detroit, including some senior executives of the auto companies and me, the lowest ranked of them all. The best-known member was Lee Iacoca, vice president of Ford and later head of Chrysler.

I stuck my neck out again and volunteered. I became vice chairman of the Advancement Committee, made up of the advancement chairmen in the council's sixteen districts.

I attended four bi-monthly meetings before the chairman was transferred by General Motors to a distant plant. I became advancement chairman of the largest Boy Scout council in the world, with 68,000 scouts at all levels. The dedicated district chairmen understood my dilemma. I chaired the committee from 1968 to 1971 and never became involved in scouting again.

EVERY NOVEMBER FROM 1965-75, I took a break to go hunting on Jim Ferguson's ranch near Eagle Pass, Texas, across the Rio Grande from Piedras Negras, Mexico. Leading our group was Luther "Bud" Reedy, manager of Washington National Insurance Co. Others were my boss, Jack Olson, and Art Diaz, circulation director of the *St. Louis Post-Dispatch*. I knew Reedy from my Tarentum days when he was assistant circulation director of the *Pittsburgh Post-Gazette*. His company handled Free Press Reader Insurance. He became a friend for life.

Ferguson had more deer than cattle on his large ranch. The deer had to be thinned out so that the cattle would have enough feed and water, particularly in times of drought. It didn't take hunting prowess to bag the limit of two bucks and a doe. The venison provided food all year for his ranch hands. Riding the quarter horses was a bonus.

I never fired a rifle or shotgun before these annual trips. One time I was up in a mesquite tree, waiting for a big buck to come near. The limb broke. I fell several feet, taking a few small branches with me. The fall didn't hurt my butt, but it cracked the butt of the rifle. Bud

Reedy never let me forget that. Too many of my friends heard about the "big game hunter's" fall from a tree.

CIRCULATION DIRECTORS of several major evening papers, including The *Detroit News*, met regularly to exchange ideas for combating morning competitors. In 1966, Roy Newborn, circulation director of the *Boston Herald-Traveler*, and I formed an organization we called Major Morning Markets. Its members were the circulation directors of the *Chicago Tribune, Cincinnati Enquirer, Cleveland Plain-Dealer, Los Angeles Times, New York Daily News, New York Times, Philadelphia Inquirer,* and *Washington Post*. Each had an afternoon competitor. The group's information exchanges helped everyone. I chaired most of the quarterly meetings.

The host member always rolled out the red carpet in grand style. At one meeting, our New York host entertained us at Toots Shorr's famous restaurant, where we met entertainer Bob Hope and Ed Sullivan, a *New York Daily News* columnist who produced television variety shows. Sullivan made a name for himself by introducing the Beatles to American audience in 1964. We couldn't match this type of hospitality in Detroit, but we always showed our friends a good time.

I WAS THE REGULAR DISCUSSION leader for seminars related to circulation at the American Press Institute at Columbia University. It was always good to get to New York. Every year I gave a few speeches at newspaper-related conventions in several cities. I also served as vice chairman of the ABC's Review and Development Committee and the Circulation Committee and Industry Affairs Committee of the American Newspaper Publishers Association (ANPA). Unless there was a schedule conflict, I never turned down an invitation to speak or to appear on a panel.

There were no paid billets in any Naval Reserve unit in Detroit. I attended weekly classes in Navy subjects, took correspondence courses, and eventually retired with twenty-one years of service as a commander, two grades below that of rear admiral. A reduced pension at age sixty would be based on points earned on active and reserve duty.

At the 1970 ICMA convention in Denver, I won my first and only golf award. In a tournament sponsored by Washington National Insurance Co., my golf balls managed to find every sand trap, pond, tree, and fence. Bud Reedy never let me forget his presentation of a statuette of a Rocky Mountain goat for having turned in the highest score, a dubious "honor." I carried a high handicap, never joined a country club, and golfed only when invited.

I was named to the executive committee of the National Council of Organizations for Children and Youth in 1970, representing ICMA, and represented Michigan at the 1970 White House Conference on Children and Youth. Unlike the first White House conference ten years before, now there was a general consensus among the 7,000 delegates that keeping young kids busy, including work on newspaper routes, was preferable to inactivity that invited various problems. My work on the ICMA Youth Affairs Committee, with members in all fifty states, appeared to have paid off.

IT WAS A CASE OF what goes around coming around. Mike Tynan had recommended me for my job at the *Free Press*. In 1967, he asked me to nominate him for president of ICMA. He was elected. Later Tynan moved from Miami to the *Pittsburgh Press* and *Post-Gazette*. At my request, he hired my niece, Nancy Pulkowski (now O'Connor), as a circulation clerk. She became the go-to person in circulation where she worked for more than thirty-five years. Nephew Leonard was hired as a route man, but left after ten years when the papers were on strike to become sales manager for a supply company.

My record-setting twelve years as secretary-treasurer of the Inter-State Circulation Managers Association was recognized at the association's fiftieth anniversary program in 1967 with the presentation of the ISCMA Outstanding Achievement Award. I was introduced as the keynote speaker at the 1982 convention in Baltimore by the association president, Richard Welsh, a former carrier-salesman at the *Valley Daily News* whom I hired before leaving the paper in 1958. He later became circulation director of the *Valley News Dispatch* before moving on to head the circulation departments of the *Pittsburgh Press* and *Pittsburgh Post-Gazette* after Tynan's retirement. There he worked with my nephew and niece.

Had I not enjoyed all these outside activities, I would not have put forth the time and effort required. Dividends always came back, often when least expected.

Chapter 17

■ ■ ■

Promotion and Change

In spring, 1970, I was promoted to business manager of the *Free Press*, a new position, to take some of the workload off of Jack Olson. In addition to circulation, I now managed the production departments, data-processing, and personnel while helping prepare the budgets. I tackled my new responsibilities with enthusiasm, bringing a fresh outsider's view of all newspaper procedures. I believed I was on track to reach my goal to become a general manager at one of the Knight papers.

Bob Cullinan took over day-to-day management of the circulation department. He was a natural choice. He was well liked and highly respected. From day one, Bob had been my loyal right-hand assistant as well as my best friend.

That year we canceled our contract with the largest out-state hauler and took over the runs with newly purchased tractor-trailers, considerably cutting costs. The next year, the garage and mechanics were added to the circulation department.

The *Free Press* circulation reached 600,000 as a three-month circulation average by January 1, 1971. Promised champagne-dinner events were held for all field personnel, drivers, and office staff to celebrate achievement of this long-sought goal. Wearing my new business manger's hat, I recommended a price increase to fifteen cents for single copies, seventy-five cents for weekly home delivery, and $1.05 for seven-day delivery, leaving Sunday at thirty cents. *Free Press* subscription losses after the price increases totaled 30,000, but we started to regain the circulation right away. The *News* did not raise prices until July 1 and had not benefited from our price increases.

While still circulation director, I chaired a special Knight committee concerned with "circulation managers of the future." Jim Knight and the chain's publishers had determined that, unlike other specialties, there was no program to select and train people for careers in circulation. Other committee members included John Prescott, publisher in Charlotte; Lee Guittar, circulation director in Miami; John Larrabee, personnel manager in Akron, and Byron Harliss, a personnel consultant.

Our goal was to hire immediately as many as twenty-five young college graduates in business administration and train them for significant careers as a circulation executives. Soon each Knight paper had at least one of the recruits. The first at the *Free Press* was John Raytis, who went on to head circulation departments on major papers and later became a publisher in Ohio.

IN DECEMBER, 1969, at the request of Alvah Chapman, *Miami Herald* publisher and future Knight president, I spent a week in Philadelphia analyzing operations of the circulation department of the *Philadelphia Inquirer* and *Philadelphia Daily News*, which the chain was buying for $55 million.

Founded in 1829, the morning *Inquirer* was owned by Walter Annenburg, the son of Moses Annenburg, who had been involved with the *Chicago Tribune* circulation operation in the early 1900s and purchased the *Inquirer* in 1936. The *Inquirer's* major competition was the afternoon *Philadelphia Bulletin*. The tabloid *Daily News*, purchased in 1957, was almost 100 percent street- and store-sales afternoon paper. Annenburg, a future U.S. ambassador, also owned Triangle Publications, publishers of the *Racing News* and *TV Guide*, which Knight did not buy.

Chapman was not impressed with the circulation executives at the papers and asked me to go to Philadelphia for six months to run the operation. Jack and I agreed that this might turn out to be permanent, but I elected instead to spend three days a week heading the circulation department in Philadelphia until we found a new circulation director. I made about twenty trips to Philadelphia, spending three days there and then managing the *Free Press* operations for four days. No two circulation operations are alike. Philadelphia's market demographics were different than Detroit's and the circulation operations of the Philadelphia papers were different, too.

An editor invited me to dinner with Police Chief Frank Rizzo. We discussed our respective Italian backgrounds. He said he would provide a police escort from the airport on my next trip. I declined, with thanks. That was a little too much. Instead, I spent a graveyard shift with a patrolman in a squad car as he responded to emergency calls on his radio and then went with him to a police station to view the night's collection of miscreants. Rizzo later became mayor of Philadelphia.

These were hectic weeks, but I enjoyed the challenge of tackling the many problems I found. The acting circulation director knew his job was temporary, so he was helpful. The staff accepted changes I made in some office and field procedures and particularly in transportation, which, like at the *Free Press* in 1965, needed many cost-saving and efficiency improvements. In four months, we made changes that would save more than $1 million a year. Sales promotions were stepped up. Chapman was pleased with the results. Enjoyable pleasures of these visits were the excellent seafood restaurants found in Philadelphia.

I THOUGHT WILMINGTON and Delaware were behind me after I left in 1965. The major move we made there by pulling away from combination distribution agents hurt the Philadelphia papers' daily and Sunday circulation in Delaware. It was ironic that now, as the temporary circulation director in Philadelphia, I was trying to increase the *Inquirer's* circulation in Wilmington and elsewhere in Delaware.

In June, we hired Russ Fangmeier, circulation director of the *Cleveland Plain-Dealer*, as the new head of circulation at the Philadelphia papers. I was glad to return to Detroit and resume a normal work week.

I joined Jack, Bob, and Larry Wallace, labor relations manager, with a team from the *Detroit News* that included Leo Kelly to negotiate all fourteen union contracts at the same time and avoid the problems caused by the Teamsters strike in 1967.

ON ONE OF MANY VISITS to the Knight headquarters in Miami, Jack and I were guests of Jim Knight on his fishing boat, the *Rerun*. We were perched on high chairs with long poles and strong lines fishing for the really "big ones." At one point, I could not resist laughing out loud. Jim wanted to know what was funny.

"My dad came to America with twenty bucks in his pocket and a dream," I told him. "If he saw a multi-millionaire like you putting a slimy fish on his son's hook, he would realize that the American dream had been realized." Jim laughed, too. He was easy to be around. He never showed off his wealth.

Jim Knight was the younger brother of John S. Knight, a giant in American journalism who looked after the news side. Jim handled the business side. They were the largest shareholders of Knight Newspapers Inc. and made a fine team.

Jim was prone to show up at a newspaper unannounced. I happened to be in my office one Sunday afternoon with no one else around when Jim walked in, surprised to find the *Free Press* circulation director at work. He noticed a small black metal box on the credenza behind my desk, decorated by about fifty tiny flashing lights. Asked what it was, I couldn't resist giving him the same answer I gave everyone else: "It's a B.S. detector and it didn't do anything until you came into the room." Ordinarily, I would not have said something like that to anyone of Jim's stature, but the joke went over okay. He had a good sense of humor.

In October, 1970, I was invited to present a comprehensive report on the circulation operations of all the Knight papers at a general managers' meeting in Macon, Georgia. I gave my report as senior circulation executive and business manager of the *Free Press*, but was disappointed that I was not invited to sit in as an observer. This did not look like a track to a general manager's job.

IN THE YEARS since the riot and the strike, some areas of Detroit became increasingly more dangerous. In two years, forty-eight *Free Press* district managers had been robbed or mugged. One was wounded, but survived. Carriers had been robbed, too. Home-delivery was discontinued in several neighborhoods that were unsafe and where it had become difficult to recruit carriers.

The downward spiral had begun. The Big Three automakers had not seen the rapidly growing threat of smaller, more efficient Japanese and Korean cars and did not act in time to compete against the wave of Asian competition. The Motor City had seen its best days.

Despite the city's problems, *Free Press* circulation kept growing. It was only a question of time before the *Free Press* would pass the *News*. (The *Free Press* took the circulation lead in 1975.)

I look back with satisfaction on my *Free Press* years. I worked with some outstanding newspaper executives and a top-flight staff, but Detroit did not look like a place where I would want to raise a family. I never actively looked for a new career opportunity, but I knew if one came along, I would consider it seriously.

Chapter 18

■ ■ ■

Family and Job Decisions

The promotion to business manager of the *Detroit Free Press* was
not the only major event in my life in 1970-71. The most important occurred in my personal life, followed by a decision to change
jobs. An earlier marriage ended long before I invested in a two-unit
income property on a corner lot on Chatsworth Street in the city's
East Side. When a long-time tenant left, I gave up my apartment
near the *Free Press* and moved to the first floor in January, 1970. A
detached garage fronted on the side street. It was an easy drive to the
office.

I had a full seven-day-a-week workload between management responsibilities at the *Free Press* and the assignment in Philadelphia. I
was seldom home. I heard that the house next door was owned by
a mother with two small sons. Several months passed before I met
the boys playing in their yard. Richard and David were polite and
friendly. Then I met Sunni. She was attractive and personable.

On a warm Sunday afternoon, Sunni and I took a drive in my new
Cadillac. We drove to Port Huron and walked along the shore of Lake

Huron. We chatted while the boys searched for fossil rocks. Sunni surprised me when she said her maiden name was DeVirgilis. For Virgilio to meet a DeVirgilis as next-door neighbors, was more than a rare coincidence. Adding more coincidences were the first names of our mothers. Sunni's mother, Carola Gloeckner, was born in Koblenz, Germany, in 1899. My mother's name was Carolina. We each have a niece named Carol. Both of our mothers died at age sixty-two. It was as if our diverse paths were destined to lead us to this meeting.

Sunni, a native Detroiter, was an architectural designer who had earned a Bachelor of Fine Arts degree in architectural design with post-graduate studies at Wayne University. She is different, in many positive ways, than any other woman I've ever met. Born in 1933, she has always been known as "Sunni" and is "Shirley Anne" or "S.A." only if necessary.

Her father, Richard DeVirgilis, was born in Mesagne, a few miles west of the Adriatic port of Brindisi, Italy in 1897. He told me the area has many surnames with variations of "Virgil," all said to be descendants of the ancient Roman poet, Virgil, author of the *Aeneid*, who is believed to be buried in Brindisi.

Orphaned at age twelve, DeVirgilis came to the United States with an uncle. He joined the Army in 1918 and served with the Army of Occupation in Koblenz, where he met his bride.

Sunni's father worked in Ford's Lincoln plant in Detroit as a tool- and die-maker and acquired some U.S. patents. His years with Ford qualified Sunni to compete with children of Ford employees nationwide for one of fifty college scholarships from Ford. She won a full scholarship to any college, but chose Wayne so she could stay at home, commute, and work part-time. Her later experience included work at architectural firms and teaching.

Having more time at home after the Philadelphia assignment ended in late June, I was able to join Sunni and the boys for dinner most evenings when in town. Richard and David were great kids. It was obvious that Sunni was a good mother who enjoyed being with her sons. We visited Detroit-area attractions on day excursions and barbequed on weekends with Sunni's dad and often with her older sister, Virginia, brother-in-law Bill Damoth, and her niece, Carol. (Sunni's father, a warm, gentle man, died at age seventy-five in 1972.)

IN JANUARY, 1971, BOB HUNT, assistant circulation director of the *Chicago Tribune*, visited the *Free Press*, ostensibly to study our systems but really to find out if I might be interested in working for the *Tribune*. I was willing to listen to any offer. Both the morning *Tribune* and the afternoon *Chicago Today* had been losing circulation for many years. Our Major Morning Markets group had met at the Tribune Tower the year before. Over lunch, several *Tribune* executives asked me many questions about *Free Press* circulation gains, which Hunt said the *Trib* had been studying for some time.

Over the next few months, I met in Chicago with Publisher Harold Grumhaus and Fred Nichols, both members of the Chicago Tribune Co. board of directors. General Manager Stanton Cook came to Detroit with the newspaper's attorney to discuss terms of a possible contract to become circulation director of both Chicago papers. Naively I told them a contract would not be necessary if I joined them—a handshake would do. Later I learned that most metropolitan papers negotiated contracts with their top executives. The *Free Press* did not. I put them on hold, promising not to divulge their identity.

Meanwhile, I had informed Jack Olson of the *Tribune*'s interest. We met with Publisher Lee Hills. I advised him that I had a substantial job offer, but wanted to know where I was headed with Knight before deciding whether to accept it. I refused to identify the paper. The next morning I received a call from Jim Knight. There was a plane leaving at noon for Miami. "I want you on it," he said. Jack wanted to know more about his own situation, too, so we both made the flight.

We met in Knight's office with Alvah Chapman, publisher of the *Miami Herald*. They saw me as someone whose entire newspaper experience had been in circulation, unaware of my *Beechview News* ownership, advertising and reporting experience, rank as a Naval Reserve commander, and a desire to become a general manager.

Chapman asked if I would consider coming to Miami as his staff assistant to learn more about the other departments of the newspaper. I said I was a line officer, a responsibility I preferred, and never had worked as staff person. He suggested I spend a week at the *Herald*, a non-union paper, to observe the production departments. That was a possibility. Meanwhile, I was offered a substantial pay increase, a vice presidency at the *Free Press*, plus some stock options. We enjoyed cocktails at Chapman's home followed by dinner at his private club. They convinced me that I had a future with Knight Newspapers. I called Stan Cook in Chicago to thank him for his offer and let him know I was staying with Knight.

A few weeks later, I attended a two-week seminar on management and cost controls in New York. A fellow attendee was Tony Ridder, publisher of the *San Jose Mercury-News*, flagship of the Ridder Newspapers chain. While Tony and I were relaxing at a bar, he asked many questions about Knight Newspapers, wanting to know about its leadership, management, editorial policies, business controls, and other issues. I gave him positive reports in all areas.

Three years later, Knight Newspapers and Ridder Newspapers joined to form Knight-Ridder Newspapers Inc. Ridder had been doing some research. I was an innocent provider. Many years later, he became chairman of Knight-Ridder, which also owned 49.5 percent of the Seattle Times Co., acquired earlier by Ridder.

MY WEEK AT THE MIAMI HERALD gave me insight into corporate politics. I wore work clothes in the composing room and in the engraving, plate-making, and press rooms, going to lunch and dinner with the foremen. Only once was I invited to lunch in the executive dining room, where I had dined frequently on previous visits. I rarely saw any of the officers. It was obvious that there were other contenders for general-manager jobs. My competition worked in Miami in constant contact with corporate management. I was way up north in Detroit—"out of sight, out of mind."

Soon I had second thoughts. The disinterested reception I received in Miami and the unwelcoming publishers' and general managers' meeting in Macon in 1970 raised serious doubts whether I ever would become a general manager in the Knight organization. Later I learned from a friendly source that some in Miami suspected I had bluffed to get a promotion and a raise when no industry announcement of a new circulation executive was made by a major newspaper.

ALTHOUGH I TURNED DOWN the *Chicago Tribune*, the paper kept sending real-estate listings from Barrington Hills, Illinois, a suburban village with minimum residential zoning of five acres, figuring the prospects of living in "horse country" might change my mind.

After Miami, the *Tribune* was looking better. I figured if moving up with Knight was turning into a long shot, perhaps I had better think twice about turning down the circulation director's job at the country's second-largest circulation operation (the *Tribune* and *Chicago Today*).

Meanwhile, Sunni and I made plans to marry. We discussed the pros and cons of both cities and respective career opportunities. It wasn't a heads-or-tails discussion. Chicago won on all counts. I knew and liked Charlie Corcoran, the long-time circulation director of the *Tribune,* and was told privately that Corcoran would be retired if I accepted the job.

We planned to visit Chicago in late October. I called Bob Hunt for help getting tickets to attractions in Chicago for a weekend trip. I'm sure they had an inkling of the real reason for my visit. Stan Cook and Bob Hunt met us. The next day, Cook drove us through Barrington Hills. I had been impressed by Cook the first time we met. He was affable, had a good sense of humor, and obviously was well-qualified. He had come up through the ranks in the production department to the general manager's job. He reiterated his earlier offer, adding a vice presidency. I thought it over for about two minutes and accepted.

I RESIGNED FROM THE *FREE PRESS* in November. Despite the riot, a record-long strike, and the frequent friction with the Teamsters, I enjoyed the job and left behind a solid organization and a record of circulation gains in one of the country's most competitive newspaper markets.

I had worked with some of the top professionals in the newspaper industry: Publisher Lee Hills; Jack Olson, a great boss; Bob

Cullinan, the best assistant I could possibly have; Frank Angelo and Derick Daniels, first-class editors; Dave Henes, the top promotion director; Mark Ethridge, editorial-page editor; Production Director Bill Coddington; Labor Relations Manager Larry Wallace, and Personnel Manager Cle Althaus. Every one of my executive peers and the managers and staff in the circulation department at the Free Press were anxious, as underdogs, to beat the competition. They were all my friends. It was a congenial group. We worked together without internal political maneuvering. I hoped I would find the same kind of associates at the *Tribune*, the long-time leader in Chicago.

SUNNI AND I WERE MARRIED on December 30, 1971. A *Tribune* lawyer worked through all the necessary legal procedures for adoption and a few months later I became the proud dad of Richard Joseph, born in 1962, and David Nicholas, born in 1964.

I started my new job at the *Chicago Tribune* and *Chicago Today* in early January and temporarily moved into a nearby apartment. For the next six months, I was extremely busy and worked long hours to get to know my staff and become familiar with *Tribune* policies while taking care of the personal matters.

I flew home to Detroit every other weekend. Weekends in Chicago were spent studying the Saturday-Sunday operation and looking for a house and acreage in Barrington Hills, about forty miles northwest of the office but an easy commute on the Chicago-Northwestern railroad. Barrington Hills was a large village with a small population. Most properties had a stable and horses with easements for riders to pass through. I always wanted to own my own horse. Sunni shared my interest. This looked like the right area.

We did not find a suitable house but bought an attractive six-acre property, backed by three small lakes, on Caesar Drive in Barrington Hills about a mile west of Barrington. It was the perfect place to build a new house, eventually add a stable, and raise a family. In the meantime, I rented a townhouse for my family in Barrington, a few blocks from a school and the railroad station.

Chapter 19

■ ■ ■

The *Chicago Tribune*

C hicago has well-earned the title of "Windy City." The morning of January 3, 1972 was bitterly cold and windy when I left my temporary apartment on State Street and walked south on a stretch of Michigan Avenue known as the Magnificent Mile to begin my new career. I had been to the Tribune Tower many times over the years and three times in December before officially starting work, but I always arrived by cab. My office was in this beautiful building.

The thirty-six-floor Tribune Tower is larger than two similar buildings in the world, both Gothic towers attached to cathedrals. This practical office building, completed in 1925, had won a $100,000 prize for its design in an international competition. The site was selected for its proximity to the center of Chicago, close by the river and a railroad siding near ships bringing in newsprint direct from *Tribune* paper mills in Canada. Most important, it was on a double-decked street, the lower level of which provided excellent facilities for distributing newspapers. A twelve-story annex stood alongside.

Col. Robert R. McCormick, publisher from 1911 until his death in 1955, was impressed with the major cathedrals of Europe. The entrance is a masterpiece of Gothic art. The tower is adorned with gargoyles and grotesques. Studded around the walls are 126 stones from twenty-six famous structures around the world. William Randolph Hearst, owner of the *Chicago American* and *Chicago Herald*, built his castle in San Simeon, California. Colonel McCormick, who carried his WWI rank, built his cathedral in Chicago. Both men were bigger than life with egos to match.

Colonel McCormick was an heir of Joseph Medill, a young lawyer and newspaperman in Ohio, who had gone west and in 1855 and, with others, acquired the *Chicago Tribune*, one of many small papers in the new city. Medill, believing the Whig Party was finished, was one of the first to propose a new party—the Republican Party—and strongly opposed slavery. He was impressed with Abraham Lincoln, the Springfield lawyer and state legislator, and was a major supporter of Lincoln's rise to the presidency. From then on the conservative *Tribune* was staunchly Republican.

The *Tribune* had a dubious history of engaging in sometimes-violent circulation battles. Many Chicago papers competed for dominance. The battles that ensued over control of the best sales locations were bloody and marked by gunfire as thugs were employed by the newspapers' circulation departments. Many years later some of those young thugs became the gangsters who fought over control of the illegal liquor trade that characterized Chicago in the Prohibition era. By then, the *Tribune* controlled the street corners and had become the leading newspaper in Chicago, its circulation growing.

It is reputed that when drivers struck the *Tribune* in the late 1920s the notorious gangster Al Capone met with Circulation Director

Louis Rose, offering to settle the strike for $25,000. Rose succeeded his brother-in-law, Max Annenburg, in 1926. Annenburg, who was lured from the Hearst papers in 1909 by an annual salary of $20,000, later left to help a McCormick cousin start the *New York Daily News*.

Annenburg and his brother, Moe, had started as corner newsboys and rose to head circulation departments. Moe eventually started the *Daily Racing Form* and then bought newspapers, including the *Philadelphia Inquirer* and *Daily News*, which Knight Newspapers bought from his son, Walter Annenburg, in 1970.

CIRCULATION DETERMINED the fortunes of each Chicago newspaper. Nobody cared how the circulation was obtained. The "how" was a mystery on most papers. The *Tribune* gained and held leadership in the market under Annenburg and then Rose. They established newspaper distributorships as they expanded into other Midwest cities and towns, installing many of their friends in business. Some distributors represented the *Tribune* only, but most were "combination" distributors handling all newspapers. The *Tribune*, as the biggest, called the shots in Chicagoland newspaper distribution.

When an agency was sold, the buyer had to get approval of the circulation director of the *Tribune* by proving financial stability, a system still in effect after I arrived in 1972. Receipts were delivered to Rose, whose large corner office (and later mine) was on the second floor facing Michigan Avenue and reached by walking through an open clerical office.

A large room behind the office had a steel door. It served as a safe and later was used for storage. In it I found old bank books noting frequent deposits of hundreds of dollars, all possibly personal payments for approval of the sale of distributorships. I was told by an

Indiana distributor that his father and other distributors occasionally attended poker parties at Rose's home, always bringing expensive gifts. Apparently the distributors were poor poker players. They always lost.

Annenburg and Rose had an uncanny sense of what news would sell. They advised the editors on edition changes. I found a button at my desk, by then inoperative, connected to the press room and used to stop the presses. The circulation mangers' judgement was unchallenged.

When Rose retired in 1951, Charles Corcoran replaced him when a sister paper, the *Washington Times-Herald*, folded. Corcoran was honest. The under-the-table deals ended. But the *Tribune* did not change. Colonel McCormick, a crusty reactionary, ruled the closely held empire for forty-four years until his death. He had molded the company in his own idiosyncratic style and used the newspaper to trumpet his right-wing political views.

Perhaps because Colonel McCormick's way of doing things continued long after his death, a decline had begun and the *Tribune* lost circulation for twenty years. For the first time in decades, the newspaper's management believed it had to find a circulation director who could reverse the downward spiral. They recruited an outsider who had set circulation records on three newspapers.

That was the situation I faced on that cold, windy January morning in 1972.

LEAVING MY FAMILY IN DETROIT was difficult when I started the new job. They joined me after the boys got out of school in June. We moved into the townhouse in Barrington Village until we finished building our new home. Sunni knew the basic layout and user-friendly features she wanted. She selected the architect, building contractor, and major subcontractors. Construction started in 1973. Sunni stayed with the project all the way and personally selected most of the materials.

We moved into our 3,400-square-foot, four-bedroom home with an attached three-car garage in mid-1974. The home was Northwest style and built for convenience. The exterior was red clinker brick with a shingle shake roof. A ridge beam stretched the entire length of the interior. A daylight basement featured a large recreation room, wine cellar, mud room, and a large workroom. It was a perfect place to live.

I bought a John Deere tractor for mowing the grass in summer and clearing snow in winter. Richard and David learned to drive (and joy-ride) that tractor. There was work to be done. The lawn needed to be mowed. The landscaping needed regular weeding. I needed the boys' help. To this day, I am reminded of how expert they became taking care of the property and how much they hated the experience. I understood, too, why my Dad had needed my help.

I HAD BEEN ON BOARD for a few months when Jack Olson resigned as general manager of the *Detroit Free Press* to become director of operations and then general manager of the *Tribune*. He would be my boss again. I had alerted Publisher Harold Grumhaus that Jack was available. A Chicago native, Jack became the second key executive hired from outside the paper. He and his wife, Virginia, moved into a townhouse in Barrington.

Jack and I commuted together on the 7:15 a.m. Chicago-Northwestern train. A *Tribune* circulation driver met us across from the station. A driver took us to the station at 6 p.m. to catch the train home. For the most part the *Tribune* management preferred written reports to face-to-face contact. The commute provided time to catch up with our paperwork. I regret that the long days did not allow me time to help my sons with sports or after-school activities.

I traveled on business often and took the family along whenever possible. In 1973, we traveled to Mexico City where I gave a speech to the International Promotion Managers Association and then flew on to Acapulco. Rich used my Argus C3 camera to take pictures at a bullfight. (He became a very good photographer, worked in camera shops as a student, and took his talent into a successful business.)

The publisher of the *St. Petersburg Times* invited me to Florida to discuss our experience in taking over distributors. While I consulted, the family enjoyed a vacation. We also attended the June, 1972 ICMA convention in Philadelphia. We visited Disneyland and afterward I drove, clenching a toothpick, up the winding coastal highway to San Francisco.

Frank Carver, the Pitt athletic-information officer who had mentored me in 1949, nominated me in 1974—my first year of eligibility—for a Varsity Letterman of Distinction Award, based on my non-athletic accomplishments after graduation. We all went to Pittsburgh, where we attended a function at the chancellor's home followed by the award dinner. I joined three other ex-athletes, all older men, for introductions at mid-field before a packed crowd at a homecoming football game against Temple. I visited my sisters and their families, too.

THE CHICAGO TRIBUNE CO. became interested in the *Wilmington News-Journal* papers when rumors surfaced that Christiana Securities, the DuPont's holding company, would have to divest. At Stan

Cook's request, I made periodic contacts with Editor Dick Sanger for updates. In the meantime, the News-Journal Co. started the *Sunday News-Journal*, twelve years after Creed Black, then editor of the *News-Journal* papers, and I had urged the owners to add a Sunday edition.

Mistakes were made implementing the Sunday paper. The circulation director had a breakdown. Fred Walter, general manager, asked if I would help. I told him to call Stan Cook, who inquired if I was willing to do it. I spent several days reviewing all systems. Many improvements I had made were changed or dropped since my departure in 1975. It was like homecoming week. My ten-page report with recommendations was welcomed by Walter and Publisher Norman Isaacs. Cook was pleased that the *Tribune* had been able to help.

During this time, I made several more appearances as a discussion leader for the American Press Institute. I made my forty-ninth and last while still in Chicago, but continued to make appearances as a speaker or panelist at several newspaper conventions, including the ANPA, regular meetings of the Major Morning Markets group, and the Review and Development Committee of the Audit Bureau of Circulations. A week-long seminar for non-technical executives at IBM in San Jose, California, was informative and gave me a chance to see Uncle Henry, Aunt Jeanette, and Cousin Maria in San Francisco.

The first week of November each year was spent deer-hunting at the Ferguson Ranch near Eagle Pass, Texas. The first night there, Bud, Jack, Art, and I crossed the Rio Grande to Piedras Negras, Mexico for a *cabrito* (goat) dinner. These trips every year were great diversions.

Chapter 20

■ ■ ■

Making Waves at the *Tribune*

My twenty years of experience in three different markets convinced me that if a newspaper starts to lose ground to a competitor, the problem is more than just circulation. It is a deeper problem that requires everyone's dedication to making a better newspaper that people want to buy and read—a better choice than the product offered by the competition.

My active involvement in strategy and planning began weeks before my official hiring as the first major department head and vice president from outside. It was obvious that as the circulation leader in Chicagoland, the *Tribune* did not seem to have the some competitive spirit—an intense desire to beat the competition—that characterized the *Detroit Free Press*.

It is not easy to convince everyone particularly editors that circulation is everyone's problem. As the saying goes, "When a newspaper's circulation increases, editors get the credit. If it is losing circulation, the circulation department is to blame." In fact, *both* were to blame.

The newspaper's top leadership including the other vice presidents, the editor, and the advertising and production directors all had started young and risen through the ranks. The *Tribune* needed someone who could provide completely new, objective, aggressive leadership—uninhibited by past traditions and personal affiliations—to straighten out a circulation operation that was as inefficient and ineffective as could be found in any metropolitan newspaper.

I came to stay, anticipating it would take five years to build a solid foundation for long-range circulation stability and growth. I hoped the editors would help to make my job easier.

The *Tribune*, with 750,000 daily and more than 1.1 million Sunday circulation, was the fourth-largest newspaper in the country, employing a circulation staff of more than 1,000 people. Its primary market covered eight counties with circulation extending throughout Illinois and into nearby Indiana, Wisconsin, Iowa, and Missouri. As planned, I took over circulation for the afternoon *Chicago Today*, adding another 453,000 afternoon and 450,000 on Sunday to make us the largest combined operation in the country with more than 1,500 employees and a truck fleet that grew to 330 vehicles.

In 1972, I also became president of Newspaper Readers Agency, a subsidiary of Tower Life Insurance, a Tribune Company that handled reader and carrier Insurance. I also managed three garages and a team of mechanics transferred from the production department.

THE CHICAGO TRIBUNE CO. purchased the *Chicago Herald-American* from Hearst in 1956, leaving the staff in place and operating it as a separate company, to prevent it from being bought by the *Chicago Daily News*, which then would have controlled the Chicago afternoon market. (Knight owned the *Daily News* at the time, later selling it to Marshall Field, owner of the *Sun-Times*.) Circulation of the *Herald-American* then was 523,000 daily and 678,000 Sunday.

The Chicago Tribune Co. changed the paper's name to the *Chicago American*, leaving the staff in place and operating it as a separate company. Circulation declined. It was converted to a tabloid in 1969 and renamed *Chicago Today*. It had not picked up *Tribune* traditions and remained "Hearst-like" until 1972. George Howell had been transferred there by Hearst from the Detroit Times in 1953.

IN BEGINNING A NEW JOB, I always made a to-do list of projects. My long list in Chicago grew longer. The year 1972 was the busiest and most productive of my short *Tribune* career. Many major projects were completed. Cost savings were more than enough to cover my own salary and bonuses. *Today's* operation were slowly integrated with the *Tribune*. The chain of command was streamlined. Programs were standardized. Suburban and country departments handled both papers, as did marketing and customer service. Both city departments temporarily remained separate. Only the drivers remained on *Today's* payroll. George Howell became my assistant with the title of circulation manager. He was a big help.

Early on, I questioned why the *Tribune* was profitable while *Chicago Today*, published by the same owner and using the same production facilities in the same building, was not. "Don't complain," was the response. There was a simple reason. *Tribune* executives received a profit-sharing bonus. *Today* executives did not. It was another of the troublesome questions I raised that did not endear me to my colleagues. Sunni often observed that "although I had studied for the diplomatic service in college, I was not very diplomatic." This was often true. I was too direct and not a good politician.

On October 1, 1972, there were ninety-one city and two suburban independent exclusive distributors of *Chicago Today*. *Today*'s Sunday edition competed with the Sunday *Tribune*. A decision was made to discontinue *Today*'s Saturday and Sunday editions on January 1, 1973, substituting *Tribune* editions on those days, creating "Super Sunday" product. We offered to buy out *Today* distributors and acquire their customer lists. All but three agreed to sell and to accept *Tribune* employment, if offered, as district managers. The buyout cost $2.2 million. Without it, most of the distributors would have gone over to the afternoon *Chicago Daily News*. In Chicagoland, each distributor's customers ("tags") had a value.

This major change was to result in some driver layoffs at *Today*. Stan Cook agreed to a solution to save these jobs.

CHARLES LEVY HAD STARTED delivering the *Tribune* sixty-seven years earlier by horse-drawn wagon. His company became the largest distributor of newspapers, magazines, and books in the Midwest. Levy hauled 44 percent of the daily *Tribune* and more than 50 percent of the Sunday paper in suburban and country, plus *Today*, the *Sun-Times*, and the *Daily News*. Chas. Levy Co. trucks hauled all distributed publications on the same trucks, charging each by the hundredweight. In effect, the *Tribune* and *Today*, the biggest publications in volume and weight, were subsidizing the distribution of its competitors.

Charles Levy Jr. called on me in January, 1972 to introduce himself and to complain about "losing money on some runs." He announced that his charges were going up, as apparently they did nearly every year. Based on my experience in Detroit, I was sure we could handle our own distribution more efficiently and probably less expensively than the more than $2 million we paid Levy each year.

That October, we terminated the services of Chas. Levy Co., effective January 1, 1973. Levy was shocked and angry. When I offered to buy his surplus trucks, he responded, "I'll back them into Lake Michigan before I would sell to you." Fearing Levy might dump us before January 1, we made a contingency plan. The *Chicago Tribune's* 300 trucks were all Fords. I contacted Sunni's brother-in-law, Bill Damoth, who worked in Ford's truck-division office in Detroit. That resulted in a promise from the manager of a Ford plant in Louisville to deliver twenty-seven trucks and tractor-trailers on a day's notice, if needed, while the plant produced a larger order. We hired several Levy drivers. No layoffs were needed.

In sheer size and scope, and with a minimum of problems, the transition was unprecedented. The *Sun-Times* and *Daily News* no longer had a cheap ride on the tail-gate of Levy trucks. The competition's distribution costs went up, while ours decreased.

I HAD BEEN A "PAPERBOY" and later headed circulation departments where I worked directly with our own district managers and carriers, who bought wholesale and sold retail, earning a profit on each newspaper. This system was new in Chicago, where the newspapers used independent distributors that hired their own carriers. Wherever possible In Wilmington and Detroit, I took over distribution agencies and installed our own in-house system.

In January, 1972, the *Tribune* owned one suburban agency and twenty-six independent city distributors, all taken over for non-payment. We converted each to an employee district- manager operation with a junior-merchant plan. (Bud Reedy's son, Reedy, was hired for Winnetka. He later became an executive for Hearst in Beaumont, Texas.)

By January, 1973, the Tribune had thirty city and twenty-one suburban district managers. *Today's* distributors also became district managers. In all, we had 182 employee district managers, seventy relief men and trainees, and 6,000 junior merchants. The numbers grew each year. An estimated 15,000 carriers worked for the combination distributors.

Fellow circulation directors in the Major Morning Markets group were amazed at the number of big projects tackled simultaneously at the Trib. Most were successful.

SOME EARLY ACTIONS created a few serious personal issues. First, I discontinued the long-standing practice, never sanctioned by the company, of some drivers delivering the *Daily Racing Form* to distributors on the side—a holdover from the Annenburg days. Second, after reviewing the high number of "returns" and "unaccounted-for" papers, I tightened the distribution accounting procedures. Both numbers dropped substantially. I had busted a lucrative racket involving drivers and mailers. No longer were papers sold off the books and/or returned for credit.

These changes did not go down well in some quarters. My circulation competitor at the Field papers, Al Von Entress, and an undercover detective he had hired, told me that some drivers were overheard discussing a $5,000 "hit" said to have been ordered on the "Big Shooter from Detroit." The *Tribune* assigned me a "shadow" for a few months. Months later, my family joined me in Chicago. One day we dined at a Barrington restaurant where the owner, a former driver, recognized my name and said, "Oh, you're the Big Shooter from Detroit." My heart sank. I had not told my family about the rumored threat.

In mid-1973, George Howell retired. He had played a crucial role in negotiating the buyouts of the *Today* distributors. It had not been easy for him to accept an assistant's role after so many years in charge at *Today*. I hired Leo Kelly to replace Howell as assistant circulation director. For the previous three years Leo had been circulation director of Knight's *Akron Beacon-Journal*, where he was hired at my recommendation. Before Akron, he was assistant circulation director of the *Detroit News*. I knew him well and knew he was just the man to help make changes.

THINKING OF PROMOTIONS that might help the *Tribune's* image, I suggested a no-cost public-relations gesture worth $1 million in national promotion. It played on the *Tribune's* most-famous front page, which had been an embarrassment. The paper had backed Republican Thomas Dewey for president in 1948. Late on election night, *Trib* editors rushed out an edition with a banner headline: "DEWEY DEFEATS TRUMAN." Dewey lost. The next day, pictures appeared in newspapers all over the country of a jubilant, smiling, newly re-elected Harry S. Truman holding up the *Tribune's* front-page. My suggestion: make a replica of the infamous front page with the picture, suitably inscribed, and present it to Truman.

Tribune brass, all Republicans, was not receptive. Eating crow isn't tasty. But persistence paid off. Months later, a large, page-size plaque was made. By then Truman had been in and out of the hospital. Our presentation was delayed until the President "felt better." A $1 million idea lost its value when Truman died on December 26, 1972. The following spring, Harold Grumhaus presented the plaque to the Truman Memorial Library in Independence, Missouri. The inscription read: "Presented with sincere admiration and affection on our 125th anniversary to Harry S. Truman, whose election victory in 1948 made this one of the most memorable front pages ever published by the *Chicago Tribune.*" I always regretted my own vote for Dewey in 1948. I had just turned twenty-one.

I had better relations with officers of Teamster Local 706 in Chicago than with Local 372 in Detroit. At a distributors' outing, I asked a union official, "What happened to Jimmy Hoffa?" Hoffa had tried to regain control of Teamsters International after serving time in prison for jury-tampering and misuse of union funds. He was heading for a lunch to meet with a few shady supporters when he disappeared in 1975. The official looked up to the ceiling and said, "I think they drove to a warehouse that had an incinerator. I don't think they're ever going to find Jimmy, but then I don't know." Hoffa is still missing.

TRIBUNE DEPARTMENT HEADS met weekly for lunch, status reports, and general conversation on the twentieth floor of the tower. I looked out at the street below and casually said, "Every time ten hearses go down Michigan Avenue, they carry seven *Tribune* readers and three *Sun-Times* readers. If enough hearses go by, we'll lose our lead." The comment was not appreciated. *Crain's Chicago Business* paper published this quote in 1980, long after I left, in a story citing the *Tribune's* continuing losses in circulation and profitability.

At one luncheon, we discussed the problem of reaching minorities and the eighteen to thirty-five age groups. *Tribune* readers were older and more conservative than readers of the *Sun-Times* and *Daily News,* which were popular in the sizeable black communities. A decision by the editors to improve coverage of these communities apparently did not get relayed to the night desk. One evening, a prominent black alderman died suddenly. The *Sun-Times* replated, making room on the front page for a prominently placed story. The *Tribune* ran its story on an inside page. There were good intentions at the top but no follow-through.

Surveys by professionals are the best way to learn about your readers and non-readers. The *Tribune's* idea of a survey was to canvass a few friends when a new feature was introduced. They were rewarded for their participation with a set of *Tribune* water glasses. However, friends don't always tell you the truth. At Wilmington and in Detroit we had found surveys to be powerful tools for improving the paper's editorial content. I pushed for a professional survey from my first days in Chicago. Finally, in 1975, the *Tribune* contracted with a well-known polling company specializing in readership surveys. As expected, the results were not favorable. Immediately, several task forces were set up to study ways to improve the newspaper.

FIVE PRICE INCREASES in three years, service charges tacked on by the distributors, and high turnover among the district managers made it hard to stop more than twenty years of decline. Unproductive and costly sales programs were streamlined. Phone sales, boy crews, club programs, apartment managers, and more important, carrier incentives, produced more new subscribers than ever. Verification procedures were tightened. Expensive sales programs were curtailed in low-income areas where residents typically did not read the *Tribune*.

Yet, even with all this effort, subscriber turnover was high. It was like throwing spaghetti against a wall and hoping some of it would stick.

The problem was not sales. We produced plenty of new customers. Part of the retention problem was that the *Tribune* could not control the service provided by the independent, combination distributors that handled most of the Tribune's circulation as well as that of competing newspapers. But a bigger problem was the newspaper itself. Colonel McCormick was long gone, but the old guard kept his legacy alive. The editor and staff were slowly, slightly changing the newspaper's antiquated philosophy, but changing the public's perception of what many viewed as a "reactionary" *Tribune* was more difficult.

A step in right direction came in 1973 when President Richard Nixon's Watergate tapes were released. Editor Clayton Kirkpatrick sent editors to Washington, D.C. on the *Tribune* jet to pick up printed transcripts. On the return flight, they prepared the material for publication. The *Tribune* published the full text of the transcripts the next morning—a major scoop.

Among other things, the tapes revealed that Nixon aides had asked the CIA director to pressure the FBI to block an investigation into a break-in at the Watergate offices of the Democratic National Committee—a burglary involving the President's aides. The *Tribune* later called for Nixon's resignation or impeachment, shocking everybody. I went to Kirkpatrick's office, pointed to the picture of McCormick on the wall, and said: "Kirk, you don't need to have him looking over your shoulder anymore."

THE MOST ENJOYABLE ASPECT of being a *Tribune* executive was the annual long-range planning meetings in June. *Tribune* officers and key managers flew on the company jet to Baie Comeau, Quebec, on the St. Lawrence River. Float planes shuttled us to the *Tribune's* lodge at Lac Des Isles. McCormick had purchased or leased hundreds of square miles of timberland decades before to supply a *Tribune* newsprint mill in Baie Comeau. Mornings and early evenings were spent fishing for trout with the help of French-speaking guides. It was easy to land more than twenty trout a day. I have never had as much luck fishing anywhere else.

Afternoons were spent in meetings. Each of us presented and discussed lengthy status reports, recounting accomplishment of the previous year, and previewing future plans. The chef from the newspaper-owned Manoeur Hotel in Baie Comeau flew over to prepare outstanding meals for the group.

Leo and I also escorted several of our best suburban distributors to the lodge each year, just for fishing and relaxation. It was good public relations, badly needed because of a prevailing concern that we would continue taking over distributorships. I addressed the City Distributors Association and the Midwest Distributors Association in my first year and annually thereafter. Relations were better than ever. The competent distributors knew they had no problem.

IN EARLY 1974, The Tribune Company closed *Chicago Today* and heavily promoted the new "24-hour-a-day *Chicago Tribune*" with delivery of an afternoon *Tribune* to all *Today* subscribers. *Today*'s best features moved to the *Tribune* and its staff was absorbed. As had happened previously with elimination of *Today*'s Sunday edition, not all of the *Today* subscribers became *Tribune* readers. Of the 364,000 circulation of *Chicago Today*, the *Tribune* gained only 107,000. The *Sun-Times* gained only 7,000 and the *Chicago Daily News*, left alone in the afternoon, lost circulation. Almost a quarter-million circulation disappeared. Losses due to duplication were substantial. *Today*'s district managers became *Tribune* district managers. The *Tribune* daily circulation showed a healthy gain at first, but daily and Sunday numbers dropped each year thereafter.

Assistant Circulation Director Bob Hunt, who transferred to circulation from advertising a few years earlier as the assumed heir to the circulation director's job, had made some improvements. He was my assistant circulation director for three months before becoming advertising director, the job he really wanted. While in circulation, Hunt realized that several key positions needed new leaders and moved a few in from advertising. However, several of the executive and supervisory staff that I inherited were not capable of handling the immense challenges and had to be retired, replaced, and-or moved into jobs they could handle.

I welcomed Hunt's offer to transfer more "stars" to circulation. Tom Clancy transferred from the New York office to be sales-promotion manager and moved to Barrington. Harold Woldt left advertising for circulation and became a supervisor. Hunt had earlier moved Mike Malheiro and others to head transportation and city street sales. Howard Hay, the personnel manager, wanting to advance his career, volunteered to join circulation. His skills were needed to train new district managers, as well as many former *Today* distributors. Many prospects washed out.

I appointed Hay as city home-delivery manager. Harold Woldt later went on to the *New York Daily News,* a Tribune company paper, as circulation director and became president of the ICMA in 1991. Hay became circulation director of the *Tribune.* He was elected a vice president of ICMA in 1991 and served one year before the association was absorbed into the Newspaper Association of America, formerly the ANPA. In all, twenty-six men who worked in departments I headed became circulation directors or general managers. A few became publishers.

The circulation operation improved steadily. The executive and supervisory staff stabilized. When the *Newark News* folded, we sent the *Tribune* plane to fetch several managers. We hired four and placed them in supervisory positions. Leo had taken charge of several areas. Our Detroit experience helped us manage the much-different *Tribune* operation. Now we were on the same page.

I HAD CONSIDERED the possibilities of further advancement in the large Tribune company organization when I joined, but did not know then how deeply the paper was rooted in tradition, nor had I anticipated the political atmosphere. As the new vice president, I became a threat to the ambitions of others.

Before I came, Bob Hunt was been in line to become circulation director. My hiring "saved" him from circulation. As director of advertising, where his skills were impressive, Hunt could pursue his plan to get to the top. Politics were important in the *Tribune* organization. Hunt was ambitious and understood how to play the game. He moved to Lake Forest, an elite suburb north of the city, where Harold Grumhaus and the cream of Chicago's business community lived. I chose to live in a country village forty miles west.

Much later, I learned that Tom Clancy, who occasionally drove me home, had shared the gist of our private conversations with his old boss. I also was unaware that Hunt had breakfast regularly with Harold Woldt and other managers to get a heads-up on current policies. I was never invited. Many of the sales programs I dropped had been instituted by Hunt. It never occurred to me that the department was being staffed with associates who wished to carry on without any more "outsiders." I would not have cared because I was always satisfied to work with anyone who was competent and worked hard.

IN 1974, STAN COOK became publisher of the *Chicago Tribune*. Bob Hunt was named president. Jack Olson resigned as general manager to become publisher of the *New York Press*, a new daily. Harold Lifvendahl was promoted from advertising director to director of sales and then to general manager in 1975. I had shown an interest in the GM job and felt I was the most qualified. Yet, though my background was well known, no opportunity to discuss possible advancement was ever offered.

Long-time associates of Hunt were positioned to move up. Other department executives with long careers at the paper had ambitions, too. It was becoming clear that advancement at the *Tribune* was no longer a possibility for me. I did not fit the mold. I was too outspoken. I rocked the boat, something you did not do at the *Tribune*.

I was hired to do a job no one in the company was considered capable of doing—reverse the circulation losses. Yet I was no miracle worker. In trying to stimulate certain changes necessary for growth, I ruffled feathers and questioned a few sacred cows. The newspaper's corporate bureaucracy was convinced that the *Tribune* was "The World's Greatest Newspaper," as claimed in the masthead, and being number one was taken for granted.

The *Tribune* was not used to my style of management and I wasn't used to its style, either. My top-management colleagues were 180-degree opposites of my co-workers at the *Detroit Free Press*. In Detroit, we were scrapping to beat the *Detroit News* and slowly winning. We frequently got together for social events, even some poker games. There was comradery and teamwork. Not so at the *Tribune*. The social events were mostly formal and usually dreary command performances.

IN 1972, THE UNVERSITY of Wisconsin presented me with the Frank Thayer Award for "Outstanding contributions to the newspaper industry in the Midwest." It was a cherished award. My family accompanied me to Madison for the presentation.

Even though many thought I had the best circulation job in the country, I knew that I would not spend the rest of my career in Chicago. I was patient. I still gave 100 percent. But I knew something better and more personally satisfying would come along.

Chapter 21

■ ■ ■

Moving to Seattle, the "Emerald City"

Jack Olson, my friend and former boss at two newspapers, knew of my discontent with the *Tribune.* He called in mid-1975 to let me know he had recommended me to Frank Bennack Jr., head of the Newspaper Division of the Hearst Corp., as a candidate for president of the San Francisco Newspaper Agency that handled production of both the Hearst afternoon *Examiner* and the independent morning *Chronicle.* Frank knew me and told Jack he would call. When the position was filled a few months later, I gave up expecting a call.

In December, however, Frank invited me to New York where he told me he was interested in bringing me into the Hearst organization. We had wide-ranging discussions about the industry and general-manager jobs at the *Los Angeles Herald-Examiner* and the *Seattle Post-Intelligencer.* I couldn't picture myself in L.A. but Seattle sounded interesting. I saw Frank in New York a few times over the next several months and we had long telephone conversations. I wondered if an offer would ever come.

In June, 1976, Frank called to suggest I spend a week in Seattle to see if I liked the city. I had visited Seattle briefly in 1969 to speak at an industry event. Jim Bonneau, who years before was my assistant in Wilmington, was then circulation director of the *Post-Intelligencer.* We lunched atop of the Space Needle on a rainy, dreary day. Visibility was limited. It was not a good introduction to the Northwest.

Sunni and the boys did not come with me, but was keenly aware of my discussions with Hearst. This time I liked everything about Seattle. Sunni agreed it would be a good move even though she never had been to Seattle and leaving Chicago meant giving up our beautiful new home. I called Frank and accepted the position of general manager of the morning *Post-Intelligencer,* starting August 1, 1976.

On June 30, I submitted my letter of resignation to Bob Hunt with copies to Harold Lifvendahl and Stan Cook, effective July 15. I told them I was pursuing "other career opportunities," though at the time I was honor-bound not to divulge details.

Hunt couldn't wait until the next morning's *Tribune* to announce that Thomas Clancy would be the new circulation director. My departure left the inevitable question, "Was Virgil Fassio fired?" Of course I wasn't, but the old guard had difficulty accepting that someone in a high position such as mine would ever resign from the *Tribune.* My logical successor was Leo Kelly, but he wasn't a *Tribune* guy, either, despite his experience and outstanding qualifications for the job. That's why he was passed over. Disappointed, Leo resigned the next day.

Clancy inherited a much-improved operation than I had found in 1972. I left him a record of circulation gains, installation of a system of district managers and junior merchants, tightened controls of sales accounting, cost reductions, and a more efficient transportation system.

Frank had wanted to issue a joint announcement with the *Tribune*, but that was not to be, so a story was rushed into the July 4 *Seattle Post-Intelligencer* announcing my hiring as general manager in charge of the day-to-day operations. At the same time, Publisher Robert Thompson added the title of editor. An outstanding journalist and long-time Hearst news executive, Thompson had been named publisher two years earlier by William Randolph Hearst Jr., but had no business background.

The *Tribune* published a terse item in a business column a few days later mentioning my new post. Vice presidents of the *Tribune* never left voluntarily, so it was not easy for the paper to concede that one was leaving for a better opportunity in another chain.

A FEW DAYS LATER, I joined Frank in Seattle. Before introducing me to the staff, he explained privately why he delayed hiring me. Hearst had been in negotiations with the *Seattle Times* for several months over terms of a proposed joint operating agreement, but walked away without reaching an agreement. I was brought in to reverse eight consecutive years of losses exceeding $1 million annually.

Hearst's research into my background had been extensive. Every previous employer except the *Tribune* was contacted. My new employers found a history of record growth combined with cost-cutting wherever I worked. They hoped I could extend that record in Seattle.

The fact that the *P-I* was unprofitable did not deter me. I assumed as much, but was surprised that the losses had persisted for so long. I was optimistic and believed a turn-around was possible.

At long last, this was the golden opportunity I had been hoping for ever since Gene Simon encouraged me to leave the news department and find a career on the business side of the industry. The chance to run a newspaper didn't come in New Kensington or Tarentum, both small markets; or Wilmington, a medium-sized market; or with Knight Newspapers, as I had hoped. This was a major metropolitan paper, the biggest morning daily north of California and west of the Mississippi. I would be working in one of the best, if not the best, cities in the country.

I returned a week later with my family. We spent a week exploring the Seattle area and looking at homes in Bellevue, across the Lake Washington floating bridge east of Seattle. Bellevue had been mostly farmland before 1950, but was growing fast with a population of about 60,000 in 1976. We did not see any homes that suited us and decided it would be wise to wait a while. It would take time to settle everything back in Barrington Hills. We had to sell our house there while waiting for the boys to finish the school year. I would continue house-hunting at a more leisurely pace.

Meanwhile, I found a one-bedroom apartment at the foot of Queen Anne hill in Seattle and made plans to fly home to Barrington Hills every other weekend. A new and exciting phase of my career was about to begin. I couldn't wait to get started.

Chapter 22

■ ■ ■

Seattle Post-Intelligencer

Named after Chief Sealth, a leader of the Suquamish Tribe, Seattle attracted its first white settlers in 1851.

Seattle was still a pioneer village when James R. Watson founded the weekly *Puget Sound Gazette* in December, 1863. It was re-christened *The Intelligencer* in 1867 and began daily publication ten years later. The *Puget Sound Dispatch* and the *Pacific Tribune*, first published in Olympia in 1863, were merged with *The Intelligencer* in 1878. Meanwhile, the *Seattle Post* appeared in October, 1876. In 1878, the *Post* and *The Intelligencer* combined forces and became the hyphenated *Post-Intelligencer*, or the "P-I" as it became widely known.

On June 6, 1889, the Great Seattle Fire destroyed the city's business district. Overnight, the *Post-Intelligencer* salvaged its type and printing press and moved them to the home of the publisher, Leigh S. J. Hunt. There, the *P-I* printed the next day's issue with coverage of the blaze that leveled much of the central part of the city. The paper then moved to permanent quarters at Second Avenue and Cherry Street.

Hunt lost control of the *P-I* in the Panic of 1893. The paper had a succession of owners, including John L. Wilson, who later became a U.S. senator. Wilson purchased the *P-I* with borrowed from railroad magnate James J. Hill. In 1904, the paper moved again, this time into a building at Fourth Avenue and Union Street.

Washington did not achieve statehood until 1889. During most of the territorial period, the paper published a weekly edition for rural and distant subscribers in addition to its daily paper. During the Klondike Gold Rush at the turn of the century, Seattle was transformed into a metropolis of 80,000 people and the *Post-Intelligencer* became a powerful voice in development of the Pacific Northwest. The paper had a succession of different owners over the years.

WILLIAM RANDOLPH HEARST purchased the *Post-Intelligencer in 1921*, adding it to his growing chain of metropolitan dailies, at that time the largest newspaper group in the country. The paper moved to spacious quarters at Sixth Avenue and Pine Street.

In 1948, the *P-I* moved yet again to Sixth Avenue and Wall Street into a three-story building occupying a full city block in Seattle's Denny Regrade area, where it remained for nearly forty years. An eighteen-ton illuminated globe of the world was erected atop the building. One of the largest neon signs in the world, proclaiming "It's in the *P-I*," the colorful, revolving globe became a Seattle landmark. From 1976 to 1986, I worked in an office directly beneath the globe.

In April, 1986, the globe was moved by helicopter to the top of the new five-story *Seattle Post-Intelligencer* Building at 101 Elliott Avenue West, where the staff occupied two leased floors. My spacious office on the third floor had an outside deck that looked out over Elliott Bay. Sea gulls used to peck at the windows.

A FAR-REACHING LABOR DISPUTE took place in 1936. Thirty-five members of the American Newspaper Guild, a fledgling union of news employees formed in New York the year before, struck the *P-I* to protest what the guild regarded as arbitrary dismissals, unfair job-assignment changes, and other "efficiency" measures. The strike attracted the support of Dave Beck, a young local Teamster leader, and other trade unions in Seattle.

The strike, one of the nation's first by white-collar workers, lasted three and a half months and established the guild as a major force in the American labor movement. The guild won higher wages, shorter hours, and the right to organize—gains that spread to other Hearst papers. Beck was a key figure in negotiating a settlement and winning additional concessions for Teamsters in the *P-I*'s circulation department.

(Beck later became president of the International Brotherhood of Teamsters and in the early 1960s served thirty months in the McNeil Island federal prison for a conviction of filing a false federal-tax return. A *P-I* editor and I once lunched with this fascinating man, who got his start delivering newspapers and went on to become a powerful West Coast labor organizer for forty years.)

WILLIAM RANDOLPH HEARST and the Hearst newspapers were harshly critical of President Franklin D. Roosevelt and the New Deal, although Hearst had endorsed FDR earlier and hired members of the Roosevelt family.

FDR's son-in-law, John Boettiger, became publisher of the *P-I* in 1935 at a salary of $38,000 a year. His daughter, Anna Roosevelt Boettiger, served as society editor. Eleanor Roosevelt visited Seattle frequently. Boettiger left to join the service in WWII and did not return to the paper. After his absence, the paper turned increasingly conservative. Anna left in 1943 to live in the White House. WRH opposed FDR's election to a third term. He changed parties and supported conservative causes and the Republican Party the rest of his life.

(FDR's eldest son, Elliott, was often pictured standing with his father, who could not walk unassisted due to polio. In 1979, I was looking at open houses in Bellevue. At one, I remarked that the tall, stately man showing the house looked familiar. He produced his card. It was Elliott Roosevelt. He was substituting for his wife, who was busy showing another property. We had a good chat after I told him I was a few publishers removed from his brother-in-law's tenure. The next day, Roosevelt's wife phoned and offered to help find a house, but I already had a Realtor.)

THE HEARST CORP. HISTORY began in the mid-1850s when George Hearst, a Missouri farmer said to have a "nose for minerals," struck out to make his fortune in mining. Within the next several decades, he became one of the wealthiest men in America. He developed the Homestake Mine in South Dakota, the richest gold mine in the world; the Comstock Lode, a silver mine in Arizona; Anaconda in Montana, a huge copper mine that also yielded gold and silver; the Ontario Mine in Utah, a silver mine; the Sheepshead gold mine in California, and gold and silver mines in Mexico.

Hearst also invested in ocean-front real estate in California and owned the *San Francisco Examiner*. He later served as a U S. senator from California. He died in 1891.

George Hearst's only son, William Randolph Hearst (WRH), was born in 1863. Expelled from Harvard for various shenanigans including organizing huge beer parties in Harvard Square, WRH returned home and took over the unprofitable *San Francisco Examiner* and quickly increased its circulation with an exciting brand of journalism. In 1895, he purchased the *New York Morning Journal,* also a money-loser. It was the beginning of a fierce and often bitter competitive battle with the leading *New York World,* owned by Joseph Pulitzer. In time, the *Journal* overtook the *World* in circulation.

When Cubans began resisting Spanish rule in 1898, WRH anticipated a war. He dispatched Frederic Remington, the famous artist, and Richard Harding Davis, a noted writer, to cover the war. Remington, soon bored, wired Hearst that he wanted to come home.

"There is no war," Remington reported.

Hearst reportedly replied, "Stay. You produce the pictures. I will produce the war."

Hearst's enthusiastic support for the Spanish-American War contributed to the extension of American power.

Hearst newspapers were also the source of huge headlines and lurid sensationalism known as "yellow journalism," a term applied by competitors after a scruffy urchin character, the "yellow kid," who appeared in a *Journal* comic strip. Hearst was the first newspaper publisher to run a full page of comic strips, content that became the norm in the industry.

A Democrat In his early years, WRH opposed Tammany Hall, the corrupt New York political machine. He served two terms in Congress and sought a nomination for president at the 1904 Democratic convention. He lost on the first ballot. Hearst ran unsuccessfully for mayor of New York and governor of the state. He was opposed to the powerful corporations and advocated for the "little man."

HEARST BOUGHT OR STARTED newspapers and other media all over the country. By 1936, the corporation owned twenty-nine newspapers in eighteen states. In addition to Seattle, there were papers in New York, Albany, Boston, Baltimore, Detroit, Chicago, Milwaukee, Los Angeles, San Francisco, Washington, D.C., and Pittsburgh, where my family was loyal to the *Sun-Telegraph*. Later, the corporation was divided into three dozen companies. Hearst also published many popular magazines and books and operated International News Service (INS), King Features Syndicate, radio stations, and movie studios. Hearst also had large mining, real estate, and timber holdings.

All these businesses earned a profit. Hearst spent all the profits and then some. He amassed the largest private art collection in the country, silver and antique furniture collections, and purchased large plots of land in Manhattan and acreage in California. He constructed the gigantic Hearst Castle at San Simeon with materials and priceless antique furniture and artifacts collected in Europe.

When the country struggled in the Depression in 1936, the Hearst empire struggled as well, but Hearst kept spending. His top executives were the highest paid in the industry and he refused to cut reporters' salaries. Soon he was deep in debt. Banks were closing in. Finally he was forced to make drastic cost-saving measures. A trustee began to dismantle the empire. Within two years, six papers were sold or closed. Eight others followed. Other companies were shut down. Executive salaries were cut. Valuable art and other possessions were sold at auction, bringing a fraction of their value. Hearst borrowed money from friends and family.

A much smaller Hearst Corp. survived. The company turned the corner in 1945. It had been reduced in size by 40 percent, having shed sixteen newspapers and eight magazines. Other assets of the empire remained largely intact. The corporation is still privately owned by the Hearst family, but is governed by a thirteen-member board of trustees comprised of eight company executives and five members of the Hearst family. The elder WRH died 1951.

William Randolph Hearst Jr. was the only one of WRH's five sons to follow his father into the news side of newspapers as a reporter and editor-in-chief. He won a Pulitzer Prize. On the business side, Randolph also became a publisher and served as chairman of the company. George was briefly a publisher. None of WHR's sons graduated from college.

The Hearst family became front-page news worldwide in 1974 when Randolph's daughter, Patricia, a nineteen-year-old college student, was kidnapped by eight self-styled left-wing radicals calling themselves the "Symbionese Liberation Army." Patricia Hearst was held hostage for several months, terrorized, ordered to tape-record tirades against her family, brainwashed, and forced to carry a gun in a bank robbery and follow the orders of her captors. After her capture, she spent two years in prison for being an accomplice to the bank robbery, though her defense lawyers insisted she was following orders to survive.

FRANK A. BENNACK JR. WAS general manager of the Hearst Newspaper Group when he hired me in 1976. A San Antonio native, Frank had a truly remarkable career. He hosted radio and television programs as a teenager. He joined the *San Antonio Light* as a classified-advertising salesman and became publisher of the paper at age thirty-four. Seven years later, he was promoted to general manager of the Newspaper Group. In 1977, he was named chief operating officer of the Hearst Corp. A few years later, he became chief executive officer, serving in that position for twenty-three years. Then, after an absence to tend to other corporate work, he returned to the post for another six years.

During Frank's tenure, the corporation grew steadily and acquired a number of media properties. Nine newspapers bore the Hearst name when I joined the *Seattle Post-Intelligencer.* At that time, Hearst operated 135 businesses and employed 12,000 people.

By 1993 when I retired, the newspapers in Baltimore, Boston, and Los Angeles had folded, but Hearst had purchased papers in the cities of Midland and Bad Axe in Michigan; Houston, Beaumont, Midland, Laredo, and Plainview in Texas, and Edwardsville in Illinois.

Hearst also owned five non-daily newspapers and was the largest publisher of monthly magazines in the nation, including *Good Housekeeping, Cosmopolitan, Harper's Bazaar, Town and Country, Esquire, House Beautiful, Popular Mechanics, Sports Afield, Connoisseur,* and various trade publications. It also owned a large company in England that published in ten languages; book publishers Avon, Arbor House, and William Morrow; King Features Syndicate; six television and seven radio stations; joint ventures in cable networks such as Arts & Entertainment, ESPN, Lifetime, and others.

Hearst also retained mining and ranching interests. The Hearst Castle was donated to the state of California and remains a major tourist attraction, though the vast property surrounding it—"the ranch"—remains in family hands.

Growing up, the Hearst-owned *Pittsburgh Sun-Telegraph* was the only paper in our home. My assistant and some of my best supervisors and district managers at the *Detroit Free Press* came over from Hearst's *Detroit Times* when it folded. An assistant and some supervisors at the *Chicago Tribune* had worked on Hearst's Chicago *Herald-American*. I had considerable experience—almost all positive—working with ex-Hearst news and circulation people.

Hearst had a reputation for promoting its top executives from within, perhaps in some cases keeping them in place too long beyond the standard retirement age. Frank was changing this. I never expected to be one of the first of many top Hearst executives hired from other newspapers. I was proud to be asked to join the Hearst "family."

Chapter 23

■ ■ ■

A Step up the Ladder

The next seventeen years were the best of my newspaper career. Gene Simon told me in 1951 that someday I would be a publisher. I never dared plan that far ahead, but understood that as vice president and general manager of the *Seattle Post-Intelligencer*, I was a step closer to fulfilling Gene's prophesy.

The day after Frank introduced me to my new staff, Business Manager William Cobb took me to dinner at Canlis, the finest restaurant in Seattle. That began a close business association and thirty-six-year friendship until his death in 2012. A Seattle native, certified public accountant, and lifelong *P-I* employee, Bill was a trusted, loyal right-hand man. He was invaluable and had the newspaper's historical background that I needed.

The first few weeks were busy as I became acquainted with department heads and key managers in the advertising, circulation and production departments, and in the business office. Bob Thompson then scheduled a newsroom meeting of the news and editorial staffs so the employees there could meet the new general manager and hear what he had to say. They were curious.

I called Sunni a few hours before the meeting. She had just learned she was pregnant. I was in a state of shock when I addressed the assembled staff. Most were Newspaper Guild members. I was not warned that there would be some tough questions. Rumors had been flying around Seattle for months that Hearst was planning to close the *P-I*.

The news staffers, knowing my background, were convinced I was being brought in to close the paper. I did my best to allay their fears by comparing the *P-I* to the *Detroit Free Press,* both morning papers trailing their afternoon rivals. The *Free Press* had caught up with and passed the *News*. The *P-I* was not second, I told the staff, it was the *morning* paper. This was our advantage. We would work together to narrow the gap between the *P-I* and the *Seattle Times*. I could see the more aggressive questioners remained skeptical.

When the skeptics learned that my family had not come with me, they were all the more convinced that I was a hatchet man with a grim task. It wasn't until the word got around about Sunni's pregnancy that everyone understood why I would not move my family until the following summer. Until then, I took a red-eye flight every other Friday night to Chicago and returned Monday morning. I treasured those weekends at home.

FRANK OUTLINED OUR GOAL: find $1.2 million a year to eliminate our losses. Bill and I, with the help of Owen Hoskinson, a young MBA grad and CPA, spent several hours a day over several weeks reviewing every nickel and dime of expense in every department. We cut a lot of "nice to have" but unnecessary expenses, both large and small. One example: we limited all future air travel to coach class, which was good enough for me. The personnel manager immediately resigned. He flew only first class. Amazingly, we came close to finding $1 million in savings, but the raging inflation of the late 1970s brought higher newsprint costs, increased transportation expenses (mostly gasoline), and rising prices across the board, taking back most of what we saved. This was going to be an ongoing struggle.

All the Hearst publishers met in Seattle a few weeks after I joined the *P-I*. When introduced, I directed my remarks to William Randolph Hearst Jr., Hearst editor-in-chief.

"My immigrant parents had studied their English reading the *Pittsburgh Sun-Telegraph*, a Hearst paper," I told him. "They could only afford one paper and wouldn't take the *Pittsburgh Press,* even though I had a *Press* route. Their paper was always the *Sun-Telegraph*. I grew up reading it."

Hearst was pleased.

THE *P-I*'S CIRCULATION was slightly fewer than 200,000 daily and 250,000 Sunday. Like all morning papers, it was strong in outlying areas with circulation extending throughout most of Washington State and into neighboring Oregon, Idaho, and British Columbia. The major competitor was the evening and Sunday *Seattle Times* with a circulation lead of a little more than 30,000. The *P-I* led in circulation until 1948, when the afternoon *Seattle Star* folded and was absorbed by the *Times*. With most of its circulation concentrated in Seattle and nearby suburbs, the *Times* consistently sold 67 percent of the newspaper advertising in the market, leaving the *P-I* with only 33 percent.

Closing that gap was the most difficult challenge I ever faced.

THE *SEATTLE TIMES* is owned and controlled by the Blethen family, but Knight-Ridder, my former employer, owned 49.5 percent.

The paper was founded in 1891 by Alden Blethen, a lawyer and teacher from Maine. It was the largest daily in the state and largest in the West north of San Francisco. The *Times* also owned the *Walla Walla Union-Bulletin* and *Yakima Herald-Republic*.

The *P-I* had most of the same union contracts as the *Times* and about the same operating costs, but the *Times* was profitable. The *P-I* was not. Before moving to Seattle, I read the Seattle newspaper labor contracts and compared them with those of the *Free Press* and other papers. Some were the worst I'd ever seen. When I mentioned this to Jerry Pennington, the *Times* publisher, he called Frank Bennack Jr. to express his fear that I might make the upcoming joint negotiations with the American Newspaper Guild and other unions more difficult. After more than thirty-three hours of intense bargaining by our negotiators in early January, 1977, Pennington and I stepped in to formalize the settlement.

In its coverage of the negotiations, the *Seattle Weekly* referred to me as "the hard-nosed general manager of the *P-I*." I accepted this as a compliment.

Bob Thompson and Bill Cobb had been actively involved with Hearst officers and lawyers from New York during the protracted negotiations with the *Times* for a Joint Operating Agreement. This took a lot of time away from our paper's other business. Meanwhile, the *Times*, having gotten a look at financial information that we shared in the negotiations, took advantage of the situation to strengthen its competitive position.

Not making the circulation battle any easier was a new entry into the morning market. In my first month, the *Bellevue Journal-American* expanded from twice-weekly to daily publication in the mornings. Soon after, the *Everett Herald* shifted its local editions to morning publication. Within the next few years, the *Times* began publishing in the morning on Saturdays and holidays.

PUBLISHER BOB THOMPSON transferred Doug Francis from promotion manager to circulation director shortly before I arrived, so my first new hire was John Joly as marketing and promotion manager. I knew John from his days in promotion at the *Detroit Free Press* and as editor of the Detroit carrier paper before he joined Knight's *Miami Herald*. He was innovative, creative, and had a keen sense of humor. He was a perfect fit for the *P-I* and established good contacts throughout the Seattle area. In my years at the newspaper until John's retirement, we conducted the best reader and community promotions in the Seattle market. John also consulted with other Hearst newspapers. He remains a close friend.

Two of our most successful annual public-service programs were started in 1977.

We participated in the Jefferson Award program, sponsored by the American Institute of Public Service. For its part, the *P-I* presented local Jefferson Awards to five to seven "unsung community heroes" who, as volunteers and with little fanfare, had in a significant way made Seattle and the surrounding region a better place to live. We presented Jefferson Award medallions to local winners at public ceremonies.

Our first local winner, Dr. Leonard Cobb, went on to win a national Jefferson Award. Doctor Cobb, a cardiologist, founded Medic One in cooperation with the Seattle Fire Department to improve survival rates for cardiac-arrest patients by promoting CPR training for the public and providing a high level of specialized pre-hospital emergency care.

I attended several of the national Jefferson Award events in Washington, D.C. At one dinner, I was seated next to Secretary of State James Baker and Supreme Court Justice Byron White. I mentioned to the justice that, as a boy in Pittsburgh, I had followed his football career as an All-American at Colorado and a player with the Pittsburgh Pirates (now the Steelers). He was famously known then as "Whizzer" White.

The second program was the Readers Care Fund. We solicited donations from readers with heavy in-paper promotion during the holiday season, raising more than $200,000 annually for distribution to charities such as the American Red Cross, Northwest Harvest, Forgotten Children's Fund, and the Variety Club's Sunshine Coach Program.

In response, a year after the start of our Readers Care Fund, the *Seattle Times* stepped up promotion of its Fund for the Needy during the holidays.

IN EARLY 1977, ADVERTISING Director Tom Gormley resigned to join the *Pittsburgh Press*. He had been a candidate for general manager. With no viable successor on the staff, we engaged Youngs, Walker, a head-hunting firm specializing in newspapers. I hired Richard "Ric" Trent, a young, up-and-coming executive from the *Washington Post*.

When the assistant advertising director also resigned, we hired Tom Smith, a colleague of Trent's in Washington, as the new assistant. We also hired a new classified manager. The staff responded favorably to the new arrivals. They tackled the competitive challenges with enthusiasm and creativity, but it was difficult to change the habits of people who bought advertising. They found it more convenient not to change.

Our circulation didn't improve either. A change from a small television booklet to a tabloid was pushed by the former ad director who was convinced he could sell more ads with a larger page size. It did not produce more advertising and cost us Sunday circulation, but it was a major cost-cutting move. Sunday circulation took a big hit when we raised the single-copy price from thirty-five to fifty cents in September, 1977.

Frank made it clear to all the *P-I* department heads that I was in charge of the day-to-day operations. As publisher, Bob Thompson represented the paper well in the community and continued to do so. As editor, he also headed the news and editorial staffs. But I controlled the budget. Hearst had an accounting system that required all newspapers to submit weekly profit-and-loss statements. I was the paper's contact with Hearst headquarters in New York. The buck stopped at my desk.

THE HAPPIEST EVENT of my first year came in late April after a meeting with other Hearst publishers and managers in Los Angeles to study operations of the *Herald-Examiner*. I flew to Chicago immediately to await the birth of our son. On May 5, 1977, Sunni and I were blessed with the arrival of Michael Anthony. Mother and baby were healthy. I returned to Seattle one happy father.

I spent most of my Seattle weekends house-hunting and finally settled on a spacious home on a high point in Horizon View, Bellevue. It had a spectacular 280-degree view facing west, overlooking Lake Washington, Lake Sammamish, and the distant Seattle skyline. I hoped Sunni would like it.

We listed our Barrington Hills property for sale and drove west in a loaded station wagon with sightseeing stops in the Black Hills, Mount Rushmore, and Yellowstone Park. It was interesting that we had driven just eight miles south from Barrington to get on Interstate

90 and then stayed on the freeway for more than 2,000 miles all the way to Bellevue. Our home was a just a mile south of I-90.

The first clue that this home was probably not our best choice came when the large moving van failed to make it up the driveway. Everything had to be carried up the steep hill. A stray basketball tumbling down the drive and across the street landed in the yard of the house below. There was snow on the driveway in the winter but little or none several blocks downhill. We moved after two years.

FRANK BENNACK JR. WAS PROMOTED to executive vice president and CEO in 1977. Succeeding him as general manager of the Newspaper Division was Robert Danzig, publisher of Hearst's *Albany Times-Union*. Danzig had come up through the ranks at the *T-U*.

In my previous executive positions on four newspapers, I pretty much ran my own show without calling my bosses to discuss every problem or initiative. I continued to operate that way with Hearst, so more often than not, Danzig would call me. I knew that the publishers of the seven other Hearst papers called to discuss most matters with him. I didn't, unless it was required or involved a corporate decision. Danzig always expected optimistic reports, especially budget forecasts. Frankly I did not look forward to our phone conversations. He was creative and frequently made suggestions, mostly promotion ideas. Many were adopted. Some were not practical.

Danzig encouraged us to look into computerization, particularly for setting classified ads, the most lucrative use of space. Most people find change difficult. Acceptance of new methods requires ample training. Many newspapers implemented new processes without adequate preparation. The result was employee resistance and, as my experience taught me, problems getting the newspaper out on time.

There were many horror stories. This was not going to happen at the *P-I*. We would pick the best system and thoroughly train everyone before implementation. Our first computer applications would be in classified, followed by the news departments.

We bought thirty-day passes on Eastern Airlines and dispatched a key editor, classified manager, production manager, and Owen Hoskinson from the business office to visit newspapers using different systems developed by the five leading vendors in the field. They all agreed that the Atex system was the best choice. We bought computers for everyone and provided two weeks of training in classified. Later, we implemented computerization in the newsroom, where it was harder to retrain some of the hunt-and-peck writers wedded to their typewriters.

The new computer looked business-like in my office, but truthfully I never learned to use a computer until after retiring. Then my sons were my teachers. I still need their help from time to time. There is some truth to the old adage that you can't teach an old dog new tricks.

We implemented many new processes in other departments, but never missed a press start by more than ten minutes. The training saved money in the long run.

IN LATE 1977, HEARST became a finalist in the bidding when the *Wilmington News-Journal* was offered for sale. I had the most experience in this market, based on seven years as a *New-Journal* executive, contact again while consulting for Knight in Philadelphia, and yet again in 1974 when the *Tribune* sent me to help the *N-J* after its unsuccessful launch of a Sunday paper.

I went to Wilmington with Frank Bannack Jr. and other Hearst executives to evaluate the circulation operation and the market in general. Hearst was outbid by Gannett Company, which paid $60 million.

BOB THOMPSON HAD open-heart surgery in early 1978. During his three-month absence, I was called upon to represent the newspaper at civic events. One of many invitations came from Walter Schoenfeld, owner of Brittania Sportswear and one of six owners of the Seattle Mariners. Various business leaders attended a dinner at Schoenfeld's home the evening before opening day. Mariner partner Danny Kaye, the comedian movie star, drew a sketch of "Thumbelina" from the Danish fairy tale on Sunni's thumb, which she later showed Richard and David, much to their delight. The Mariners were a business with Kaye. He did not use his movie star status to promote the team.

The guest of honor that evening was Joe DiMaggio, the celebrated Hall of Fame New York Yankee, who would throw out the first pitch the next day. Joe had been my childhood hero. After learning that an Italian-American publisher, a rarity in the newspaper industry, was in attendance representing the *Seattle Post-Intelligencer*, DiMaggio invited Sunni and me to join his table. The next day, he spoke to Seattle Rotary and offered me a ride back to my office.

A HEARST PUBLISHERS' MEETING was planned for Seattle in late June. Sunni was asked to organize events for the spouses, including an outing to Snoqualmie Falls and the nearby lodge. When Thompson returned to work in early June, however, his wife immediately took over, substituting some of Sunni's planning with plans of her own. Bob was a nice guy, but apparently had not told his wife that I was in charge of the P-I. I told Bob Danzig that the situation was not acceptable and asked for a transfer to another Hearst paper. He asked me to be patient. We would talk further when he came to Seattle.

The day before the publishers' meeting, Danzig and I took a long walk, something he liked to do when he came to Seattle. He said that when the meeting ended and everyone had left town, he would inform Bob Thompson that he was being appointed chief of the Hearst Newspapers' Washington, D.C. bureau, a post he held before William Randolph Hearst Jr. named him publisher of the *P-I* in 1974.

On June 30, 1978, I was appointed the new publisher of the *Post-Intelligencer*, effective immediately, with full control of the news and editorial departments. I called Gene Simon to thank him for believing in me.

Chapter 24

■ ■ ■

First Two Years as Publisher

In naming me the new publisher of the *Seattle Post-Intelligencer* on June 30, 1978, Frank Bennack Jr. of the Hearst Corp. said, "Virgil Fassio is acknowledged by his professional associates as one of the nation's most outstanding newspaper executives. The quality of his leadership as general manager has been underscored by his laying the foundation for future strengthening the newspaper in every way."

I faced a big challenge. Beyond the immediate goals of increasing revenue and reducing expenses, my implied mission was to convince the public that the *P-I* was not a failing newspaper. This would take the dedication and best efforts of every employee.

Senator Robert Dole of Kansas was the first person outside of the staff to offer congratulations. He had read the announcement in the paper that morning before coming in for an editorial-board interview. He was making the rounds of newspapers seeking support for his bid for the Republican nomination for president in 1980. (Dole's effort fell short that year, but he became the GOP nominee in 1996, losing to Bill Clinton.)

A second call came from Senator Henry "Scoop" Jackson, one of the most powerful leaders in the U.S. Senate. I had met him casually on a previous occasion. He wanted to become better acquainted. When I offered to come to his office, he said, "No. I'll come to yours." We had a far-ranging discussion about a variety of issues.

That's when I came to understand the power of the publisher of a metropolitan newspaper. Up to that point, my entire managerial experience had consisted of doing the best-possible job as a department head and a team player, working with others to make the newspaper successful. I understood that no matter what, the publisher would get the credit or the blame.

SENATOR WARREN G. MAGNUSON, Washington's senior senator (like Jackson, a Democrat) was one of the first national leaders I met. At the time, "Maggie," as his friends called him, was president pro tempore of the U.S. Senate and chairman of the powerful Appropriations Committee. Maggie had been our guest at the 1977 *P-I* Sports Star of the Year banquet. Afterward, we had a few drinks in the lounge. He was able to put away vodka like it was water, never showing any effect. He told marvelous stories of the early years of his long Senate career. President Lyndon Johnson had been his best man when he married his wife, Germaine.

Maggie sent his driver to pick me up me for the 1979 Touchdown Club dinner in Washington, D.C. I had been invited by Herman Sarkowsky, managing partner of the Seattle Seahawks. The long reception area of the hotel was full of people gathering for the event. Most knew Maggie. They greeted him as if he was royalty. His popularity and power were evident.

JANUARY 25, 1979 was a memorable day. I was among twenty publishers and editors invited to interview President Jimmy Carter at the White House. I chatted with the President before the questioning began. Carter was calm, flashing his familiar smile throughout and showing a keen knowledge of the minutest details as he responded to questions.

We spent the rest of the day with cabinet officers, staff experts, and presidential advisors, including Zbizniew Brzezinski, the President's national security advisor. Most of the briefings concerned our diplomatic and other relations with China and future relations with Taiwan. I met Carter again in 1988 at a Hearst meeting at the Carter Library in Atlanta.

The President was aware of the breakfast meeting I had arranged with Premier Teng Hsaio-ping of China for the premier's upcoming visit to Seattle.

The Southern Publishers Association had hosted an interview breakfast for Teng in Atlanta. Through channels, I invited him and his party to take part in a similar interview over breakfast with members of the Pacific Northwest Publishers Association (Allied Dailies). Every publisher and most editors in Washington, Oregon, Idaho, Montana, and Alaska attended.

Unfortunately, Teng came down with a cold and did not come. Chairing the event, I was seated at the head table between Vice Premier Feng Yi and Foreign Minister Huang Hua. I allowed the *New York Times* and wire-service reporters to join us, but the questions were restricted to our members.

In a slow, difficult interview, Huang warned that "all peoples and countries should be on guard against Soviet ambitions to control the world." Every question and answer had to be laboriously translated, even though Huang spoke excellent English. He and I had a friendly chat.

Huang had been the chief Chinese negotiator at Panmunjom where the Korean Armistice Agreement was signed in 1953 suspending the Korean War. I had been a Naval Reserve officer at the same time.

A few days earlier, I attended a reception for Henry Kissinger, who was President Nixon's emissary to China prior to establishment of diplomatic relations in 1972, and a luncheon attended by political and business leaders honoring Teng the day before our scheduled interview.

In 1980, former President Gerald Ford was the guest at a small reception in Seattle. He had been a long-time congressman from Michigan and then vice president. He succeeded a resigned Richard Nixon, but was defeated by Jimmy Carter in 1976. We chatted about the *Detroit Free Press* and our mutual friend, Frank Angelo, whom he considered a fine editor.

DIXIE LEE RAY WAS GOVERNOR of Washington from 1976-80, following two successful terms by Republican Dan Evans, one of the state's most capable public servants. Evans later became a U.S. senator. Governor Ray, a Democrat, was unlike any governor I ever met. The *P-I* was justifiably critical of her from the start.

Once Sunni and I arrived early for a Christmas party in the Governor's Mansion in Olympia. The governor took us to the kitchen, where she had two parakeets, and pointed to the bottom of the cage. There was that day's front page of the *P-I*. She changed it every day.

On another occasion, I was serving myself at the food buffet during a Mariner's pre-game party in the Kingdome when Governor Ray entered, saw me, and charged across the room to berate me, loudly, about the *P-I*'s criticism. The governor's supporters were shocked.

Shortly afterward, the governor and I shared the podium at a banquet for national travel writers. She called herself "the *P-I*'s favorite governor" and informed the group that "any relationship between the *Seattle Post-Intelligencer* and intelligence is coincidental." Ray presented me with a small urn made of Mount St. Helen's ash, describing it as a symbol of learning and mercy.

Most politicians are smart enough to "never pick a fight with someone who buys ink by the barrel," as Mark Twain once put it. The smart ones tend to ignore criticism, understanding that it comes with the job. Governor Ray lost a re-election bid to John Spellman, a moderate Republican. He served one term and was defeated by Booth Gardner, a Democrat, in 1984. All Washington governors since then have been Democrats.

EX-GOVERNOR ALBERT ROSELLINI invited me to lunch at Rosellini's 610 Restaurant, owned by his cousin, Victor, in early September, 1980. Albert's son, John, was a candidate for Washington attorney general. He requested that we cover his son's campaign without rehashing his own career as governor. John Rosellini is the candidate, he said, not his father. This seemed to be a reasonable request that I promised to pass on to our editors.

A few weeks later, I was the featured speaker at the annual banquet of the Bellevue Sons of Italy lodge. John Rosellini sat at the head table and was asked to say a few words to a then-friendly audience. However, the *P-I*, investigating a tip, broke a story a few weeks later reporting the younger Rosellini's questionable financial dealings as the honorary Italian consul. He had misappropriated funds from the estate of an Italian citizen that were supposed to go to relatives in Italy. He lost the election.

In the winter of 1979, Bob Danzig and I flew to Alaska to visit Robert Atwood, owner-publisher of the *Anchorage Times*. Hearst was interested in buying the *Times*. Atwood, a genial host, appreciated our visit but the paper was not for sale. Before leaving, we toured Anchorage. Brrrr! I had no regrets about not having accepted a job Atwood offered in Bagdad in 1958.

EDITORIAL BOARDS of metropolitan papers are "must" stops for candidates running for office. In 1980, we met with Congressman John Anderson, who had enough support to qualify as an Independent candidate for president. He was accompanied by Secret Service agents who searched my office bathroom in advance of his visit. Anderson received our endorsement, but lost to Ronald Reagan. We met with countless primary candidates before making endorsements and always made an honest effort to select the best one. Anderson aside, we had a good record of picking winners.

I regret not keeping a log of all the interesting newsmakers, not just politicians, who met with the editorial board during my fifteen years as publisher. Among the many newsmakers who visited were Supreme Court Chief Justice Warren Burger; Secretary of State Alexander Haig; Major League Baseball Commissioner Peter Ueberroth; Evangelist Pat Robertson; Jacques Cousteau, famous French underwater explorer; CBS television anchor Dan Rather; cable-television magnate Ted Turner; labor leader Cesar Chavez, who organized California farm workers; civil-rights leader Rev. Jesse Jackson; Secretary of Defense Casper Weinberger, and dozens of local, state, and national political leaders and elected officials. It was our privilege and duty as journalists to question them all in depth.

I never wanted to add the title of editor to my publisher's role, as Bob Thompson and many publishers did. I did not feel qualified. This turned out to be a wise decision for another reason, too. Being editor would have restricted my ability to work with business and political leaders. It was important to be able to talk in confidence and to be trusted.

During my time as general manager, I frequently sat in on editorial board interviews but rarely participated in editorial decisions. My political-science major and previous editorial experience were valuable assets when I headed the editorial board and had the final word to decide the paper's positions on vital issues.

I had to be prepared to defend our editorial positions as well as our news coverage if challenged by those in the community who disagreed. I participated, when not otherwise occupied, in discussions at the daily editorial board meetings and in interviews with the most news-worthy guests. If unable to attend, I met with the editorial-page editor afterward to form our opinion. I also reviewed each day's editorials and offered direction on subjects with which I was familiar.

I rarely exercised my veto overruling a staff consensus, and only then when I was more familiar with an issue or candidate. The editorial-page editor, Jack de Yonge, managed a department of six excellent, thoughtful writers. When de Yonge left to write a history of his native Alaska in 1981, he was succeeded by Jean Godden. Charles Dunsire, who accurately and fairly covered the JOA litigation from 1981 to 1983, took over the position in 1983 and continued to write editorials for several years after my retirement. Dunsire and I were on the same page most of the time.

Among our other stars were Shelby Scates, a veteran political reporter and columnist; David Horsey, the best hire I ever made, who later won two Pulitzer Prizes for political cartooning; Nancy Hevly, Sam Sperry, Solveig Torvik, and others for short periods. *P-I* editorials were well written. Our positions were respected.

The *P-I* determined its own editorial positions without direction or interference from Hearst headquarters, even though our opinions frequently differed. In the 1980 Presidential Election, I bowed to the unanimous vote of the editorial board to endorse the aforementioned independent, John Anderson, over the Democratic incumbent Jimmy Carter, and Republican challenger Ronald Reagan.

Every other Hearst paper and our corporate headquarters in New York endorsed Reagan, who won. Danzig's comment: "You wasted your endorsement." On our own, we endorsed Reagan for re-election four years later. We agreed he was the better candidate.

On many issues, Hearst was conservative with the *P-I* taking a more liberal position, in line with the demographics of Washington state and our readers.

There is a distinct separation between the responsibilities of the editorial board, which articulates the newspaper's opinion on issues, and the news department's role to report the news accurately and without bias. The public doesn't always understand this.

Historically the *P-I* had been a newspaper with feisty, vigilant reporters on the news side and a left-of-center outlook on the editorial pages. Personally I tended to be a middle-of-the-road independent, more conservative on international issues but more liberal domestically, and aimed to make the *P-I* more of an "editors' paper" and close to the middle editorially.

IN ADDITION TO PRODUCING a lively newspaper to attract more readers, there was the daily challenge of increasing the volume of advertising, which typically accounts for 60 to 70 percent of the revenue. Major local advertisers had to be sold on the value of the *P-I* as a good buy. Innovative promotions were invented to accomplish this.

Our advertising executives worked hard to sell space to major buyers. I had frequent lunch meetings with the individual heads of retail businesses. A slight increase resulted. We put the same number of salesmen on the street as the *Times*, but ours returned with only one-third of the advertising. Another daily battle was containing costs. The number of news columns and pages is governed by advertising volume. I met every morning with the ad-layout man. Sometimes, a decision had to be made either to go up two to four pages or cut back pages to tighten the paper. Each editor had a "budget" of allotted space for news, opinions, features, and sports. With limited space, we favored a high story count to cover as wide a variety of content as possible.

Communication among department heads at weekly meetings was good. Frequently I met one on one with members of my team.

The *P-I* had the second-highest circulation gain in the country, 6.3 percent, in 1978 over 1977. We wanted to keep the momentum going, despite the resignation of Doug Francis as circulation director. His successor did not last long. And with a good economy, it was becoming difficult to find morning route carriers. Stability in the circulation department was returned when David Perona took over.

In 1979, circulation gains were erased by price increases: from $5 to $6 monthly for daily and Sunday delivery; $3.50 to $4.35 for daily delivery only; and from fifteen to twenty cents for single copies of the daily and fifty to sixty cents for single Sunday copies. Single-copy sales represented a large proportion of our circulation.

More price increases in 1980 raised the cost of daily and Sunday delivery to $6.75, daily-only to $5.10, and Sunday single copies to seventy-five cents. The increases were encouraged by corporate in an attempt to raise new revenue to balance against cost increases, but each increase cost us circulation. Still, New York's direction regarding revenue was taken very seriously.

The bottom line improved slightly, but fixed costs grew. The only real profit the *P-I* made in its years of losses came from the annual Seattle Home Show, one of the biggest events of its kind in the country. The newspaper received 25 percent of the net profit in exchange for heavy promotion space.

An important part of my job was representing the newspaper in the community. I attended weekly meetings of Seattle Rotary, the world's largest Rotary Club; the Community Development Round Table with off-the-record speakers; the 101 Club within the Washington Athletic Club; and monthly meetings of Greater Seattle Chamber of Commerce, the Seattle/King County Convention & Visitors Bureau, and the Downtown Seattle Association. It was helpful, too, to be a member of the prestigious lunch clubs, Rainier and Columbia Tower, where I promoted the newspaper as a successful business. I also attended quarterly meetings of Hearst publishers and annual meetings of the ANPA, the ABC, and the Allied Newspaper Publishers Association.

THE UNIVERSITY OF PITTSBURGH played the University of Washington at Husky Stadium in September, 1979. As a Pitt alumnus, I hosted a Gray Lines tour for the official delegation and welcomed the visiting football team at a breakfast in the Westin Hotel. I accompanied Chancellor Wesley Posvar to several functions and was interviewed on a Pittsburgh radio station.

After the game, I walked with Posvar whose custom was to escort the players to the locker room. While passing the fifty-yard line, in front of some of the most dedicated, long-time UW fans, my five-foot-six stature seemed to shrink considerably when some friends yelled my name and teasingly demanded to know, "What are you doing there?" Pitt won for the third time in four games against the UW in a series dating back to the 1936 Rose Bowl, giving me bragging rights with my Husky friends.

IN DECEMBER, 1979, OUR FAMILY moved into a six-year-old waterfront home on Lake Washington in Bellevue. The boys did not have to change schools. The daylight basement faced the backyard and a dock offering perfect moorage for a boat.

We had happy experiences buying four boats in succession ranging in length from nineteen to forty-four feet—and even happier days when we sold them. We enjoyed several cruises on the lake, through the Lake Washington Ship Canal and Ballard Locks to Elliott Bay, and on to the San Juan Islands and Victoria, British Columbia. But I have to say we never really became a boating family.

IN SUMMER, 1980, I took an overseas trip for the first time in twenty-two years. I was invited by the Israeli Journalists Association with seven other U.S. journalists to spend two weeks in Israel. Security for the El Al Airlines flight, New York to Tel Aviv, was tighter than I have ever seen. The male flight attendants were built like heavyweight wrestlers. We never saw the host journalist group after an opening reception. After the first night, we were escorted by a government representative, Rafael Horowitz, our genial host and guide to places most Israelis and few tourists ever see.

We visited Palestinian cities on the West Bank and left notes in the Western (Wailing) Wall; interviewed Deputy Prime Minister Viguel Yadin and the chief justice of the Israel Supreme Court; went inside bunkers on the Golan Heights from which Syrians had fired on Israeli fields below before losing the six-day war with Israel in 1973; slept in a kibbutz; visited several Maronite Christian villages in Southern Lebanon, accompanied by armed guards; saw castles remaining from the crusades; and got a look at the refugee situation on the Gaza Strip.

We also traveled to the Israeli-made city of Yamit on the edge of the Sinai Desert, which Israel was turning over to Egypt; swam in the Sea of Galilee; floated in the Dead Sea; took a gondola to ancient Masada; witnessed shouting in the Israeli Knesset over a no-confidence vote for Prime Minister Menachem Begin; and visited Beersheba, Seattle's sister city, where Jewish emigrants were learning Hebrew, as required of all newcomers.

Best of all, we saw historic sites in the Holy Land—walking where Jesus walked, performed miracles, was crucified, and died. This experience was especially moving.

One evening, I was a dinner guest at the home of a couple born in New York who had become committed Israelis, like many other citizens I met. Like all Israeli men, the husband was an army reservist, prepared for a call to duty at a moment's notice. The ruins of an ancient structure were exposed to view underneath his home, a common sight in Jerusalem.

The trip offered a good look at the Israeli side of the Middle East.

I had seen the Arab side in Egypt and Iraq in 1958 and heard Arab leaders denounce the creation of Israel. Israel was more impressive. It had gone through three wars with its Arab neighbors. It was relatively peaceful at that time and it was safe to travel almost everywhere in the occupied West Bank. This was after President Carter brokered the historic Camp David Accords between Israel and Egypt and before Israel began to build settlements on the West Bank, adding another complication to the already-serious difficulties that were deterrents to peace despite many years of failed effort by the United States, Israel's closest ally, and other nations to resolve the many differences that made peace so elusive.

On the way home, I took a detour to Rome where I boarded a train for Torino. Enroute I practiced my Italian, rusty after so many years, on my seatmate, a schoolteacher. I was greeted at the station by two aunts. That began a joyous reunion with relatives in Torino and Asti. Everywhere I was welcomed with typical Italian hospitality by uncles, aunts, and cousins from both sides of the family. I had not seen them since 1956.

JACK DOUGHTY, A VETERAN newspaperman who had reported from Vietnam, was the *P-I*'s executive editor under Bob Thompson. Bill Asbury, the managing editor, had lobbied extensively for the executive-editor position. Impressed by some of Asbury's progressive ideas, I named him executive editor and made Doughty managing editor. This seemed like a good move at the time.

In fall, 1980, Bob Danzig recommended a trip to the *San Antonio Light* for Bill Asbury and me to find out how the paper had cut the news department staff by 10 percent, substantially reducing expenses. On our return, Asbury told me he could not do his job properly if we made the same cuts.

Danzig also recommended hiring an expert in newspaper design to oversee a makeover of our news and feature pages, believing an improved look would attract more readers. Ted Bolwell, a Canadian, proposed some attractive redesigns. However, the changes did not sit well with Asbury. I understood that it was difficult for an editor to accept someone else's ideas for changes when he believed he was doing a good job. Bolwell also recommended taking on two layout editors who had successfully implemented makeovers elsewhere. I interviewed and hired Jim Rennie for the news side and John Reistrup for features.

The combination of requested staff cuts, major changes in the newspaper's design, and addition of two experienced editors hired to work under him prompted Asbury to request reassignment as editor of the editorial pages to replace Jack de Yonge. This plan seemed like a solution.

My first two years as publisher were an amazing learning experience. At the end of 1980, even though we were still struggling to break even, I did not expect the major surprise that would derail our efforts in January.

Chapter 25

■   ■   ■

Joint Operating Agreement Litigation

On Sunday morning, January 3, 1981, I reached for a piece of wood from the garage rafters to finish a project and fell twelve feet from a ladder, severely breaking my left arm near the shoulder. Dr. Leo Burnett, a neighbor and head of radiology at Virginia Mason Hospital, came at Sunni's urgent request and intervened in time to prevent surgery and literally put my arm back in place, strapping it to my torso like a mummy. Only my fingers showed for more than two months.

I canceled a trip to New York for a meeting hurriedly called by Hearst for Thursday, January 8. It apparently was urgent enough for Bob Danzig to come to Seattle and meet me at home on Friday morning. Without a clue, I had invited department heads to come to my home with updates for Danzig. Their reports were not needed.

Danzig swore me to secrecy before reporting on the success-ful conclusion, after months of negotiations, of a Joint Operating

Agreement with the *Seattle Times.* In 1975-76, Bob Thompson and Bill Cobb had squandered valuable time from other duties while engaged in lengthy, unsuccessful JOA negotiations. When I joined the *P-I,* I requested that I not be included in any future negotiations.

The federal Newspaper Preservation Act of 1970 grandfathered twenty-four existing JOAs, including one in San Francisco between Hearst's *Examiner* and the independent *Chronicle.* The federal law allowed future JOAs to be negotiated in markets where one or more daily newspapers was in "probable danger of financial failure."

The *Seattle Post-Intelligencer* had been losing money for twelve consecutive years, 1968-80. Despite major changes and hard work, we had not been able to improve the bottom line.

Under a JOA, our advertising, circulation, production, and most business functions would be handled by the *Seattle Times.* Both papers would remain separately owned and independently edited. The *P-I* would publish mornings Monday-Saturday, the *Times* evenings Monday-Friday and mornings on Saturdays and holidays. The Sunday paper would display a joint masthead, but all the news content would be provided by the *Times.* The *P-I* would have its own Sunday editorial section.

Term of the agreement was fifty years. The *Times* would receive 6 percent of the net profits as a management fee. Of the remaining profit, 66 percent would go to the *Times,* 34 percent to the *P-I.*

Given its record of financial losses, the *P-I* definitely qualified as a newspaper at risk of failure. Hearst expected quick Justice Department approval. A JOA would mean drastic changes for the *P-I* publisher. Hearst preferred that I stay in Seattle. If this was not agreeable, I was told, Hearst would find me another publisher's job elsewhere. This was an easy decision. Sunni and I liked Seattle. This was home. We wanted to stay.

BOB DANZIG RUSHED back to Seattle the following Tuesday, a few weeks earlier than planned, after a clerk copying the agreement in the *Times*' law firm tipped off a radio station. Before meeting with department heads, Danzig, without consulting me, assured Bill Asbury that the JOA would not change his job. This scuttled my plan to transfer Asbury to the editorial page. He balked at a transfer.

Accompanied by Danzig and with my arm under my shirt, I stood atop a desk in the newsroom to make the surprise announcement to the assembled *P-I* employees. Danzig assured everyone that our newspaper would remain independently edited even as the *Times* assumed the other functions. Staffers were stunned, having been unaware of the gravity of our financial situation. Our positive moves had dispelled rumors of imminent closure. The general public could not believe we were a failing newspaper, either. Apparently we had worked too hard to give an impression of success.

Approval didn't come quickly. Joining calls for a public hearing were Seattle Mayor Charles Royer, Senators Jackson and Magnuson, members of Congress, most local politicians, and the unions. Opposition groups with vested interests were soon organized.

A group of employees, concerned with the loss of jobs and worried about news and editorial independence, formed the Committee for an Independent P-I (CIPI). A People Opposed to a One Newspaper Town (POINT) committee was chaired by David Brewster, editor of the *Seattle Weekly* (which had applied for Associated Press membership). M. Lamont Bean, major owner of Pay-n-Save's retail companies, organized other retailers and business people to form the Committee for a Free Press (COFP), which expressed concern about advertising rates under in a JOA. Ironically, Bean's companies bought 75 percent of their advertising from the *Times* and pulled their advertising from the *P-I*. The groups joined forces to engage a well-known attorney, William Dwyer, to make their case for a public hearing.

A year earlier, I had written the Hearst's chief lawyer requesting that we change law firms in Seattle because I believed our current firm was not properly handling an equal-opportunity and discrimination case filed before I arrived. I recommended we engage the law firm of William Dwyer. The decision not to change firms proved to be very costly for Hearst. Dwyer, an outstanding lawyer and expert in anti-trust litigation, was a tough opponent. He later became a federal judge.

I felt that we had good cause to fire the advertising staffer who was bad-mouthing the company to advertisers while collecting a paycheck. Our lawyer recommended we not do so. He suggested we tolerate the situation in anticipation of prompt approval of the JOA, after which the employee would no longer be needed.

THE *TIMES* AND THE *P-I* formally applied to the Department of Justice for approval of a JOA on March 28, 1981. Supporting documents from the newspapers were made available for public viewing. The application was under review by the agency's Anti-Trust Division. A few months later, Attorney General William French Smith appointed David Hanscom, retired chief administrative law judge at the Federal Trade Commission, to conduct a public hearing.

A three-week hearing was held at the U.S. Courthouse in Seattle in November, 1981. The government was represented by Anti-Trust Division lawyers. Hearst and Times attorneys joined forces. Bob

Danzig, Bill Cobb, and I attended every day. Opponents had requested 16,000 pages of documents, including all minutes of negotiations. Every session was covered extensively by both dailies, several suburban papers, and the *Seattle Weekly*, which opposed a JOA. Stories appeared in the *New York Times* and *Wall Street Journal*.

"The *Times* was a sleeping giant ready to explode like the *Detroit News* in my earlier career with the *Detroit Free Press*, but I found there were many differences with the *Times*," I said in my opening statement. "The *Times* changed to morning on Saturdays and holidays and launched a morning edition in 1980. I've always been an optimist. I thought I could turn it around. We were a fiercely competitive newspaper but the picture didn't change."

I pointed out that gasoline alone cost the *P-I* almost $1 million a year more than it had in 1980.

"You still have to put a million bucks into the gas tank and get nothing for it," I testified. "It would take more than a miracle to restore profitability. The *P-I* was state of the art in all areas except presses. Replacements would cost $20 million."

In twelve years, 1968-80, *P-I* losses totaled $14.5 million. In 1980, operating revenue was $39.9 million. Operating costs were $41.5 million, for a loss of $1.6 million. Advertising revenue was 71.3 percent of revenue. The *P-I*'s share of retail advertising was 30.2 percent. Our classified share was 30.7 percent. Seattle was the most competitive market in the United States with four suburban morning papers.

I spent five full days, plus rebuttal sessions, fielding aggressive questions from Dwyer and lawyers from the Anti-Trust Division, which opposed a JOA. Surprisingly I enjoyed being on the stand. The other side had been given a lot of false information and misleading innuendos from employees who didn't have the facts. I was able to correct the record. I was asked to comment on my letters to Hearst headquarters, mostly optimistic, that did not hint of imminent failure. I had been encouraged by Danzig to be positive. Questions were also raised about my optimistic statements at employee meetings.

"As chief executive of the paper, I had to have a voice of optimism," I responded. "I can't be a pessimistic leader of enthusiastic people."

Dwyer was relentless. He kept coming at me. At one point, I stood up and said, "Mr. Dwyer, if wishes were horses, beggars would ride." The gallery laughed. Judge Hanscom laughed. Dwyer did not. My protest wasn't pertinent, but it sure felt good.

OPPONENTS TRIED TO MAKE a case that Hearst could support the *P-I* and that the charges to the *P-I* for syndication, among others expenses, were excessive and financially draining. John Morton, a leading newspaper analyst, said the *P-I* would have failed financially long before had it not been for assistance from the Hearst Corp.

Frank Bennack Jr. testified about the aftermath of failed negotiations in 1976. "We conducted an extensive search for talent and lured Virgil Fassio from the *Chicago Tribune*," he said. "I knew it was a long shot, but we had to give it another shot."

Frank promised that the *P-I* would remain a strong news and editorial voice in Seattle, saying, "The leader and executive staff is the best the paper ever had." That statement made us all very proud.

Harrison Mitnick, treasurer of the Hearst Corp., testified that *P-I* losses by 1985 would total $21 million. In the sixty years under Hearst ownership, the paper had been profitable in only twenty-seven years with its net loss in Seattle totaling $8.6 million.

Bob Danzig, Bill Cobb, and Circulation Director Perona also testified, as did a few other expert witnesses for Hearst. The opponents brought forth several expert witnesses, too, but none made any convincing points.

Meanwhile, after several months of increasingly difficult relations, Bill Asbury accepted a severance settlement and left to become editor of a group of business publications. He surprised us by surfacing during the JOA hearings as a witness for the opposition. He claimed that Hearst and I thwarted his plans to make the paper competitive and complained that he had been asked to cut 10 percent of his staff. He conceded I was an "excellent publisher, but a good soldier who did not fight enough to get things we needed." In fact, I had gotten everything we really needed from Hearst. Asbury also had told me earlier he believed that he believed a JOA was the only thing that could save the *P-I*.

Another ex-executive editor, Lou Guzzo, also testified. He claimed that Hearst had made insufficient improvements in the *P-I* to make it competitive. Guzzo had been fired in 1975. He admitted that he had sued Hearst. We assumed both Asbury and Guzzo had been approached by prospective buyers promising jobs at the paper, if it were sold. They were among several current and former employees who asserted that the *P-I* was overcoming past mismanagement but had a brighter future. They offered no proof to back up their statements.

Hearst's lead lawyer, John Thackeray, was a master of cross-examination. He was able to pin down opponents' claims and to ask all the right questions. Other Hearst lawyers were equally competent.

James Rosse, a Stanford economist, testified that "the *P-I* is in the grip of virtually an irreversible downward spiral that will lead to its ultimate demise if there is no JOA." The decline, he said, had started before 1965. Reflecting on Rosse's testimony, I knew that had I been aware of the long history of losses, I still would have joined Hearst. An opportunity to manage a metropolitan newspaper was too tempting.

Judge Hanscom ruled that the paper had to be judged as a single entity, not as part of a larger profitable media company. During the course of the hearings, a few offers to buy the *P-I* surfaced. Among others, Rupert Murdoch, the Australian-born media mogul, was said to be interested if the JOA was turned down. However, the judge ruled that offering the paper for sale was not a requirement for a JOA. In any event, Frank indicated Hearst had no interest in selling.

The hearings ended the day before Thanksgiving. On January 18, 1982, Judge Hanscom submitted his report to the attorney general recommending approval of the JOA. The attorney general then had to decide to approve or disapprove.

Throughout the long process, I was the public face of Hearst and the *P-I*. I held a widely covered press conference to comment on the judge's recommendation and said that, if approved, the joint operations would begin in mid-March. I promised, once again, that the P-I would remain a fiercely competitive newspaper. I regretted that many employees would lose their jobs. The alternative was *all* employees would lose jobs.

In order to keep our employees from jumping ship, we offered a cash bonus to everyone who stayed until the JOA transition was completed. Still, we had a few resignations. Some left for good jobs elsewhere, including General Manager Ric Trent, who became head of a group of weeklies in California. David Perona became circulation director of the *Buffalo Evening News*.

On June 16, 1982, the attorney general approved the JOA. The *P-I* scheduled June 28 for the first papers to come off the *Times* presses. The next day, the opponents filed suit in U.S. District Court challenging the federal decision. It asserted that the Newspaper Preservation Act was unconstitutional and violated anti-trust laws and First Amendment protections.

WHILE THE LITIGATION was pending, I experienced chest pains and arm-tingling at a Seahawks game on August 13. Noticing my discomfort, my sons Richard and David took me to nearby Virginia Mason Hospital, where I had double-bypass surgery a few days later to repair blocked arteries leading to my heart. I spent the next three weeks at home. Then I returned to the office, working half-days for six weeks and finally resuming a full-time schedule.

I was recuperating at home on August 28 when U.S. District Court Judge Barbara Rothstein blocked the JOA, ruling that the AG's decision was invalid and that the *P-I* must be offered for sale before an agreement could be approved. While considering an appeal, Bennack and Danzig flew to Seattle to meet in my home to discuss our next move. On September 3, the *P-I* and *Times* asked the U.S. Ninth Circuit Court of Appeals for an expedited emergency review of Rothstein's ruling, asserting that further delays would more seriously jeopardize the future of the *P-I*. The paper already had lost more than $1 million that year.

On December 18, 1982, a panel of Judges in San Francisco heard our appeal. Four months later, the appellate court ruled that the JOA should proceed as the only way to save the *P-I*. Our cheers were somewhat subdued, however, because the opponents immediately asked for a review by the U.S. Supreme Court. The high court declined to review the case.

On May 23, 1983, the first Sunday edition with a joint *Times* and *Post-Intelligencer* masthead rolled off the presses at the *Times* plant, twenty-eight months after the JOA was announced.

Finally, the Joint Operating Agreement was a reality.

Chapter 26

■ ■ ■

New Era at the
Post-Intelligencer

A satisfying part of my job from day one after I became publisher was representing the *Post-Intelligencer* in the community and occasionally representing the community to visitors. I enjoyed lending not only the newspaper's editorial support but also my own personal time and energy to organizations and projects that contributed to the vitality, livability, and economic health of Seattle.

In one of my earliest civic ventures outside of the office, I was installed as president of Seattle/King County Convention & Visitors Bureau in December, 1981. A few months later, I headed a delegation to Tokyo, Japan to promote the Pacific Northwest as a travel destination. There, we hosted a reception featuring Washington and Oregon wines for key leaders in the travel industry and spent several days calling on the principals of each of the five leading travel agencies that booked the majority of vacationing Japanese tourists.

When we returned home, Hartley Krueger, director of the bureau, resigned to take a job in Alaska. Suddenly I had to find a successor. The hotel managers were insistent that the new director be able to fill their rooms. A good friend and neighbor, Gene Pfeifer, vice president of Pacific Northwest Bell Telephone, headed a search committee that found a replacement.

In my role with the visitors' bureau I urged Washington legislators to help market tourism, which would create jobs and bring in more new tax revenue than the marketing would cost. The state ranked forty-ninth nationally in tourism promotion. The prevailing attitude was that Washington had it all—ocean beaches, lakes, boating, mountains, spectacular scenery everywhere—and would attract visitors without spending any money.

In 1987, Governor Gardner appointed me co-chair of the Washington Tourism Industry Assessment Committee (TIAC), comprised of public- and private-sector officials from diverse backgrounds around Washington. The committee made twenty-one recommendations in the areas of market research, product and market development, education, training, and management. Several tourism regions were formed and funds were appropriated to promote each region. This approach was politically necessary to get conservative Eastern Washington legislators to come aboard, even though some regions had little to attract out-of-state visitors.

QUEEN ELIZABETH II and Prince Phillip of Great Britain visited Seattle on March 7, 1983. Governor Spellman and his wife Lois hosted a reception at the Westin Hotel where about fifty local couples stood behind a circular corral waiting to welcome the royal couple. Sunni and I were among the first to be introduced by the governor.

Her majesty was well-attired and shorter than we imagined. She extended her gloved hand. I welcomed her to Seattle and told her that the *Post-Intelligencer* was covering her visit and that we would deliver newspapers to the royal yacht, which was anchored in Elliott Bay. She graciously smiled, repeating practically every word I said. So went my "conversation" with Queen Elizabeth. Prince Philip came around the other side with Lois Spellman. His greeting was a perfunctory "pleased to meet you."

In a speech at the annual visitors' bureau meeting in 1983, following the recommendation of the board of directors, I urged that the proposed Washington State Convention Center be built over the Interstate 5 freeway, within walking distance of several thousand hotel rooms. The site was ultimately chosen, despite a recommendation by Mayor Charles Royer to select a site near the Seattle Center.

In April, 1983, Japan Airlines and United Airlines began service to Seattle. We organized a reception for JAL officials at which our guests presented us with a symbolic cask of sake. I was honored to be invited to tap the top of the cask in a *kagami-biraki* ceremony. I hit the cask too hard. Sake splashed over our visitors. Needless to say I was embarrassed. But the JAL folks were unerringly gracious and my invitation to join JAL's inaugural flight to Tokyo was not rescinded. In Tokyo, we boarded the bullet train to Kyoto, the ancient capital; visited Kobe, Seattle's sister city; and toured Nagasaki, where an atomic bomb hastened the end of WWII. The Japanese were perfect hosts.

THERE WAS CIVIC DISSATISFACTION with the nickname "Queen City" given to Seattle during the Klondike Gold Rush. So the visitors' bureau ran a contest to select a new one. The winner, "Emerald City," was quickly embraced and widely used by businesses and the general public. Soon no one remembered the old nickname.

The visitors' bureau experience had been fun. An easy, pleasant duty was addressing meetings of convention-planners where I bragged about the Seattle area. As a thank-you for my service after two terms as president, board members presented our family with a trip to Hawaii and week-long stay at the Mauna Kea resort on the Big Island. Richard, David, and I golfed, went deep-sea fishing, and rode horse-back up into the hills.

I was at a Hearst publishers' meeting in Baltimore on Sunday, May 18, 1980 when Mount St. Helen—an active volcano in southwest Washington that had been dormant since 1857—erupted with such a powerful force that the top 1,500 feet of the mountain blew off, spewing volcanic ash and gas twelve miles high. Ash was detected almost 300 miles to the east in Spokane.

I'll never forget a helicopter tour arranged for Executive Editor Jim Rennie and me by the Weyerhaeuser Co. in mid-1981. The flight took us over the dome crater and an eerie gray landscape of ash and flattened and buried trees around the mountain. A house on the shore of once-serene Spirit Lake was buried under thirty feet of ash.

The American Legion held its annual national convention in Seattle in 1983. Representing Hearst, I presented an award to the legion. Admiral Hyman Rickover, father of the Navy's nuclear sub program, was the guest of honor.

SUNNI AND I BECAME WINE importers in 1982. Our enterprise was inspired by my first cousin, Giuseppe Berzano in Asti, Italy. He was a member of the Asti Provincial Council in charge of economic development. Wine is the principle product of Asti in the Piedmont Region and my cousin wanted to send us samples produced by a winery looking for distribution to the United States.

Sunni and I incorporated Virsun Inc. and secured all the necessary state and national permits and licenses. We became the sole U.S. agent for fine wines produced by Bava, under the label Casa Brina, and other labels. Giuseppe and Piero Bava, a distant cousin, came to Seattle with a small shipment of samples. After a special tasting for prospective customers, we presented samples of twelve wines including Barolo, Barbaresco, and Asti Spumante, and later Grappa, a liquor, to the Washington State Liquor Control Board. We ordered 800 cases to start. As I kid I didn't like helping Dad make wine, but here I was in the wine business!

Over the next several years, we sold 13,000 cases of wine from Bava and Tuscany producer Luigi Cecchi under the brand name Sardelli. As agents, Virsun worked with distributors in the Seattle area and in Michigan and Arizona. On vacations, I made several trips to Italy on business, stopping in at a wine exposition in Torino featuring Piedmont wines and attended by international wine writers. I attended the International Wine Exposition in Bordeaux, France in 1987.

I introduced a writer for the leading British wine magazine to Roberto Bava. That began a friendship and expanded Bava markets in Great Britain. On one trip, I was interviewed on television discussing Americans' tastes in Italian wines. This was seen by relatives who were amused by my accented Italian.

Richard and I also promoted Casa Brina at wine expositions in San Francisco and Boston on vacations. Unfortunately, our local distributor, G. Raden & Sons, discontinued handling Casa Brina due to pressure from the larger wine-producers. Virsun's new distributor went bankrupt in 1989. That was the end of our wine business, which had been moderately profitable.

Italian wines, the leading U.S. wine import at that time, were facing stiff competition from new, cheaper wines of many countries, not to mention the fast-growing wine industry in Washington. Our relationship with Bava and the wine industry was a satisfying experience, but to be successful in the business, one had to devote full-time to it. I could not do that. What started as an enterprise to fall back on in case the JOA failed to win approval became more of a hobby toward the end.

With our eye on the future, Sunni and I invested in an apartment building in 1982 on the north side of Queen Anne near Seattle Pacific University. With her architectural background and general expertise, she managed the apartments and another property added later, working from home.

Chapter 27

■　■　■

A Publisher's Dream Job

When the first issue of the combined Sunday *Seattle Times/ Seattle Post-Intelligencer* rolled off the presses in the *Times* plant on May 23, 1983, the job of *P-I* publisher changed from several years of being one of the toughest and most demanding in the country to what many in the newspaper industry considered to be a dream job.

After years of tight fiscal constraints in a battle to keep a long history of losses from getting worse, suddenly we no longer were responsible for the expenses of the advertising, circulation, and production departments. The *Times* hired most employees not retained by the *P-I*. Those neither retained nor hired received a bonus for staying through the long JOA-approval process. We kept the entire news and editorial staff, despite the loss of our Sunday edition, and a small staff for business, personnel, promotion, and technical issues.

The *Times* took responsibility for marketing and producing both papers, but the Hearst Corp. owned the *P-I*. Many referred to the arrangement as a "merger." It was not a merger.

Starting Monday, May 24, the *P-I* was printed six days a week on pages two inches deeper to fit Times presses. Advertising rates were kept separate. Combination ads were discounted 15 percent. The *P-I* had a four-page Focus section with editorial/opinion content in the Sunday paper, but no news or features. The *P-I* comic section and *Parade* magazine were added to the Sunday edition.

Jerry Pennington had negotiated the JOA for the *Times*. When Pennington drowned in a boating accident, Frank Blethen, a member of the *Times'* founding family, succeeded him as publisher. Blethen had not been actively involved in the earlier negotiations and litigation. It was no secret that he disliked the JOA. Moves by the *Times* over the next several years indicated that its long-range aim was to end the agreement.

At regularly scheduled meetings of the JOA committee, Bob Danzig and I represented the *P-I* and Hearst. The Times publisher, at first Pennington and then Blethen, along with two other executives, represented the *Times*. We received financial updates, our share of the profits, and monthly figures for advertising lineage and circulation. But we were never asked for our input.

Bill Cobb and I believed that Hearst should have requested periodic outside audits of the JOA because some of the agency charges appeared excessive. No audits were requested. Under terms of the agreement, both papers were to receive equal promotion. This did not happen. I wrote to the *Times* publisher to complain of instances where the *Times* was promoted and the *P-I* was not, such as only the *Times* logo appearing on delivery trucks, only *Times* subscriptions solicited at stadiums, and readers having to ask supermarkets clerks where to find the *P-I*. These JOA issues were not pressed by Hearst, which was satisfied as long as the *P-I* made a profit.

In many areas, our experiences could have improved operations. But the *Times* did not want to hear our ideas, despite Cobb's experience and the high regard of his peers on the financial side of the industry and my many years as circulation director of four papers, two in competitive markets larger than the Times; discussion leader at the American Press Institute, and work as a circulation consultant for the Hearst newspapers. We wanted both papers to be successful and would have welcomed an opportunity to contribute.

The JOA returned the *P-I* to profitability. From day one, it became a better newspaper. We invested in product content with a larger "news hole" and hired excellent reporters. We wanted to beat the *Times*, and often did, with a news staff of between 160 and 180—little more than half that of the competition.

JIM RENNIE, EXECUTIVE EDITOR since 1981, implemented our improvements and oversaw the news and features departments. As publisher, I made it my policy not to interfere with news coverage, except to insist that our reporting be fair and objective, while reserving the authority to make final decisions on new hires, the budget, and setting the paper's editorial policies. In order to assume a leadership role in the community, a proper role for a publisher, I could never act as a reporter. I had to earn and keep the trust of newsmakers and did so with active involvement in many areas, sometimes working behind the scenes.

We could state truthfully that we did not get editorial direction from Hearst, even when the corporation disagreed with our position, nor did Hearst ever criticize our news coverage.

The *P-I* was the first West Coast paper to dedicate a reporter to cover the Pacific Rim. Jack Swanson, our first reporter on the new beat, arranged for an exchange program with the *China Daily* in Beijing, the country's only English-language newspaper. Two of its reporters visited the *P-I* in 1985 and I accepted an invitation for a return visit the next year.

Because the Puget Sound area is home to several major military establishments, we hired Ed Offley to cover military affairs. The *P-I* was the only West Coast paper between San Francisco and Minneapolis to staff the Gulf War in 1991. Offley and Washington correspondent Chris Hanson sent back dispatches, many of them tailored to our readership. Other reporters traveled extensively to cover news around the country and abroad, including the Olympics Games, which we had not been able to staff previously. We assigned our own reporter to cover our congressional delegation, politics, and relevant events in Washington, D.C., working out of the Hearst News Bureau. We rotated this assignment every few years. (One star, Joel Connelly continued to write a thoughtful, well-received column years later for the *P-I* online edition.)

Rennie, a Canadian with a quick temper, abruptly resigned in August, 1985 after a disagreement. The editors' grapevine works fast. Within two days, I received calls from several editors interested in applying. After interviewing three candidates screened by a head-hunting firm, I got a call from J.D. Alexander, managing editor of the *San Diego Union*.

I had met Alexander several years before when he was associated with Jack Olson as part of a group setting up staffs for the *New York Press*, which never got off the ground. An experienced newsman, Alexander had reported on the long-running Watergate story for the *Washington Post*. He was hired as our new executive editor, knowing he would have a shot at being the publisher after I retired.

Soon after implementation of the JOA, it became obvious that the publisher's increasing involvement in the community required an administrative assistant who would double as secretary. Myrna Casad had managed Henry Jackson's Seattle office prior to the senator's death. She knew the community well and filled a vital role very capably until I retired and afterward. Among many projects that Myrna arranged was the annual holiday party for employees at a different location every year. She was helpful, too, in setting up informal discussions in my office with seven or eight staff members. Over time, most employees came together in my office for these talks.

WHEN FRANK BENNACK JR. hired me in 1976, I was assigned the collateral duty of circulation consultant for the Hearst chain. I always had proxies of all the Hearst papers at annual Audit Bureau of Circulations conventions, but not until the JOA was approved did I have time to do much consulting. Over a decade beginning in 1983, I visited all but two Hearst papers at least once and several more than once, reviewing each paper's circulation operation. No two were alike. After each visit, I submitted detailed, written reports to the paper's publisher and to Bob Danzig.

The visits were enjoyable opportunities to pass on my twenty-five years as a circulation director of different-sized newspapers to young executives. Hearst papers included the metropolitan papers: *Los Angeles Herald-Examiner, San Antonio Light* and *Albany Times-Union*; medium-sized papers: *Beaumont Enterprise*, Midland, Texas; *Reporter-Telegram*, Midland, Michigan; *Daily News*; and the Laredo, Texas, *Morning Times*; smaller-market papers: Plainview, Texas *Daily Herald*; Bad Axe, Michigan *Huron Daily Herald*; Edwardsville,

Illinois *Intelligencer*, and the Clearwater, *Florida Sun*. I did not consult with the *San Francisco Examiner* (in a JOA) or the *Houston Chronicle*.

George Irish was the publisher of three of these papers that I visited. Later he succeeded Bob Danzig as general manager of Hearst Newspapers. At this writing, he was the head of the Hearst Foundation.

In Midland, Texas, I was a guest of the publisher at an annual gathering of the Midland Chamber of Commerce. The speaker, George W. Bush, a Midland native, was then president of the Texas Rangers Baseball Club. Bush did not impress me. I was surprised when he became governor of Texas and even more surprised when he was elected president of the United States in 2000.

I met George H. W. Bush at two functions in Seattle when he was vice president. I was reintroduced to the first President Bush by Attorney General Richard Thornburg, a fellow Pitt alumnus, at the Gridiron Club dinner in Washington, D.C. in 1991.

I joined Bennack, Danzig, and other Hearst executives in Des Moines, Iowa in 1985 to take a close look at the *Register* and *Tribune*, which were to be sold. I had visited the papers many years before and still knew a few people there. Hearst was unsuccessful in its bid to buy the papers.

IT WAS GRATIFYING when the *P-I* was singled out by *Adweek* magazine in 1987 as "the strongest paper in the Northwest with an aggressive news staff." We did everything we could to promote and improve ourselves. We sent eighteen staffers to seminars at the American Press institute, supported training programs, and presented annual awards to editors and reporters. Other improvements included more suburban reporters, addition of a technical writer, expanded Boeing coverage, and a "reader representative" column to engage in a dialogue with readers.

The community became increasingly aware of the *P-I*'s commitment to excellence and leadership in striving to make the area a better place to live and work. Each January, starting in 1986, the *P-I* published a list of ten key issues that the state and region needed to address and that we covered extensively with editorials and news stories. These included Pacific Rim trade, state tax reform, the future of the Seattle waterfront, clean air and water, environment protection, infrastructure development, quality education, child welfare, low-income housing, mass transit and transportation, tourism, regional government, and nuclear-waste disposal. This annual initiative was well received and often imitated.

We always tried to beat the competition even with our smaller news staff and lacking a Sunday paper in which to showcase investigative stories. One investigative story exposed Superior Court Judge Gary Little as a pedophile. As a well-known attorney, mentor, and jurist, Judge Little had victimized many young boys. He committed suicide when we broke the story. I wondered why two of my acquaintances, a lawyer and a banker, called to protest our coverage. We also ended the political aspirations of a teachers' union leader by exposing him as a pedophile while he was a candidate for Congress.

In another investigation, we uncovered mismanagement of the Washington State Investment Board, saving the state millions of dollars. And James Wallace uncovered a long-standing practice of hauling liquid foodstuffs in the same truck tankers that carried toxic chemicals. The story quickly resulted in new regulations.

ONE OF THE BIGGEST STORIES, covered by Joel Connelly and others, concerned the Washington Public Power Supply System. WPPSS (or "Whoops," as it came to be known) was building five nuclear power plants with construction flaws and management boondoggles. The series of investigative stories culminated in cancellation of the plants and the worst government bond failures in history, costing bondholders billions.

The Hanford Nuclear Facility, near Washington's Tri-Cities and the Columbia River, where work on the first atomic bomb was carried out, was found to have become a serious health hazard. Connelly reported that an unusually high number of people in the region had developed cancer. Even the tumbleweed in the area showed radioactivity. Because the area's economy depended on Hanford, many locals were unhappy with our coverage.

Before the Hanford stories were reported, I had informed Hearst that the *Tri-Cities Herald* might be for sale. Sometime later, Danzig inquired what we were up to in the Hanford area. When I told him, he instructed me not to back off, to keep our reporter on the story. Hearst had been negotiating to buy the paper when the publisher took exception to our coverage. This was another example of the freedom of news coverage and editorials we had, even when the effects ran counter to Hearst's corporate interests. Another newspaper group bought the *Herald*.

Several years later, I spoke at a Tri-Cities Chamber of Commerce luncheon, expecting a hostile crowd, but receiving a surprisingly gracious reception. Later, I toured the Hanford plant, site of the infamous "bubbling" underground nuclear-waste tanks. After my retirement, Gov. Mike Lowry asked if I would chair a volunteer committee to deal with Hanford cleanup, a state priority. With no scientific background or interest, I declined.

Hearst publishers and advertising directors met in Seattle with their spouses in August, 1986. No Hearst city matched Seattle as a desirable destination. We organized a water tour to Kiana Lodge for a salmon bake, a Seattle Mariners game viewed from a special suite, dinner at the top of the Columbia Tower—the tallest building north of San Francisco—and an optional side trip to the world's fair in Vancouver, British Columbia.

CIRCULATION GAINS WERE reported for the two newspapers from 1984 to 1992: the *P-I* increased from 195,000 to almost 207,000; the Times from 225,000 to 238,000; Sunday Times/P-I from 473,000 to 522,000. The *P-I*'s daily advertising share prior to the JOA was 33.1 percent in 1982, increasing to 47.2 percent ten years later. Clearly, the JOA was good for both papers.

I made several trips each year to Hearst headquarters in New York for various reasons. Once a year, Bill and I presented the budget for next year. *P-I* operating costs were easier to project than the anticipated revenue from the JOA. The *Times*' figures always required revisions.

The *P-I*'s distribution of the JOA profits was good most years, but eventually this changed. The *Times* built a new plant in suburban Bothell at a cost of more than $150 million. Then it installed a pagination system to which the *P-I* was forced to adapt at a cost of $870,000. Special charges to the *P-I* were just over $5 million in 1984 and $13.6 million in 1991. The JOA experienced a loss in 1988 and another loss was predicted for 1991.

In response, Hearst directed a 10 percent reduction in our operating costs, which meant a staff reduction of eighteen. The only place we could cut was news-editorial. Most of our employees were members of the American Newspaper Guild. Seniority ruled in cases of layoffs. In early 1991, I called a staff meeting. It was difficult to announce the cuts. We offered a bonus on top of severance pay to anyone who accepted a voluntary layoff. Some of our older employees took the buyout, as did enough others so that we did not have to dismiss anyone arbitrarily. We made a profit in 1992, my last full year, but projected another loss for 1993.

We lost two of our best writers. Shelby Scates, a well-connected political columnist and editorial-board member, left to write several books about political figures. Jean Godden, also a columnist with a long record at the *P-I*, took retirement and then joined the *Seattle Times* to write a column. After retiring a second time, she was elected to the Seattle City Council in 2003, serving until 2015.

Earlier, we lost another star as the JOA was being implemented. Emmett Watson, the area's most popular columnist, had retired but was still contributing two columns a week as a freelancer. While we were being sued for libel over a Watson column about the county assessor, Watson submitted a column highly critical of Seattle Mariners owner George Argyros. Rennie and I believed that it contained factual errors and bordered on libel, so the column was killed. When Rennie cut Watson to one column a week, Watson quit. A short time later he joined the *Seattle Times*, the paper he had referred to as "Fairview Fannie" for many years in his *P-I* column

IT WAS IMPORTANT THAT the *P-I* be perceived as separate and independent from the *Times*. The newspaper encouraged this perception by assuming a greater leadership role in the community, in addition to my own personal involvement. Traditional public programs were continued and enhanced. The oldest promotion was the P-I Sports Star of the Year, one of the longest-running such recognition programs in the country. It drew more than 1,000 fans to a dinner every January.

Our Reader's Care raised more than $250,000 during the holiday season for carefully selected charities. The Jefferson Awards honored five or six local citizens who performed outstanding volunteer service without recognition or reward. Divas and Diamonds, a fashion show, drew more than a 1,000 attendees each year. The *P-I* had sponsored the Seattle Home Show for nearly half a century.

John Joly, whose duties as promotion manager prior to the JOA included advertising campaigns, became our community-affairs director. He was instrumental in establishing several of these and other programs, all carefully aimed at enhancing the *P-I*'s image by reaching out to each of the paper's constituencies in the Puget Sound region.

Several other promotions developed by John were the Olympic Scholar Awards, co-sponsored with a local television station, which saluted outstanding high-school students who set an example for others by demonstrating leadership, scholarship and concern for local communities. Awards included medallions, certificates, and $25,000 in cash prices. The Honor Student Awards, co-sponsored by the Seattle Mariners, provided free tickets to baseball games. Each year, as many as 10,000 hard-working students attended baseball games. "News for Kids" invited local non-profits, museums, schools, and businesses to support a series of community-service programs aimed at families and youth. A sixteen-page, all-news supplement was designed for young readers. Subjects included dinosaurs, space exploration, Boeing, energy conservation, rain forests, and health issues.

Big Climb for Leukemia was a fund-raiser. Participants collected pledges and climbed or raced up the 1,146 steps of the Columbia Tower. One popular promotion was Steak and Burger Night, which raised money for Boys and Girls Clubs of King County and featured

Seattle Seahawk players. Adult attendees hosted tables of kids, who ate steak. The adults ate burgers. I received the clubs' Service to Youth Award at one event. Lectures with big-name speakers were sponsored for the World Affairs Council. We supported the Chamber Music Festival. Lots of kids left the Kingdome with gloves or bats from giveaway nights co-sponsored by the *P-I.*

The newspaper was involved constantly with some kind of community program and was consistently more active than the *Times.* John and his staff assistant, Kathryn White, were always on the run and sometimes had more than one program going at the same time.

Chapter 28

■ ■ ■

Elephants, Chinasaurs, Sports Stars

I n the early 1980s, due to the failure of a bond issue, the dete-
riorating condition of the sixty-year-old Elephant House at the
Woodland Park Zoo was a civic embarrassment that threatened the
care and continued existence of the zoo's four female elephants. The
three Asian and one African elephants were a major attraction for
more than 750,000 visitors a year.

Just repairing a leaky roof would cost $60,000. I called Mayor Royer
and told him the *Post-Intelligencer* wanted to help. After some discussion,
it was agreed the newspaper would make a $60,000 donation (funds di-
verted from our television advertising budget) to be applied to the cost of
developing a new five-acre Asian Elephant exhibit, ten times larger than
the existing facility, to represent the habitat of a Thailand logging camp
with a demonstration area, outdoor bathing pool, and barn.

I should have remembered the old English expression, "in for a
penny, in for a pound." Somewhat reluctantly at first, I agreed to

co-chair a committee to raise $3.5 million, to be matched by the city—but only if I could find a banker to be the other co-chair. I soon warmed to the challenge.

I found a banker at a Rainier Bank reception honoring Edward Heath, former prime minister of Great Britain. I ambushed Rainier Chairman G. Robert Truex Jr. and asked him to co-chair the fundraising committee with me.

I caught Truex in a weak moment. He was not familiar with the elephant problem, but said, "For you, I'll do it."

I called Truex the next day to make sure he had not gotten cold feet overnight. "If I said I would, I will," he told me. I'm sure he wondered what I was getting him into.

Truex and his assistant, Dave Williams, did an outstanding job. With the help of volunteers, a professional fund-raiser, and an advertising agency, the "Save Our Elephants" campaign took off with heavy support from the *P-I*. (The *Wall Street Journal* later published a profile of Truex, prominently mentioning his work on the elephant campaign.)

We discovered that everyone loves a zoo, especially Woodland Park Zoo, which began as a small menagerie kept on the private Woodland Park estate of Guy Phinney between Green Lake and what later came to be known as Phinney Ridge. In 1899, the City of Seattle bought the property. Four years later, the celebrated landscape designer John C. Olmsted began the planning for permanent "zoological gardens."

The *P-I*'s interest in elephants dates back to 1920-21, when the newspaper fronted the money for purchase the zoo's first elephant, an Asian named "Wide Awake," for $3,122.

Support was widespread for the "Save Our Elephants" campaign. Contributions poured in from individuals, groups, and businesses throughout the region. Mayor Royer and I visited schools where kids handed over boxes and bags filled with coins. School children contributed more than $50,000. Other contributors included the Hearst Foundation ($345,000), Rainier Bank ($250,000), Boeing Co. ($250,000), Pacific Northwest Bell ($150,000), Burlington Northern ($100,000), Seafirst Bank ($75,000), the *P-I* ($60,000) and other companies. A KIRO-TV telethon brought in a wave of donations from the public.

The $6.5 million goal was reached. When completed in 1986, the elephant exhibit was rated the best new zoo exhibit in the country that year.

The *Seattle Times* never mentioned the "Save Our Elephants" Campaign. It was a *P-I* project.

In 2015, however, the *Times*, a leader in covering animal-rights groups, called editorially for the transfer of the zoo's three remaining elephants to an elephant sanctuary. They were moved to the Oklahoma City Zoo instead. I had always assumed elephants would be a lasting legacy of my tenure as publisher. It wasn't to be.

"CHINASAURS," SO-NAMED by John Joly, were three large, 150-million-year-old intact dinosaur fossil skeletons from Szechuan Province in China, where more dinosaur fossils are found than anywhere else in the world. Bringing them to Seattle became another ambitious project for the *P-I*, which paid $60,000 to the Natural Museum of Chongqing for a six-month loan.

I went to China in 1986 at the invitation of Feng Xiliang, editor of the *China Daily*, with which we had an exchange program. I was met in Shanghai on October 31, the evening before Liberation Day, a national holiday. Two local *China Daily* staffers escorted me to the famous Jin Jiang Hotel, reserved exclusively for western guests and famous for housing heads of state.

Exhilarated, I strolled alone down the main street, the only westerner among thousands of Chinese. I started passing out red balloons, left over from our move to a new building, to curious kids. Before long I felt like the legendary pied piper. Adults wanted to practice their English. I've never felt safer. My hosts took me on a city tour and boat ride through the busy harbor. It was strange to see the same warships I had seen at Pearl Harbor forty years before. At the time they were being transferred to Nationalist China, but at some point in the aftermath of World War II had fallen into the hands of Communist China's navy.

In Beijing, I consulted with the *China Daily* staff, which including two American expatriates and several senior editors who had been educated in America. There wasn't much I could tell them that they didn't know already about newspapers, though they did not enjoy freedom of the press as we do in America.

Two days later, I was joined by Fred Burrow, president of the Seattle/King County Convention & Visitors Bureau, Jim Wright of the Space Needle, and travel agent Connie Swanson. We walked the Great Wall and visited the Forbidden City, Ming Tombs, Temple of Heaven, and Mao Zedong's embalmed body in the Hall of the People at Tiananmen Square. We observed heavy bicycle traffic. The pollution was noticeable.

We had been invited to Chongqing, Seattle's sister city, to advise locals how to attract American tourists. We visited Xian, famous for the terra cotta army discovered after being buried for centuries; Dazu with its scores of Buddha statues carved into the valley walls; and other sites in and near this large city. After leaving Chongqing, we sailed down the Yangtse River through the Three Gorges, later submerged by dams. Along the way we saw a few floating bodies.

The Chongqing parks director, whom I had met earlier in Seattle, invited me to a special Szechuan hot-pot dinner at the zoo. We were served "delicacies" on a lazy susan intended to be dipped in boiling oil or water. Strange dishes I did not recognize could not be described in English, the interpreter claimed. Szechuan food is my favorite Chinese food, but this was not "special." My colleagues, meanwhile, were treated to a sumptuous, multi-course dinner. While at the zoo, I relayed a request from Woodland Park Zoo Director Dave Towne and Mayor Royer to borrow a pair of giant pandas, but to no avail.

The fossils had been loaned previously to Toulouse, France, for hard currency. With earlier encouragement from the mayor's office, I verbally agreed that the *P-I* would pay the required $60,000 if we could secure an airline co-sponsor and provide twenty-five round-trips for museum experts to assemble, dismantle, and care for the fossils. Eddie Carlson, chairman of United Airlines, agreed to provide transportation. The Burke Museum at the University of Washington was delighted to host the exhibit. Bill Cobb and John Joly traveled to Chongqing to finalize the deal. Local families housed twenty-three Chinese experts.

When the exhibit opened, attendance in the first week equaled the Burke's annual attendance. Record attendance continued for six months before the fossils were returned to Chongqing. This was another blockbuster promotion that excited the general public. Yet, the "Chinasaurs" were never covered in the *Seattle Times* and mentioned only in terse museum schedule listings without identifying the sponsor.

THE P-I SPORTS STAR of the Year awards banquet was one of the most popular events in Seattle, a tradition started in 1935 by Royal

Brougham, legendary sports editor and columnist who worked sixty-five years at the *P-I*. John Joly and the sports department staff managed the promotional aspects and details.

Ten male and ten female athletes were nominated by the *P-I* sports staff. The nominees were members of the Seattle area's professional and college teams as well as individual athletes who starred in other sports. Sports fans attending the banquet selected the winners in a vote. In the years before professional sports came to Seattle, the winners were wide-ranging, including high-school coaches and some representing relatively minor sports. Later, fans of the SuperSonics, Seahawks, and Mariners fans had better-known athletes with outstanding records to choose from.

Originally, the ten nominees were a mix of men and women, but later the event was reorganized so that ten men and ten women would be nominated, with a winner chosen from each group.

Royal Brougham was a deeply religious man, unlike many newsmen in his day. He didn't drink, smoke, or cuss. He retired several years before I came to Seattle, but continued to write a weekly column and maintained a museum-like office across the hall from mine. It was packed with photos, personal mementos, historic artifacts, and souvenirs of events Brougham covered. In 1977, I was honored to serve as the master of ceremonies for a black-tie banquet held by civic leaders to honor his achievements.

Brougham died suddenly at his typewriter in the Kingdome press box at a Seattle-Broncos game October, 1978. Seattle Pacific University named a building in his honor. Royal Brougham Way, which runs on the north side of Safeco Field, became another fitting tribute to the man who left an indelible mark on the *P-I* and Seattle sports history.

In 1991, the *P-I* established an annual Publisher's Award. I presented the first award to Harold Reynolds, Mariners second baseman, for his local foundation that benefited inner-city youth. In 1992, it was a pleasure to present the award to the three new local directors of the Seattle Mariners: John Ellis, chairman of Puget Power; Frank Schrontz, chairman of Boeing, and Howard Lincoln, president of Nintendo of America. Lincoln represented Hiroshi Yamauchi, chairman of Nintendo, who had bought majority interest in the team so that it would remain in Seattle. In 1993, the award went to a young man, Tony Volpentest, a champion Special Olympics runner who had persevered despite being born with deformed legs and arm.

Above: Virgil Fassio hosted and moderated a group interview with Feng Yi, vice premier of China, far left, at a breakfast meeting of the Pacific Northwest Newspaper Association in Seattle in 1979. At the far right is Huang Hua, the Chinese foreign minister who helped negotiate an armistice in the Korean War.

Below: The author chats with President Jimmy Carter at the White House in 1979.

An earnest discussion with President Gerald Ford in Seattle in 1980. Ford, then vice president, became president after the resignation of Richard Nixon, who had become mired in the Watergate scandal. But Ford failed to win election to the White House in 1977, losing to Jimmy Carter.

From left, Frank A. Bennack Jr., president and CEO of the Hearst
Corp.; Robert Danzig, general manager of Hearst Newspapers; and the
author at a November, 1981 U.S. District Court hearing on an anti-
trust challenge of the proposed joint operating agreement.

The author greets President Ronald Reagan and the First Lady, Nancy Reagan, at a White House briefing on drug-abuse prevent programs. Despite some gains, the War on Drugs was not going well.

Virgil Fassio presents the *Post-Intelligencer's* second annual Publisher's Award to John Ellis, chairman of the Seattle Mariners, in 1992. The author, a lifelong baseball fan, co-founded the RBI Club and is credited with having helped save the Seattle Mariners from being moved to another city.

Sunni and Virgil Fassio, 2005

Richard, Michael, and David Fassio with their father, 2013

A mock front page of the *Seattle Post-Intelligencer* was created as part of
the sendoff for Virgil Fassio, who retired as publisher in 1993.

Chapter 29

■ ■ ■

Domestic and
International Travel

I was invited to the White House by President Ronald Reagan and the First Lady for a drug-abuse prevention briefing on March 7, 1988 attended by about twenty newspaper executives, including several CEOs of major chains. I represented Hearst newspapers. The Reagans' report on the War on Drugs was both sobering and encouraging.

Reagan cited a study suggesting that 50-75 percent of all domestic crime was drug-related. "There is also lost productivity, increased health-care costs, continuing threats to worker and public safety, the transmission of AIDS, and an overall degradation of our society," he said.

Yet, Reagan was optimistic overall. He pointed to a recent survey of the nation's high-school seniors revealing that "one-third fewer seniors acknowledged current use of cocaine in 1987 than the year before (and) almost all the students said it was wrong even to try a drug like cocaine."

The President praised private efforts, including those supported by the media and the entertainment industry, to combat one of America's most serious problems. "Let's remember that our actions today are an investment in the future," he said.

"I hope you will keep up your tough reporting on this story," Reagan said. "This means holding government officials accountable, of course, but it also means keeping a close eye on trends in drug use in America and reporting to your readers fully and fairly about those efforts."

A reception followed in the East Room, giving everyone a chance to talk with Reagan. He was warm and friendly. It was easy to see why he was so popular. At one point, I stood with three other newspaper people casually chatting with the President. We asked how he had gotten into politics. He said he had been asked by Republican Party leaders to run for governor of California in 1967. He thought he would give it a try, expecting to be defeated by the two-term incumbent, Edmund G. "Pat" Brown. Reagan won. (In the campaign, Reagan had vowed "to send the welfare bums back to work.")

I had met Ronald Reagan twice before. Once he had spoken at a chamber of commerce dinner in Wilmington representing General Electric. Later, as governor of California, he had been the honored guest at a Hearst reception in San Francisco. But there was nothing like meeting and talking with the president of the United States in the White House.

This was one of several stand-out events in the decade from 1983-93.

BERLIN/USA INITIATIVE, a private group in the American Zone ᶠWest Berlin, was dedicated to maintaining contact with the United

States. A divided Berlin was divided into English, French, and Soviet zones, and was surrounded by Communist East Germany and Soviet troops. In 1987, the group invited several publishers to observe the 750th anniversary of Berlin's founding.

Bill Taylor of the family-owned *Boston Globe* and I were the only publishers who accepted the invitation. Our ten-day visit was instructional and eye-opening. The schedule included a boat ride down the Wansee River dividing East and West Germany; a meeting with the mayor and a city legislator who later became mayor of Berlin after Germany was unified; an excursion into East Berlin through "Checkpoint Charlie"; a luncheon with top diplomats in both Berlins; a meeting with journalists from *Der Spiegel*, the weekly news magazine; and courtesy calls on several bankers and business leaders.

We took a good look at the Berlin Wall, erected in the early 1960s to prevent East German citizens from escaping into the West. Markers showed where people had been shot and killed by East German guards while trying to flee. The most memorable experience was a flight aboard a U.S. Army helicopter inside the entire perimeter of the Berlin Wall. I returned home with a photo of my feet sticking out of the open-sided helicopter with the walled-in city below.

AFTER THE BERLIN WALL was torn down, the Conrad Adenauer *Schtiftung* (foundation), set up by the first chancellor of the Federal Republic of Germany (West Germany), invited ten journalists to the newly unified Germany in 1991. We were recommended by our local Lufthansa Airlines representatives. The massive, complicated unification process was expected to take five to ten years. East Germans had lived under communism in third-world conditions for more than forty years. Sweeping changes were coming.

We were briefed on the *Treudhandt*, a program to convert 3,100 East German state-owned companies into private enterprises. Twenty companies a day were being sold or returned to qualified former owners. The smallest had twenty employees. The largest had 40,000. Everyone had to be trained to operate in a new economic system.

Combining the two halves of Germany was creating unemployment. Under communism, everyone had a job; under West Germany's capitalist system, not everyone was needed. An example was heavily polluted Bittefeld, the chemical capital of Germany. One plant had 17,500 employees under communism. It would need only 5,000 under private ownership and modernization. Silver nitrate from the AGFA film plant covered the bottom of a small lake with contaminated water flowing into a river and then on to the North Sea. Not far away, Dresden, almost completely destroyed by Allied bombs, had been rebuilt.

East Germans had lived in fear of *Stasi*, the dreaded secret police considered worse than the Nazi Gestapo, which had a force of 100,000 agents and support personnel and as many as 400,000 informants. A person never knew if one of his neighbors, or a co-worker, was spying on him, but the odds were good that they were. It was estimated that if *Stasi* documents were laid end to end, they would stretch 202 kilometers.

WE VISITED THE SOVIET ARMY headquarters at Wansdorf, fifty kilometers outside of Berlin. We were among the first American journalists to visit. Col. Vladimir Strelinikov, commander of the Soviet Western Ground Forces in East Germany, ticked off the number of Soviet planes (633), helicopters (615), tanks (4,100), armored vehicles (7,950), military personnel (380,800), and families and civilian workers (208,800) still in East Germany. The equipment was being shipped back to Russia or sold. Military personnel and civilians were being returned to the Soviet Union more slowly because of a critical housing shortage at home. But all were to be out of Germany by 1994.

When asked about the accuracy of his inventory, Strelinikov responded, "The Germans pay us for every item and they are good accountants." He said that, as a boy, he had worn a U.S. Air Force jacket given to his father, a Soviet hero, by an American pilot. He told us he had received a pay raise, adding, "I no longer have to pay dues to the Communist Party." As we left, several Soviet officers flashed us the peace sign. We welcomed the gesture after more than forty years of the Cold War.

German military leaders in Potsdam described the integration of former East German soldiers (none above the rank of captain) into the German army. We toured drab Soviet-style East Berlin and vibrant West Berlin. We met with officials in Bonn, West Germany's capital, who were making plans to move the seat of government to Berlin.

TRUDGING THROUGH THE STREETS of Beechview in 1940-42 delivering the *Pittsburgh Press* I never dreamed that the job would land me in the International Newspaper Carrier Hall of Fame as its 105th member. Famous members, too many to name, included Presidents Dwight D. Eisenhower, Herbert Hoover, and Harry S. Truman; Supreme Court Justices Warren Burger, William O. Douglas, and Earl Warren; astronaut John Glenn and WWI flying ace Eddie Rickenbacker; entertainers Bing Crosby, Walt Disney, Bob Hope, and John Wayne; athletes Jack Dempsey, Willie Mays, Wayne

Gretzky, Jackie Robinson, Julius Erving, and Duke Snider; literary figures Carl Sandburg and Isaac Asimov; and other leaders in several categories, including a handful from the news media.

Having no idea how the selection was made, I accepted the award at the International Circulation Managers Association convention in San Francisco in 1990. Billionaire Warren Buffett was honored the next year.

AL NEUHARTH, CHAIRMAN of Gannett Newspapers, called in August, 1984 to discuss the presidency of *USA Today*. Gannett, the country's largest newspaper chain, had founded *USA Today* a few years earlier. Its circulation exceeded 1 million nationwide. Neuharth and I had been acquainted for more than twenty years, having appeared together a few times at industry conferences.

Running *USA Today* was a huge, demanding job. The downside was relocating to Washington, D.C. and extensive travel to Gannett plants where the paper was printed and distributed. We had no desire to move. Sunni and I loved Seattle and I loved my job at the *P-I*.

Neuharth hired Lee Guittar, who had been circulation director at the *Miami Herald* and a member of the Circulation Manager of the Future committee that I had chaired for Knight Newspapers. He had succeeded me as business manager of the *Detroit Free Press* before becoming a publisher in Denver and Dallas for another chain. After a short time with Gannett, he joined Hearst to become Bob Danzig's assistant in charge of the metropolitan papers, including the *P-I*. Guittar was a good newspaper associate and a friend.

In the years leading up to my retirement, I was never without an assignment to serve on a committee of the ANPA, to join a panel at an industry conference, or to give a speech at a newspaper association meeting. This was good for the *Post-intelligencer* and Hearst. I became even more active after the JOA was implemented. This work was a pleasure.

An early ANPA assignment included membership on the Circulation Committee and, as publisher, chairmanship of the Readership and Retention Committee and organizer of two symposiums, one on single-copy sales and the other on distribution and marketing. In 1982-86, I was vice chair of ANPA's Industry Affairs Committee and in 1987-93 a member of the association's Government Affairs and Public Policy Committee. Quarterly meetings were held in Washington, D.C., where guest speakers included presidential advisor and former Senator Howard Baker, Assistant Secretary of State Lawrence Eagleburger, Supreme Court justices, and various members of Congress.

At one breakfast meeting, I sat at a table with our guest speaker, a young congressman from Wyoming. I considered him to be just another congressman among many a newspaperman meets. He was not particularly impressive and gave no inkling of a major announcement to be made later that day. Hours later, Richard "Dick" Cheney was appointed secretary of defense by President George H. W. Bush. In 2000-08, he served as vice president with President George W. Bush, exercising a strong, sometimes controversial influence on the course of events, including wars in Iraq and Afghanistan.

Chapter 30

■   ■   ■

Robust Activity in the Seattle Area

S eattle is a young city. The first white settlers didn't come to the Puget Sound area until 1851. The Washington Territory did not become the forty-second state until 1889. Seattle remained a small, remote outpost until it became the major jumping-off point for the Klondike Gold Rush that attracted tens of thousands of gold-seekers north to the Yukon in 1896-1899.

As it turned out, the Seattle merchants who sold supplies to the prospectors were the real winners. They struck "gold" without leaving town. Most of the thousands of prospectors who rushed to the Klondike found none.

A high percentage of Seattle's movers and shakers are native-born Washingtonians and graduates of the University of Washington or its cross-state rival, Washington State University, or the smaller Seattle University. People who transferred to the city often did not want to leave. It was not so easy for newcomers to become accepted in Eastern and Midwest cities where established, old-line families controlled much of the political, business, and social life. Seattle was different. It seems anyone who wanted to dive into the local scene was welcome. There was room for all.

Never being able to say no when asked to volunteer or assume a leadership role can get one involved in one's community. I was willing to help as long as my involvement was good for the paper and also personally satisfying.

AN ONLY-IN-SEATTLE EVENT occurred in May, 1990 when a first-generation American and Seattle-area resident for only fourteen years accepted the gavel as president of the 700-member Downtown Seattle Association from Joshua "Jay" Green III, chairman of U.S. Bank of Washington and a prominent member of a distinguished Seattle banking family that had been active in the community for more than a century.

"Why would a newspaper publisher take such an involved role in a downtown business association?" I asked rhetorically in my acceptance speech. "I am not a banker, a retailer, a developer, or a lawyer, as many of my predecessors have been, but I am someone who cares about this city. Seattle is the heart of the Northwest and downtown is the hub and the heart of Seattle."

Our featured speaker that day was Jack Kemp, secretary of housing and urban development and a former congressman. Kemp had been a star quarterback on the Buffalo Bills when "Cookie" Gilchrest played for the team. We reminisced about Gilchrest, a newspaper carrier in Tarentum, Pennsylvania years before whom I had encouraged to stay in school when he was on the verge of dropping out. Kemp was Senator Bob Dole's running mate when Dole ran for president in 1996.

The *P-I* did not engage in any international trade, except for the sale of newspapers in British Columbia, but we did support and cover the state's considerable international trade. After several years on the executive committee of the Washington Council on International Trade, I was elected council chairman for the 1992-93 term.

One of the highlights was a high-level conference, "From the Inside Out," focusing on domestic policy and international trade. The sessions were held at a resort in Port Ludlow, Washington and attracted business and government leaders from seven Pacific Rim countries. Among those attending was Indiana Congressman Lee Hamilton, chairman of the House Foreign Affairs Committee. I asked for his help on behalf of the Cruise Ship Alliance and later exchanged letters with him on the subject of amending federal law to make it easier for cruise ships to start and end cruises in Seattle. Also on hand were Bill Frenzel of the Brookings Institute and Bob Samuelson, business editor at *Newsweek*.

My active involvement, the *P-I*'s coverage of trade issues, creation of a Pacific Rim news beat at the paper, a *China Daily* journalism exchange, our funding of the "Chinasaurs" project, and sponsorship of a series of programs for the World Affairs Council earned me the council's World Citizen Award in 1992.

BOB WALSH, SEATTLE PROMOTER, organized the second Goodwill Games in Seattle in 1990, featuring athletes from the United States and the Soviet Union to promote peaceful relations between the two countries. Ted Turner had organized the first games in Atlanta in 1986. The 1990 Goodwill Games were another positive step in thawing the Cold War.

Sunni, Michael, and I watched a few swim meets, and Michael and I attended a reception for host committee members and dignitaries. Poor photographer that I am, I did not get a clear picture of Michael with former President Reagan, but he did get a handshake and better pictures with actor Arnold Schwarzenegger and with Turner and his wife, actress Jane Fonda.

GOVERNOR BOOTH GARDNER was chairman of the National Governors Association when it met in Seattle in August, 1991. Members of the host committee were invited to several social functions. Among others, I met the governor of Arkansas, Bill Clinton. Our paths crossed again in 1992 at an informal reception at KOMO–TV after Clinton became the Democratic candidate for president. A third time was at the Asian-Pacific Economic Conference (APEC) in Seattle in 1993, when Clinton led the American delegation and welcomed heads of state and trade representative from most of the twenty Asian-Pacific member nations.

During my term as chairman of the trade organization, council President Bob Kapp and I had persuaded a delegation from the State Department to hold the 1993 APEC conference in Seattle.

IMPRESSED BY FATHER William J. Sullivan, SJ, president of Seattle University, I readily agreed to serve for several years on Board of Regents and later on the board of SU's Albers School of Business. All three of our sons earned degrees from the university: Richard, a bachelor's degree in marketing; David, a master's degree in financial management, and Michael, an advanced degree from the Sullivan School of Law. David and Michael had received their bachelor's degrees from the University of Washington. Father Sullivan performed wedding ceremonies for Richard in 1993 and Michael in 2005. When he retired, Father Stephen Sundborg, S.J. became president and continued to expand the Jesuit school.

DR. LESTER SAUVAGE, internationally famous heart surgeon, was the first to perform an arterial coronary bypass on a pig several years before the first bypass was performed on a human. By the time I met him, Doctor Sauvage had performed several thousand such surgeries at Seattle's Providence Hospital and was the founder of Hope Heart Institute, which was dedicated to education and research. Recruited to the institute's board in 1985, I later served as board president in 1994 and 1995 after retiring and spent many hours at the institute.

A much longer affiliation with the Medic One Foundation, begun in 1985, lasted for twenty-three years. Dr. Leonard Cobb, a University of Washington and Harborview Hospital cardiac specialist, had been the winner of a national Jefferson Award as co-founder of Medic One, which trained Seattle firefighters as emergency medical technicians. The first responders and others received 2,000 hours of specialized training as paramedics, paid for by the private foundation.

Pioneered in Seattle, Medic One and units like it spread throughout the country. Survival rates for out-of-hospital cardiac arrests in Seattle was twice that of other American cities. The aim was to get help for a victim at the scene within minutes of a 911 call.

Soon, Seattle was recognized as the best place in the world to have a heart attack. In 1983, while visiting my Uncle Giuseppe Pia in the hospital in Asti, Italy, my cousin, a nurse in the cardiac unit, introduced me to a doctor. When he learned I was from Seattle, he said, "You're from the city with the best emergency response for heart attacks."—a welcome endorsement.

Because of my personal and family history of heart issues, serving on the MOF board was one of the most satisfying things I ever did as a volunteer.

FROM MY FIRST DAYS IN SEATTLE, I had been active as well on the board of the Greater Seattle Chamber of Commerce. I participated in meetings, discussions, committee work, and the group's annual visits to neighboring cities, but I never assumed a leadership role. The chamber sponsored the Community Development Round Table that met weekly with off-the-record speakers. It was the only organization where publishers and editors of the two dailies and heads of the local broadcasting companies, all permanent members, met in the same place on a regular basis.

Other non-profit board memberships included the Museum of History and Industry, Woodland Park Zoological Society, and Seattle Goodwill Industries. I was involved, too, in the formation of the lesser-known Odyssey Maritime Museum and Foundation for Russia-America Economic Cooperation. The Hearst Foundation was one of the first to make a major contribution ($50,000) to build the Museum of Flight, which has become one of the finest aviation museums in the country.

As *P-I* publisher, I was invited to speak to almost every Rotary Club and several Lions and Kiwanis clubs within fifty miles of Seattle and other clubs as far east as Moses Lake and as far south as Centralia. I saw these invitations as opportunities to discuss the importance of a free press, the fascinating history of the Hearst Corp., and our newspaper's policies and editorial agenda for the state. I found sincere interest wherever I spoke.

I served as the program committee chairman and as treasurer for one-year terms and received the Rotary Vocational Service Award in 1989. I was surprised and honored at a Rotary meeting in 1994 by the appearance of Sam Beard, head of the American Institute of Public Service, who came from Washington, D.C. to present me with a national Jefferson Award for Community Service.

I served on the board of governors of the Washington Athletic Club (WAC) for six years. For three years, I headed the board's marketing committee. Yet I never took advantage of the club's excellent exercise facilities until after I retired, my poor excuses being that I was too busy. I should have taken the time. A special unit within the WAC, the "101 Club," promoted local athletic programs. Most of its 101 members had been college athletes, the majority of them alumni of the University of Washington, or professional athletes.

In October, 1990, more than 200 people were invited to "come see one of Seattle's true human meddlers greatly dishonored" at Seattle's fourth annual Roast and Toast Gala, a tradition of "saluting those valued local leaders who have made a unique contribution to the community." I was the "dishonored" recipient. The proceeds benefitted the Medical and Health Education Association. Honorary co-chairs were Gov. Booth Gardner and his wife, Jean, who served with a committee of fifty government and business leaders. I was royally roasted by some of my good friends before being recognized as a "Seattle Goodwill Ambassador." It was great fun.

On four occasions, I was the headline speaker at large gatherings of local and state Italian -American organizations. I since have learned that many local Italian-Americans were disappointed that I never joined any local group, especially since it was known that I had visited Italy many times, had relatives there, spoke and understood the language, was a first-generation American, and probably remained closer to my Italian roots than many others who were grandchildren of immigrants. I am immensely proud of my Italian heritage. I might have joined under different circumstances, but I believed that as publisher of the newspaper, my membership in an ethnic group could create a possible conflict of interest or the appearance of one. I did not need this kind of problem.

Chapter 31

■   ■   ■

Politics, Tourism, and Ports

The two national political conventions were must-see events, at least once, for a life-long newspaperman. With two sets of press credentials, I attended both party conventions in 1992 with *P-I* Executive Editor J. D. Alexander and political writer Joel Connelly

My assigned hotel in Houston for the Republican convention in August happened to be the headquarters for the Louisiana and Mississippi delegations. I rode to the Astrodome each day on the convention shuttle, listened to delegates' conversations, and observed the placards that some carried. These were mostly evangelicals concerned more with abortion than with more serious problems facing the country. Their criteria for selecting a presidential candidate were much different than mine.

Watching from the press gallery, I listened to speeches by Vice President Dan Quayle, a far-right conservative whom many of President George H. W. Bush's advisors believed should have been dropped from the ticket; Pat Buchanan, an arch-conservative who had challenged the President in earlier primaries; evangelist Pat Robertson, and many others.

I had attended the convention as a political independent, more conservative on national and international issues, but more liberal domestically. The *P-I* had endorsed the elder Bush in 1988. I had voted for him and thought he had done a fairly good job in his four years. He was a moderate Republican who could work with the opposition, though he was being challenged on many issues by members of his own party, including future House Speaker Newt Gingrich.

Until that year, I had voted for Republican presidential candidates in most elections, dating back to Thomas Dewey in 1948. I voted three times for Richard Nixon. But the Republicans lost me in 1992. I no longer could identify with the party's philosophy. At Senator Slade Gorton's invitation, I sat in on a meeting of Washington Republican leaders for a post-convention review. I warned that the party had a problem relating to the average voter.

I had felt more comfortable with the atmosphere and the delegates at the Democratic convention a few weeks earlier in Madison Square Garden in New York City. The people and atmosphere was completely different. New York Gov. Mario Cuomo had stood out among several positive speakers. Bill Clinton and Al Gore were nominated. I left New York impressed. The Democrats had a heart, something I didn't sense at the Republican convention. Clinton won. In my youth, I had argued politics with Dad and Uncle John, both blue-collar, naturalized Americans. They were proud to be citizens and voted in every election. It took me several decades to understand and appreciate why they were Democrats.

Prior to the inauguration of Clinton and Gore, I happened to be in Washington, D.C. for a meeting when an ANPA staffer invited me to join him at a holiday party next door to Gore's home. A few of us chatted with a relaxed Gore in the kitchen. I invited him to visit the *P-I* but he never came.

(In 2000, after Clinton's two terms, Gore ran for president himself. He won the popular vote, but lost the final Electoral College tally when the U.S. Supreme Court ruled for George W. Bush after a few recounts of Florida's controversial ballots. Had Al Gore been elected president then, the United States likely would not have invaded Iraq and perhaps seen a better outcome in Afghanistan. Many tens of thousands of lives might have been saved and the billions of dollars dedicated to these wars could have repaired a lot of bridges and roads in the United States. Fifteen years later after Gore's defeat, peace remained elusive, the Middle East was in turmoil, and Islamic terrorism was spreading.)

THE PORT OF SEATTLE, which included the Seattle-Tacoma International Airport (Sea-Tac) midway between Seattle and Tacoma, served the entire region. But the Port of Seattle and the Port of Tacoma, busy seaports equally vital to their local economies, were miles apart as strong competitors for the same business. Tacoma lured away SeaLand, a major shipper at the Port of Seattle, in a price competition. Any move to merge the two ports for the common good was not going to happen given the conflicts of elected boards of commissioners, particularly the Tacoma commissioners. Historically, Tacoma had always felt like a stepchild, politically and economically, and was gratified to better Seattle in every way possible.

We always considered the *Seattle P-I* as a regional newspaper. As publisher I worked behind the scenes to bring the two ports together to harness the strengths of each to benefit both cities. In 1987, I hosted lunch meetings away from both cities with the executive directors of each port, Jim Dwyer of Seattle and Larry Killeen of Tacoma, Sealand executive Jack Helton, and a few business people.

The plan was to form a committee of ten influential business leaders drawn from the two counties to work on a draft agreement merging the two ports. To make it palatable to Tacoma, the chairman would be a Pierce County business executive. I did not intend to be one of the ten members. Discussion would take place in secret. Publicity would scuttle any negotiations.

George Weyerhaeuser, president of Weyerhaeuser, the major employer in Pierce County, agreed to head an informal committee. Unfortunately, the *Tacoma News-Tribune*, an opponent of anything favoring Seattle, published a story about "secret" meetings held by Weyerhaeuser, the *P-I* publisher, the two port directors, and Sealand. Weyerhaeuser, understandably, backed off and the project died. For nearly two decades thereafter, the two ports were like dogs fighting over a bone. In 2015, however, the ports joined in a marine cargo-operating partnership known as the Northwest Seaport Alliance, becoming the third-largest cargo port in the United States.

THE PASSENGER SERVICES ACT of 1886 forbids foreign-flagged vessels from carrying passengers between U.S. ports. It was designed to protect the domestic shipbuilding industry and American maritime jobs. Passenger liners operating in the United States had to be American built and crewed by Americans. However, there no longer were any U.S. cruise ships in operation. Thus, almost 250,000 "room nights" were booked each year in Vancouver, British Columbia, most of them by Americans who flew into Sea-Tac, transferred by bus, train, or plane to Vancouver where they boarded ships making 200 cruises annually to Alaska.

A study commissioned by the Seattle Chamber of Commerce showed the city and the state would receive tremendous economic benefits if a waiver could be obtained allowing cruise lines to use Seattle as a home port for one-way cruises to Alaska ports.

As a founding member of the Puget Sound Cruise Ship Alliance, I co-chaired a community leaders' lunch in 1990 to raise funds for a lobbying effort in Washington, D.C. and then traveled to the capital with Jim Johnson of Alaska Airlines; George Duff, head of the chamber of commerce; and Jim Dwyer of the Port of Seattle. We called on every Washington and Alaska congressman and senator, handing out a list of products their constituents could sell cruise ships calling on the Port of Seattle: grain, produce, and beef from eastern Washington; wine from central Washington; flowers from Skagit Valley; seafood from the shore, and a variety of goods and services from Seattle—all of which were being supplied by Canadians in Vancouver.

We received a cordial reception, but no change occurred for some time. However, a waiver was obtained eventually for sailing between West Coast ports and Alaska. As a result, the cruise-ship industry is flourishing in Seattle. (The Jones Act of 1917 had the same restrictions as the Passenger Act, but it was not waived for cargo vessels.)

MY INTEREST IN AND RELATIONSHIP with Port of Seattle business and tourism continued. After retiring in 1993, I was encouraged to run for the Port Commission if a seat opened. Fortunately, I was spared the decision to be, or not to be, a politician when incumbent Paige Miller chose to run again. This was a relief. I had not looked forward to having to raise money for a campaign and would not have made a good politician. I did not get off the hook completely, however. The League of Women Voters drafted me to moderate a debate between Miller and her opponent. Miller won.

In 1995, seeing a need to reassess its economic impact on the region, the Port Commission appointed a committee of interested industry, labor, and business leaders to conduct a study. I was asked to chair the committee, a fitting role for someone without a vested interest. We commissioned a professional firm, met regularly over a period of time, and produced a highly significant report.

My final role with the Port of Seattle in the late 1990s was as one of three members of the Board of Ethics serving a six-year term. Occasionally I had to recluse myself from issues involving officials who were friends.

Chapter 32

■ ■ ■

Representing Seattle Abroad

The Seattle-Chongqing Sister City Committee sponsored a trip
in 1988 for more than twenty-five people, mostly political and
business leaders, to one of China's largest cities. It was a first trip to
China for many.

In addition to renewing acquaintances from the 1986 visit, I met
with journalists from newspapers in Chongqing and other areas of
Szechuan Province. Our discussions with provincial journalists required interpreters, unlike contacts with the *China Daily* in Beijing
where everyone spoke and wrote in English. Two of our hosts had
been exposed to our press freedoms in an exchange program with
the *P-I.*

There is no such thing as freedom of the press in the Peoples
Republic of China. The press is controlled by the communist government. All stories must be submitted for approval by the "editor," a party official. In no case was criticism of any public official or the party
permitted. None ever appeared in print. The local journalists could
not understand why American reporters didn't have to submit copy to

a government official or censor. U.S. reporters and editors were free to cover and print the news as long as it was accurate and publishers and editorial writers could exercise their opinions freely, even if critical of the government and the president of the United States.

Our discourse had no effect on China's policy, of course, but gave the journalists something to think about.

A DELEGATION OF THIRTY Seattle and state officials, business and trade representatives, and the popular Junior Cadillac rock band visited the Soviet Union in 1989 to participate in trade meetings and a conference in Tashkent, capital of Uzbekistan, involving thirty-two U.S. cities and their Soviet Sister City counterparts. Our delegation was the largest. The Seattle-Tashkent Sister City exchange was the first between the two countries. A year earlier, the Seattle group had built a Peace Park in Tashkent. The city even had a Seattle's Best Coffee shop. Heading the Seattle delegation was Mayor Royer and his wife, Rosanne, who was fluent in Russian, and former Congressman Don Bonker, an expert in U.S. trade policy.

Before flying to Tashkent, a city of more than 2 million, our group stopped in Moscow for meetings with Soviet businessmen. The long Cold War was nearly over and *glasnost* (openness) and *perestroika* (political reformation) was on the rise thanks to reforms backed by Premier Mikael Gorbachev. We met with Russian businessmen (communist officials, no doubt) interested in joint ventures, though none had any private business experience. Similar meetings were held in Tashkent and Leningrad where some business relationships were established.

At a luncheon at which vodka and toasts flowed freely, a *Pravda* newspaper editor invited me to his home for dinner that evening. It never happened. I waited and waited. I learned in a call to the newspaper that there had been a "news emergency." The editor never responded. Everyone else in the delegation had a delicious dinner. I had cold leftovers.

Moscow's Rossia Hotel, adjacent to the Moskva River near Red Square, the Kremlin, and St. Basil's Church, was considered one of the city's finest. But it lacked soap and stoppers in bathroom sinks, making it necessary for this light traveler to stuff socks into the drain while doing his wash-and-wear laundry. Fascinated hotel staffers were glued to television sets watching political leaders engage in a public discussion, an event never viewed publicly before.

Like everyone else, we joined the crowd lining up to see the glass-enclosed body of Vladimir Lenin, the communist "father" of the Soviet Union, preserved for public adoration since his death in 1924. I had seen the preserved remains of the two most famous communist leaders—Lenin in Moscow and Mao Zedong in Beijing, China.

A morning stroll on nearby streets, crowded with civilians and military officers heading for their offices, was a clear reflection of life in the communist Soviet Union. There was no conversation between associates. Most looked down as they hurried along, silent except for the shuffle of shoes on the pavement.

The Russian *ruble* had a fixed exchange rate, 1.60 *rubles* for $1. The unofficial street rate was seven to eight times higher. Russians could not shop in *beriozkas*, state-run stores that accepted only foreign currency and stocked vastly superior merchandise. Flush with *rubles*, but having no place to spend them, Russians were anxious to buy U.S. dollars and persuade Americans to shop for them. An evening walk on the streets netted a nice profit and a reminder of deals in Karachi and Rangoon in 1958.

We received a warm reception in Tashkent, a southern city with a majority Uzbek Muslim population, though most top officials were ethnic Russians. During the Nazi invasion deep into Russia, many Russians sent their children to Tashkent and other remote areas far removed from the war. They stayed. The crowds in Tashkent for three concerts by the Junior Cadillac band were as enthusiastic as the audience for the single concert in Moscow.

I met Andrew Young, the charismatic mayor of Atlanta, whose sister city was Tbilisi. We talked several times about the press, particularly conservative Atlanta newspaper editors who were giving him a hard time. Young had a distinguished career and later served as ambassador to the United Nations in the Clinton administration

One of my *P-I* missions was to arrange a journalist exchange with a Tashkent paper. Viktor Sumin, an ethnic Russian reporter, came to the *P-I* for the 1990 Goodwill Games.

A side trip to Samarkand, midway between Tashkent and Afghanistan, provided a rare glimpse at the oldest city in central Asia. Founded in 2000 B.C., it was an important trading center on the ancient Silk Road between China and the Mediterranean. Our last Soviet airline flight was to Leningrad (later renamed to the original St. Petersburg). The former Russian capital was under siege by the German army for many months in WWII, but never surrendered. More beautiful than Moscow, Leningrad was built by western European architects in the days of Peter the Great and is famous for its Grand Palace and the Hermitage museum.

Our Leningrad hotel was limited to foreign guests. A City of Seattle engineer, an ethnic Russian who was an American citizen, was denied re-entry to the hotel one night until he produced his

American Express credit card, giving credence to the Amex slogan, "Never leave home without it."

Our *rubles* had to be spent inside Russia, so an ample supply of our leftover Soviet currency was spent for vodka, adding to the enjoyment of our train ride to Helsinki, capital of Finland. From there we flew home.

A EUROPEAN STUDY TRIP in 1992 on the inaugural Lufthansa flight of a new Boeing plane took a Seattle contingent of business executives, government officials, educators, and civic activists to the Dutch port city of Rotterdam and capital city of Amsterdam and then on to Bonn and Stuttgart in Germany. The cities were selected because they possessed the ingredients necessary to compete in the global market.

Some other impressions: first, European cities are old in history but new in infrastructure. American cities are new in history but old in infrastructure. Second, building and maintaining the infrastructure necessary to attract international business is a major government function. European projects are planned and completed with much less opposition and difficulty that we seem to experience with almost every project. Third, health and social services are available to everyone.

Our mission was to study port operations, international traffic, transportation, light rail, education systems, government, and industry. In each city, we got the impression that the government cooperated closely with business interests. This was particularly true in Holland, where we were told specifically that the "business of government is business." We took an eye-popping stroll through one of

Amsterdam's famed red-light districts where the sexual attractions were on display in the full-length windows.

Bonn had been the capital of West Germany before unification when Berlin again became the national capital, but elements of the federal government were still located there.

Stuttgart, an industrial city, was the home of Mercedes-Benz. Phil Smart, owner of the largest Mercedes-Benz dealership in the Northwest, was treated like royalty on our visit to the M-B plant. Our dinner speaker was the Stuttgart *burgermeister* (mayor), son of famous German Field Marshal Erwin Rommel, the "Desert Fox," who was implicated in a plot to assassinate Hitler near the end of WWII. We honored Mayor Norman Rice, our own "burgerking," with an appropriate chain necklace benefitting his rank.

THE DEPARTMENT OF DEFENSE conducted a Joint Civilian Orientation Conference in 1992 for fifty-nine civilians from states with military establishments. We received briefings from Defense Secretary Richard Cheney, General Colin Powell, and chiefs of the Army, Navy, Marine Corps and Coast Guard. We flew to Norfolk Navy Base for a tour of a few ships and rode underwater in a nuclear-powered submarine. We were strapped aboard a military transport for a flight out to sea for an abrupt, bumpy landing on the flight deck of the aircraft carrier USS *John F. Kennedy*, with a catapult-launch return to the air. Both were unique thrills.

Our next stop was at Fort Campbell, Kentucky, home of the famed 101st Airborne Division. We were invited to rappel down the side of a fifty-foot building. I almost backed out, but didn't want to lose face. On the way to Fort Campbell, we witnessed an aerial refueling operation involving a tanker plane with a long boom that approached our aircraft from the rear.

Seymour Johnson Air Force Base in North Carolina was our next stop. Every type of airplane in the U.S. Air Force was on display. We had a hands-on experience in a flight simulator. Our last stop was Camp Lejeune, the Marine Corps base in North Carolina, for a display of fire power by armed Marines who demonstrated the latest weapons and conducted demonstrations of ground-warfare tactics and aerial assaults from helicopters.

The orientation allowed us to see first-hand our nation's military capabilities in the four service branches. It was particularly interesting for me to see the Navy side of the military, having spent more than twenty years on active and reserve duty in the Navy. Much had changed since I retired from the Naval Reserve more than a quarter-century before.

Chapter 33

■ ■ ■

Family and Personal Travel

During the holiday season in 1987, Sunni and I traveled with our sons to Australia and New Zealand, flying to Sydney for few days, driving a rented car on the left side of the road across to Canberra, the capital, and then south to Melbourne. It was a new experience celebrating Christmas and New Year's Day on hot summer days in the southern hemisphere, but otherwise the holidays were celebrated in much the same way as at home.

On Christmas Eve, we flew to Auckland, capital of New Zealand, and rented another car. Almost everything was closed on Christmas, except the hotel. The next day, a Sunday, was the same. Monday was Boxing Day, a Commonwealth holiday on which gifts are exchanged, so it wasn't until Tuesday, December 28, that the stores reopened and activity returned to normal. We could truthfully say that we went to New Zealand and it was "closed."

A drive south on the North Island took us to beautiful Rotarua with its mineral springs. New Zealand has more sheep than people, and they were everywhere—the sheep, that is. The trip was a satisfying family get-together in two very fascinating countries down under.

A YEAR LATER, CONTINENTAL Airlines began service to Cairns, Australia, and invited several Seattle-area business leaders on the inaugural flight. A side trip from Cairns to the Gold Coast and Brisbane gave us a good look at the northeastern region, which was much different than anything I had seen on the family trip to Sydney, Canberra, and Melbourne on the south coast. A highlight was a boat ride out to the Great Barrier Reef and an underwater view of the colorful sea life. Many younger people swam. I watched through the glass.

SUNNI, MICHAEL, AND I spent three weeks in the summer of 1990 driving from London west to Winchester, Salisbury, and Chester and then to Cardiff, Wales, where we took a ferry to Wexford, Ireland and made our way to Dublin. From there we took a ferry back to Wales, drove north to Edinburgh and Glasgow in Scotland, and then returned to London. We followed the same route featured by a British tour-bus company. During our travels we stopped at nearly every cathedral and castle and roadside attraction including Stonehenge, Hadrian's Wall, and the Blarney Stone, which we kissed. Everywhere except in London we stayed in bed-and-breakfast homes and inns. Each was different but always charming. Our hosts were interesting.

Our last family trip while I was still at the *P-I* was made over the holiday season in 1992, again taking advantage of accumulated air miles. We flew to Tokyo for a change of planes to Singapore, the city-state island at the tip of the Malay Peninsula, with a one-day side trip to nearby Malaysia. Singapore had been a British Crown Colony on my visit there in 1958. Since then, it had become an international business success story.

Singapore was probably the cleanest city in Asia. Signs at the airport warned of severe penalties for drug possession. It was a crime to spit or leave chewing gum on sidewalks. The population looked prosperous and was split between ethnic Chinese and Malays, but the Chinese were in charge.

The Singapore Sling was a famous drink at the Raffles Hotel. I had tried one in 1958. Our family had to try it on this trip, too. It was good but very pricey.

Dave Towne of the Woodland Park Zoo had arranged with the director of the Singapore Zoo for a personal tour. The zoo was home to some truly exotic species. We also enjoyed a tour at the Hong Kong Zoo, thanks to Towne.

Hong Kong was still a British Crown Colony, but not for long. China was slated to take over the colony in 1997. A series of three treaties had given Britain a ninety-nine-year lease that would soon expire. Many believe the transfer of Hong Kong to the Chinese marked the end of the British Empire.

A mall below our hotel was jammed with shoppers and the restaurants were full of people celebrating much more exuberantly than in Australia and New Zealand. We took a Boeing-built hydrofoil to the tiny Portuguese colony of Macau, which also was to be returned to China in a few years. Macau could be toured on foot. It was much different than Hong Kong. The main attractions were casinos.

We had booked and paid for a two-day tour to Guangzhou, China, to the north. On arrival, we waited in the train station a few hours before a tour guide, then required for foreigners traveling in China, arrived to help us through customs. By then the office was closed, so we entered the Peoples Republic of China without a passport check. Our guide took us to shops and restaurants we didn't like.

MY LOVE FOR BASEBALL dated to my youth when I was a fan of the Pittsburgh Pirates and played ball into my mid-twenties. Major League Baseball made Seattle a big-league city when the Seattle Mariners entered the American League in 1977.

The Mariners' spring training attracted me like a magnet almost every March to Tempe and later to Peoria, Arizona. Richard, David, and Michael at one time or another came with me, although only Michael became a true baseball fan. In 1993, at age sixteen, he lived every boy's dream when he worked a season as a Mariners bat boy for the home games.

VIRSUN INC. AND CASA BRINA wines were good reasons to travel to Italy every few years to visit with the producer, Cantina Bava, near Asti. Travel to Italy continued after we got out of the wine business and I retired. Even after many visits, when I was no longer a novelty, the welcome from relatives was always heart-warming.

On one trip, I scheduled a layover in Copenhagen, Denmark and enjoyed the attractions of the Danish capital. On another layover, I took a train ride across a bridge over the Strait of Oresund from Denmark to Malmo, Sweden to add a true Scandinavian smorgasbord to my culinary experiences.

In 1987, Sunni and Michael joined me on a trip. When I went to Bordeaux, France for an international wine exposition, they traveled to Locarno and Lugano, Switzerland, where Sunni's father had lived as boy before coming to America. Then we drove to Florence and Rome to see the sights and visit the Vatican. It was oppressively hot, however, so we did not see everything we wanted to see.

THE UNIVERSITY OF PITTSBURGH, founded in 1787, honored a select group of alumni from among 160,000 living graduates with a Bicentennial Medallion of Distinction in 1987. To be recognized in the communications category was an honor, especially given that I'd had no contact with the university after graduating in 1949, except for receiving a Varsity Letterman Award in 1974 and hosting a visiting delegation on a Seattle bus tour when Pitt played the University of Washington in 1979.

I was unable to accept the award in Pittsburgh until April, 1989, when I appeared as part of a series of Distinguished Alumni Lectures. Diligently I researched the topic, "The American Newspaper—Its Present and Future." In retrospect, I realize it had to have been boring for the 150 or so attendees who had little interest in the newspaper business but paid $5 to hear me, including my sisters' families and old friends. I also missed completely in my vision of the future of newspapers. The electronic age, internet, and digital technology soon swept over the country with adverse effects on the newspaper industry.

I also spoke to a journalism class, a faculty group, and a few Pittsburgh reporters. A feature story in the *Pitt* magazine brought letters from some old classmates. For the next few years, I served as a member of Pitt's Board of Visitors but, except for visiting family, I had few reasons to make the long trip from Seattle where all my interests were, including Seattle University.

RICHARD BECAME A MANAGEMENT trainee with Sears, Roebuck in Los Angeles after graduating from Seattle University, but later worked for a video-production company learning the business. An excellent photographer, he returned to Seattle in early 1988, bought some equipment, and set up business in the lower level of our home with the aim of shooting wedding videos. Then fate stepped in.

Richard's former business and marketing professors at Seattle University invited him to join them to shoot a video in San Sepulchro,

Italy, marking the 500th anniversary of double-entry bookkeeping, which was developed by a monk, Luca Pacioli. The video was to be the basis for a film to be sold to publishers of financial textbooks. The publishers liked the video and asked Richard to make the film. Richard's brother David joined him with considerable gear, a staff of writers, and other support people for the filming in Italy. The documentary film ran on the Discovery Channel and launched Richard's career. He never made a wedding video.

David, a business graduate of the University of Washington, left his job as a stock broker to join Richard. Virsun Inc. was no longer in the wine business by 1990, so Sunni and I turned the corporation over to our sons. Richard was president and David vice president, doing business as Modern Digital. Both were naturals.

Modern Digital grew, bought out a larger competitor, and moved to Minor Avenue in the Denny Triangle. The enterprise became the leading, award-winning creative broadcast and multi-media production company in the Northwest with a staff of twenty-eight at its peak, serving national and regional clients ranging from NBC and Disney to Boeing and Microsoft. Its television commercials were classics, including those of the Mariners.

Michael was in elementary, junior high, and then in high school during these years. All three sons graduated from Newport High School in Bellevue and went on to earn university degrees.

Chapter 34

■ ■ ■

Seattle Weekly,
Mariners, RBI Club

After living in five cities across the country, I came to love the Seattle area and may have appreciated it more than many native-born residents. I believed it was important that Seattle avoid what happened to Pittsburgh, Detroit, and other rust-belt cities whose best days were left behind them. The *Seattle Post-Intelligencer* and its publisher could help make a great city even greater. Yet it was important that the *P-I* be regarded as independent and not a stepchild of the *Seattle Times*. Everything I did was for those reasons.

It was inevitable that my personal involvement in community activities, both in public view and behind the scenes, would be subject to scrutiny. It was imperative that no conflict of interest exist between the *P-I*'s editorial policies and news coverage and my involvement in various organizations.

THE TABLOID SEATTLE WEEKLY had always looked for clinks in the armor of local leaders and institutions, the *P-I* and its publisher included. *Weekly* Publisher David Brewster had led one of the four community groups opposing the JOA.

Cognizant of the *Weekly*'s biases, I agreed in 1988 to be interviewed by Eric Scigliano, the paper's star reporter. With or without me, a story was going to run. I had no illusions about its thrust and thought it better to respond to questions rather than to stonewall.

Scigliano had done much research. It was a long, in-depth interview. Much of it covered background on my early life and career, but I sensed the real purpose was to determine how much pressure, if any, I put on the news staff to cover particular stories or politicians in a certain way. My involvement in the community was more extensive than that of any other publisher I had known. I did not expect to be exempt from the *Weekly*'s scrutiny. According to the *Weekly*, *Times* Publisher Frank Blethen was on the board of the Downtown Seattle Association and was about to become chairman of the United Way campaign. Brewster was active in arts organizations. None of these were controversial roles.

I had not expected to find my picture covering the front cover of the *Seattle Weekly* on July 6, 1988 with this big, brash headline: "VIRGIL FASSIO. Is the publisher turning the *P-I* into a bully pulpit?"

Inside was a double-page spread with another headline set in old-English type that alluded to *Citizen Kane*, a 1941 film about a powerful newspaper publisher: "Citizen Fassio: Hearst-style boosterism and hardball live on in Virgil Fassio, the *P-I*'s pushy publisher." The article was spread over six more pages with several photos. A caption referred to me as a "power-broker and civic crusader."

The story started with a fairly accurate account of my youth, education, and career. No problem there, but Scigliano had interviewed many people in politics, business, and on the *P-I* staff in a search to uncover proof that would confirm the *Weekly's* pre-conceived notion of conflicts of interest involving news coverage of organizations and projects in which I was involved personally.

Although crediting the Save our Elephants campaign and "Chinasaurs" as community benefits, the *Weekly* questioned several other activities it considered controversial and, in its view, outside the accepted role of a newspaper publisher. Many initiatives I championed were opposed by the *Weekly*, which frequently conducted journalistic search-and-destroy missions aimed at several business organizations and community projects.

The *Weekly* had favored a Seattle Center site for the convention center in 1983. As chair of the Seattle/King County Convention & Visitors Bureau, I proposed another site closer to downtown Seattle and nearer to the city's hotels. My advocacy for development of the Westlake Center ran counter to the *Weekly's* proposal that a park should be created instead.

The *Weekly* also took issue with my work on international trade matters, tourism, and waterfront development, and criticized the secrecy of my effort to get the Seattle and Tacoma ports to merge. The article was critical, too, of my role as prospective chairman of the Downtown Seattle Association in 1990, viewing the Downtown Seattle Association as favoring developers.

"What's good for business has to be good for the city," I said in an interview. "What was good for Pittsburgh were the steel mills and what was good for Detroit was General Motors. A lot of those big cities had it made and they didn't hold on to it."

The *Weekly* apparently had interviewed several editors and reporters, but found no instance of any story being ordered, altered, or killed by me. There were none. The *Weekly* took the shaky position that a reporter, aware of my involvement, *might* feel pressure to cover a story about an issue in a certain way. But the *Weekly* found no incident to back up even this feeble assertion.

One of my remarks included in Scigliano's story had to do with Seattle complacency. "Many people born and raised here," I said, "believe it is God's country. It is. The only fault is that some believe we shouldn't change anything. If we don't, we slip back. Seattle is just touching its greatness."

PART OF THAT GREATNESS, according to the *Weekly*, had to do with my passion for baseball and my leadership role in efforts to keep the Seattle Mariners in town. I believed, I said, that "Seattle has to have Major League Baseball if we're going to be big-league quality. One of the saving graces of Pittsburgh is that it is a big-league city. Big-league presence is what makes a city first class."

Seattle was represented by the Seattle Pilots in the major leagues for just one year, 1969, but then lost the team when the owners filed for bankruptcy. The franchise was moved, becoming the Milwaukee Brewers. The City of Seattle, King County, and state of Washington represented by then-Attorney General Slade Gorton sued the American League for breach of contract. The suit was dropped in exchange for a league promise that Seattle would get a new team.

The Mariners began play in 1977. The owners were five successful Seattle-area business leaders and actor-comedian Danny Kaye, a business partner of Les Smith, who also had an interest in the team.

They invited business leaders to a reception in the owners' suite for the Mariners' first game on April 6, 1977. It was a good opportunity to meet the new owners. The Kingdome was sold out. The M's were shut out by the California Angels 7-0.

Attendance declined after the initial enthusiasm of having a big-league team back in Seattle wore off. If Seattle lost its second MLB team, it was doubtful big-league baseball would ever return to Seattle.

After the 1979 All-Star Game in Seattle, Jay Porter, president of Unigard Insurance Co.; Andy Smith, president of Pacific Northwest Bell; and I formed the Mariners RBI Club (Real Baseball Involvement) with the stated mission of supporting the Seattle Mariners and keeping Major League Baseball in Seattle. Porter was the RBI "commissioner" (president). Smith and I were "league presidents." We "drafted" community leaders as team managers and filled out teams with local business people committed to sell season tickets. To join, members had to be season-ticket holders or represent a group that was. The owners enthusiastically welcomed our efforts.

THE FAN BASE HAD IMPROVED only slightly when George Argyros, a wealthy California real-estate developer, bought the team prior to the 1981 season. He was even more supportive of RBI members, showing his appreciation in many ways, including hosting social events and sponsoring spring-training trips. I became a close friend of Argyros, viewing him as an owner who could afford to keep the Mariners in Seattle and had been willing to do so when no local buyers stepped forward. I was asked to join the team's eight-member Community Advisory Board, all CEOs of major companies, and became commissioner of the RBI Club in 1992.

It was my active support for Argyros, who had many detractors, which made my baseball interest a target of the *Seattle Weekly*. The newspaper reported on some of my activities that were public, but many were behind the scenes.

I had played a leadership role in resolving the tangled dispute over the Mariners' Kingdome lease. It was probably the most controversial role among all my community activities. Working with Andy Smith and George Duff, we arranged meetings with King County Executive Tim Hill, and two council members in an effort to negotiate on behalf of Argyros. The team owner was willing to extend his lease beyond its 1996 expiration and to remove an escape clause, which allowed him to move the team to another city if annual attendance fell below 1.4 million, in exchange for about $2 million a year in increased revenue from concessions and parking.

The *Weekly* opposed the deal. At one point, I carried the financial books of the Mariners to Tim Hill's office to show Hill why additional revenue was needed by the Mariners. Sparks would fly if Argyros and Hill were in the same room.

In 1987, I convened a breakfast meeting with Mariners President Chuck Armstrong, business leaders, and four King County Council members in an effort to delay a Mariners exit invoking the escape clause. It was supposed to be an off-the-record discussion, but due to the extra presence of eight county council staff members, the meeting was not secret for long. A story wound up in the *Seattle Times*, causing me grief with my own staff that was embarrassed by having been beaten on the story.

George Duff, John Ellis of Puget Power & Light (Later to become Puget Sound Energy), John Mangels of Rainier Bank, Jim Thorpe of Washington Gas Co., and I were leaders on the Safe at Home committee, formed in 1987 to find a local buyer for the Mariners when Argyros expressed interest in buying the San Diego Padres, a team that was closer to his home and businesses. I arranged for Dave Sabey, the *P-I*'s landlord, to meet with Argyros about a possible sale, but it didn't work out. That "secret" meeting also made the *Seattle Times*.

These efforts took place prior to publication of the *Weekly* story. Some detractors believed my negotiations with county officials and the county executive had been "threatening." Tim Hill denied that they were.

Perceptions are not always accurate. It was hard for some to understand that my motive in trying to preserve a community asset, the Mariners, had nothing to do with Argyros. He happened to be the owner. I would have done the same no matter who owned the team.

Argyros grew weary of the effort to find a local buyer and put the Mariners up for sale again in 1989. We mustered our group to look for a local buyer, again without success. One Saturday morning, Argyros phoned me from his plane (he owned AirCal) to give me a heads up that he was enroute to Seattle to announce a sale of the team, but he personally assured me the new owner was not going to move the team.

JEFF SMULYAN, OWNER of a chain of radio stations based in Indianapolis, brought in his own executives when he bought the Mariners. He was an open and likeable guy. It was easy to become well-acquainted with him and to believe that he intended to make a success of the Mariners, which had not had a winning season since 1977 and still had not built an adequate fan base. I always responded to Smulyan's question of whether Seattle would ever become a "baseball town" by telling him he had to field a winning team first. Still, I supported him, personally and editorially, as I had Argyros, because Seattle could not afford to lose the team.

Smulyan became increasingly concerned in 1991 that baseball might not make it in Seattle. He was not able to negotiate lucrative television contracts. A big loan was coming due. There were ominous signs that he might move the team to St. Petersburg, Florida, which had built a domed stadium expecting to get the Chicago White Sox whose owner, Jerry Reinsdorf, wanted a new stadium and threatened to move if the city didn't build one. Chicago built a new stadium. The White Sox stayed. The stadium in St. Petersburg remained empty.

Smulyan was ready to move in 1992 if a local buyer was not found within 120 days. Our "Safe at Home" group went back to work again.

I received phone calls from two prospective buyers: Wayne Huzenga, owner of Blockbuster Video, who later bought the Florida Marlins; and Charlie Finley, controversial former franchise owner who moved the Kansas City Athletics to Oakland. Finley said he represented others prospective buyers when I told him I doubted MLB owners would approve a sale to him. Besides, we were not interested in any out-of-town buyers.

Slade Gorton, who by this time had been elected to the U.S. Senate, persuaded Hiroshi Yamauchi, owner of Nintendo in Japan and the Kirkland-based Nintendo of America, to become the majority owner of the Mariners. Sixteen local partners including Microsoft and McCaw Cellular executives comprised the minority ownership. Opposition was voiced by some MLB teams, including the Chicago Cubs (owned by the Tribune company), who were skeptical about a Japanese owner in "America's national pastime." Stan Cook, my old *Chicago Tribune* boss, had become president of the Cubs. I lobbied Cook extensively. He voted for approval.

John Ellis and Frank Shrontz, Boeing chairman, joined the board. Howard Lincoln, president of Nintendo of America, represented

Yamauchi. Chuck Armstrong returned as president. The new ownership took over on June 28, 1992.

The Mariners were saved.

BECAUSE SMULYAN'S ORGANIZATION had not recognized
the value of the RBI Club, the club became inactive and nearly folded. I proposed a revised RBI Club to the new owners. It would be
an independent, dues-paying club maintaining its original mission of
supporting the team. The new owners welcomed the plan. I became
commissioner in 1992 before retiring.

Chapter 35

■ ■ ■

Goodbye *P-I*, Hello Retirement

Hearst publishers are supposed to retire at age six-five according to a policy established when Frank Bennack Jr., publisher of the *San Antonio Light*, was promoted to general manager of Hearst Newspapers. Previously, publishers stayed on until they were ready to retire, no longer could work, or died. I personally agreed with the policy. There has to be opportunity for aspiring, younger executives to reach the top. The industry was constantly changing. New ideas were needed.

My last two-year contract expired in December, 1992, five months past my sixty-fifth birthday, but my relationship with Hearst in New York continued with no mention of retirement. Nothing changed. For several months I thought of myself as a lame duck, though none of my associates were aware of the situation. Finally, I wrote to Danzig and Bennack in June, 1993 to advise them of my wish to retire on August 1, and to recommend that Executive Editor J. D. Alexander take over as publisher. They flew to Seattle to make the announcements.

On Thursday, July 29, nearly 500 well-wishers attended a "Good Luck, Virg" luncheon-roast at the Sheraton Hotel. Gov. Mike Lowry proclaimed the date "Virgil Fassio Day" in Washington State. Mayor Norm Rice did the same for Seattle. President Bill Clinton sent his best wishes.

Roast-masters were ex-Mayor Charles Royer, who had moved on as director of the John F. Kennedy Institute at Harvard, and Cliff McGrath, soccer coach at Seattle Pacific University. Other roasters were George Duff, director of Seattle Chamber of Commerce; Rev. William J. Sullivan, SJ, president of Seattle University; Pat Davis and Paige Miller, Port of Seattle commissioners; Chuck Armstrong, president of the Seattle Mariners; William B. Stafford, director of the Seattle International Trade Alliance, and Seattle Mayor Norm Rice.

Everyone received a four-page *P-I* section filled with articles and pictures summarizing my life and career with flattering quotes. My favorite was from Chuck Armstrong, who said, "The Seattle Mariners would not be in Seattle if it were not for Virgil Fassio."

That afternoon, a reception was held in the newspaper's executive offices where almost every staffer came by to pay respects and to wish me well. It was heart-warming that so many of these fine men and women wanted to have their pictures taken with me. I was touched, too, that so many referred to me as "Virg," which I preferred to "Mister Fassio." It was a memorable day that I will treasure forever.

I reflected on all the fine people on the best news staff I had ever worked with. The credit for continuing to make the *P-I* the most influential newspaper in the state belonged to editors and reporters whose work brought about important changes.

A few who deserved credit readily come to mind: Charles Dunsire, editorial-page editor; David Horsey, cartoonist and columnist; Shelby Scates and Mike Layton, political writers and columnists; John Owen, sports editor, columnist, and cookbook author; Bill Knight, sports editor; Tom Read, assistant editor; Art Thiel and Jim Moore, sports columnists; Dan Raley and Jim Street, sports writers; Janet Grimley, lifestyle editor; Nancy Hevly, Solveig Torvik, and Sam Sperry, editorial writers; Joel Connelly, environment and political writer; James Wallace, environment and aerospace; Susan Paynter, Jon Hahn, and John Marshall, columnists; Phil Webber, photographer, and a newsroom full of other excellent journalists; Myrna Casad, my valuable administrative assistant; Bob Swearengin and Bob Roach in business and systems; Kathryn White in promotion; and my closest associates, Bill Cobb, business manager; and John Joly, public-relations director. I could name everyone.

Shortly after retiring, Sunni, Michael, and I went to Cooperstown, New York to visit the national Baseball Hall of Fame on a vacation trip that J.D. Alexander, the new publisher, gave me as a parting gift. It was an all-baseball trip. We went to a Yankees game and a Mets game in New York, an Orioles game in Baltimore, and a Phillies game in Philadelphia. Sunni doesn't care much for baseball, but she was a good sport and enjoyed the sightseeing.

IT HAD BEEN FORTY-SIX YEARS since I struck up a chance conversation with a printer sitting next to me in a bar in a Pittsburgh neighborhood. The conversation put me into the newspaper business for the next forty-six years. Newspapers had been good to me. My seventeen years at the *P-I*, fifteen years as publisher, was the highlight of my career.

A new challenge, retirement, was about to begin on August 1, 1993.

I looked forward to it because I had things to do.

Chapter 36

■   ■   ■

Adjusting to a Busy Retirement

After retiring I was often asked if I missed my job at the *P-I*. The publisher's job at any newspaper inherently comes with the power to influence community events in many positive ways. I thought I would miss it all, but truthfully the answer was, "No. Been there, done that."

Still, it took a while to adjust. No longer were there any (or perhaps fewer) 7:30 a.m. power breakfasts, no weekly community-development lunches, no monthly Chamber of Commerce or Downtown Seattle Association meetings. I still attended weekly Rotary Club lunches and Washington Athletic Club 101 events when the program sounded interesting. Eventually I resigned from both clubs.

I no longer came home from the office every evening with a briefcase full of homework after a nine- or ten-hour day. I did not miss that at all. The fifty- to sixty-hour work weeks were history. I could enjoy more family and leisure time and more travel.

ALTHOUGH LACKING EXPERIENCE in banking, I was invited by Pat Patrick, chairman and CEO of Metropolitan Savings and Loan in Seattle, to join his board of directors in 1992. This was the only paid directorship I ever accepted and I did so only because my retirement was imminent. The board met monthly. I'm not sure how much my newspaper background helped, but it was an informative experience. The bank was sold to Washington Federal in the late 1990s.

Little by little over the next few years I gave up seats on the boards of a diverse group of organizations. I stayed connected with a few. My association with the Medic One Foundation continued. The foundation has been one of the most satisfying of all my community activities. I also remained on the board of Hope Heart Institute until 1999 after serving as president for two years, 1994 and '95.

I REMAINED ACTIVE in the RBI Club, too, which I co-founded in 1979. After its reorganization in 1992, I served as commissioner (president) until 2006 and later remained on the board as commissioner emeritus. A lot of time was spent in the Mariners offices during those fourteen years, scheduling our monthly speakers. Notable guests were Hall of Fame members Bert Blyleven, Bobby Doerr, Paul Molitor, Gaylord Perry, and Don Sutton. Hall of Famers Pat Gillick, a Mariners executive, and Dave Niehaus, popular Mariner broadcaster, were frequent speakers as were Lou Piniella and Jamie Moyer. Edgar Martinez a future Hall of Famer, appeared a few times.

I felt honored in 2009 when the Mariners designated me their "Fan of the Year" in 2009 at a pre-game, red-carpet ceremony with an award presentation by Manager Don Wakumatsu.

When I stepped down as commissioner, Bob Simeone took over. He did an excellent job expanding the scope of the club beyond monthly luncheons and, frankly, doing a better job with younger board members while I continued participating as commissioner emeritus.

Meanwhile, outdated or ill-suited stadiums were being replaced in several cities. The Kingdome was made for football, not baseball, and the Mariners ownership argued that the aging facility should be replaced with a baseball stadium. In 1994, King County Executive Gary Locke appointed a twenty-eight-member Stadium Task Force to explore the need for, cost of, possible locations for, advisability of, and funding options for building a facility. I was one of the appointees.

After studying all alternatives, we recommended construction of a new baseball stadium with a retractable roof on a site immediately south of the Kingdome. That summer, Kingdome ceiling tiles fell just before the start of a game, forcing cancellation of all home games for the rest of the season. This strengthened our case that a new stadium was needed.

In 1995, when the long-range future of the team in Seattle seemed at risk without a new stadium, RBI Club members lobbied county council members and state legislators, registered voters as they arrived for weekend games, and contributed financially to the campaign for a new stadium. However, King County voters narrowly rejected an initiative for a one-tenth of one percent sales tax increase to build one.

Then, the Mariners won their first Western Division championship in a dramatic come-from-behind series in 1995. That shifted public opinion and brought the state legislature into the picture.

Fast forward: the first game was played in the new Safeco Field, one of the best baseball stadiums in the country, on July 15, 1999. San Diego Padres beat the M's 3-2 before 47,000 fans.

RICK RIZZS, MARINER BROADCASTER since 1983, and former outfielder and broadcaster Dave Henderson formed Toys for Kids in the 1990s initially with funds donated by the players. In

2000, backed by the RBI board, I offered the club as the sponsor for a fund-raising dinner and auction to benefit this good cause.

We raised about $10,000 in 2000. The proceeds grew each year. More than $375,000 was raised in November, 2016, benefiting nearly 8,000 homeless, hospitalized, and needy children through twenty-four local agencies. It has been a distinct pleasure to be involved with Rizzs.

The RBI Club also initiated the annual "Moose" Clausen Award for Community Service to honor a Mariner player or executive. Moose, an RBI charter member, is a former Mariners sales executive beloved by all.

THE ANNUAL AUCTION of Northwest wines at the St. Michelle Winery in Woodinville is a major fund-raising event benefitting Children's Hospital. I served as the second co-chair in 1993 and enjoyed meeting Northwest wine-makers and participating in related events. A year later, I was the lead co-chair with Mercedes-Benz dealer Phil Smart. The honorary chairman that year was Ernest Gallo from the famous California winery whose family, like mine, had come from the Piedmont region of northern Italy.

Gallo had been touched by what he saw on a visit to Children's Hospital. When introduced at the auction that evening, he held up a three-liter bottle of cabernet sauvignon, declaring it to be the best wine he had ever produced. He offered to donate $50,000 to Children's Hospital if someone would match his gift. Two bidders offered $25,000 each, effectively raising $100,000 for a bottle of Gallo!

SEATTLE SEAFAIR, SAID TO BE the largest city festival in the country, encompasses a wide variety of neighborhood celebrations every summer and several major citywide events such as the long-running hydroplane races on Lake Washington, a popular milk-carton derby, and the thrilling Navy Blue Angels flyover.

In 1997, I was asked to serve as the forty-eighth "King Neptune" to preside over Seafair. Frankly, I was reluctant to put myself on display wearing a colorful, custom-made costume befitting a king and waving to crowds at Seafair events and promotional appearances throughout the region. My family, however, was enthusiastic so I consented to perform the royal duties.

It turned out to be fun. I participated in numerous programs, "knighting" people with a symbolic sword, and rode in more than twenty parades in cities as distant as Portland and Spokane. I became expert at waving at the crowd, as did Jim Johnson, Washington Athletic Club manager, who was "prime minister" of SeaFair; and Ann Slaugh, Miss SeaFair. The biggest procession was the televised Seattle Torchlight Parade that started at Seattle Center and wound through downtown to the Kingdome. Many in the crowd of 300,000 people lining the parade route had been waiting since early morning, having positioned themselves at curbside in their own comfortable chairs. It was uplifting to see all the happy children.

IN 2002, I JOINED a 24-Hour Fitness Center in Bellevue and met some retired acquaintances, mostly Italian and all a few years younger than I. After a one-hour workout three to five mornings a week, we enjoyed coffee and conversation at Tully's, which is probably what kept us going.

Our group included Tony Petrarca, a retired Boeing manager who had invited me to speak to the Bellevue Sons of Italy in 1979; Daryl "Lefty" Burke, who once struck out twenty-two Pacific Lutheran

University batters while pitching for the University of Washington Huskies; Chuck Maletta, a mortgage-broker and former owner of a beauty-supply company, and Lou DiLaurenti, former owner of a well-known store in the Pike Place Market, when he is in town. We observe birthdays at an Italian restaurant with Mariner broadcaster Rick Rizzs. We made Burke an honorary Italian.

I have never been bored in retirement.

Chapter 37

■　■　■

Have bags, Will travel

The retirement years have gone by in a blur. I was always ready to pack a bag and go somewhere. Finally I had the time to visit even more exotic and interesting places at my own pace, especially with my family. I had traveled extensively, but wasn't finished yet. Many friends vacationed every year in the same places. This never appealed to me.

Not long after hanging up my publisher's hat, I embarked on the first of six trips as a tour leader for Connie Swanson Travel Agency. A tour leader is needed, not as a guide, but as an experienced traveler who makes sure that arrangements are handled along the way and problems are resolved, not unlike my experience on the around-the-world editors' tour in 1958.

Sunni had no interest in cruises, but didn't mind if I traveled. My boys and I would travel later.

My first trip with the travel agency was a Mediterranean cruise from Athens, Greece to Kusadesi, Turkey with a side trip to Ephesus, the ancient city with its famous temple, one of the Seven Wonders of the Ancient World.

The cruise stopped at several Greek islands, including Rhodes, where the Colossus of Rhodes was built in the first century B.C., and Crete, the fifth-largest island in the Aegean Sea, its history dating back to 3,000 B.C. when it was the center of the Bronze Age. Crete is referenced in Homer's *Odyssey*. We also visited Mykonos and Patmos, then sailed to Messina in Sicily with a visit to nearby Taormina, site of an ancient amphitheater; and on to Naples, Rome, and Genoa. After my group of thirty left for home, I stayed behind to visit relatives in Asti and Torino, as I did every time my travels took me to Italy.

An Egypt and Nile River cruise in 1994 was a fascinating first-time experience with a group of twenty-five. We assembled in London, then flew to Luxor and the Valley of the Kings, the land of ancient pharaohs' tombs. It was essential to have a native Egyptologist guide with us to explain the hieroglyphics and the Muslim culture. We had a good one. A close look at the countryside and a variety of small boats added to the wonder of our cruise up the Nile aboard the *Nile Romance*.

At the dock in Aswan, where a large dam was built with Soviet help in 1957, we saw a newspaper vendor on the shore displaying *USA Today* and the *International Herald-Tribune* in the last place in the world you would expect to find them. A flight to Abu Simbu to see the large statues of pharaohs was followed by a return to Cairo. In 1958, the Great Pyramids and the Sphinx were far outside the city. By 1994, the urban sprawl had crept close to these ancient treasures.

The only problem I ever encountered as a tour leader was in Cairo. A couple frequently imbibed from a copious supply of gin in their luggage and as a result the woman was injured in a fall. I spent most of a day, with a guide's help, searching for a walker. Back in London, I sent the couple home three days early.

BARCELONA, SPAIN WAS the departure port in 1995 for a twenty-one-day "Mediterranean to Africa and South America" cruise aboard the *Pacific Princess*, on which scenes of the fictional *Love Boat* cruise ship were filmed for the popular television series of the same name. I discovered that textbook Castilian Spanish was a little different than the Catalan dialect in Barcelona.

The cruise ship stopped briefly in Gibraltar, the massive rock at the entrance to the Mediterranean Sea—a British possession—before reaching Casablanca, Morocco, site of one of the three Allied invasions of North Africa in 1942. Morocco became independent of France in 1956. The bazaars, casbah, and a view of the Atlas Mountains were highlights in Marrakech before we sailed down the Ivory Coast to Dakar, Senegal, the northernmost point in Africa, giving us a view into Africa. Senegal still reflects the French influence of its colonial period.

The next few days crossing the Atlantic was what cruising is all about—relaxing days with a variety of activities, evening entertainment, and always-excellent food.

We reached South America at Recife, the "Venice of Brazil," a city laced with waterways. Portuguese-speaking Brazil occupies almost half of the South American continent. Two days later, we were in Rio de Janeiro, the country's second-largest city and its capital until 1960. It is one of the world's most beautiful cities with lush forests, spectacular mountains, and sparkling beaches. A tram ride up Sugar Loaf Mountain to the majestic statue of Christ the Redeemer looking down on the city followed by a stroll along Rio's exotic Ipanema and Copacabana beaches were vivid experiences. Rio is a city of contrasts—racially diverse, beautiful, and glittering but also poor with its ramshackle, cluttered, unsanitary barrios.

Our next port of call was Montevideo, capital of Uruguay, which is similar to a European city in style and culture. My Spanish worked well here.

Highlight of the trip was Buenos Aires, Argentina—a city with a metropolitan population of 11 million, about one-third of the country's population. It is a beautiful, European-style city, but more modern than Europe and having an almost entirely white population of 3.9 million. My Spanish worked well here.

I considered trying to learn more about my namesake uncle, Virgilio Fassio, who had immigrated to Argentina from Italy and settled in a small town in the interior. He was hunting on a large ranch in 1940 when his party was accosted by ranch guards. Fassio fled, apparently fearing he would lose a borrowed gun, and was shot dead. The sketchy news was relayed from Italy. We knew little more than that.

A CARIBBEAN CRUISE has to be on an itinerary for any American who enjoys cruises. I led a twelve-day tour in late 1996 through all the islands stopping at Coco Bay, Bahamas; St. Barts in the French West Indies; St. Lucia in the British Windward Islands; Grenada; Dominica (discovered by Columbus in 1493); St. Maarten, Dutch West Indies; St. Thomas, U.S. Virgin Islands; and San Juan, Puerto Rico. The islands blended the cultures of the Caribbean, Africa, France, Spain, and England.

We toured several islands but Grenada was of special interest to me because the United States had invaded the island several years earlier to counter growing Cuban influence. It was a very brief "war."

Complementing an earlier side trip to Nassau, Bahamas (arranged while I was on a *Free Press* business trip to Miami) and my Naval Reserve cruises to Cuba and Haiti, this trip rounded out my Caribbean experiences.

In 1997, I helped the travel agency by escorting part of a large group to London for a few days and then to Venice where my charges joined a Mediterranean cruise. This provided another opportunity to visit uncles, aunts, and cousins in Asti and Torino. As always, the American relative was treated royally with an abundance of food and Piedmont wine.

A THAILAND TOUR in January, 1999, co-sponsored by the Washington Athletic Club with forty-five members signed on, was the largest group I traveled with during my tour-leader "business." As with all Swanson trips, the hotel accommodations were first class. By way of Tokyo, we flew to Bangkok, capital of Thailand, a constitutional monarchy I had visited decades before. Buddhism, the dominant religion, was evident everywhere in Bangkok. Prominent must-see sights were the Emerald Buddha in the Wat Phira Keo pagoda, the Royal Grand Palace, the ancient capital of Ayuthaya, and the city's many canals with simple homes built on the water.

Chiang Mai, a flight north, was much different. It was in Hill Tribes country, famous for its elephants, which attracted me because of the Save Our Elephants campaign. I rode a quarter-mile atop one of these magnificent beasts at a logging camp. Our final experience was a tour of a Hill Tribe village, where we were served a meal prepared with local ingredients, much different than that of Bangkok and Thai restaurants in the United States, which I enjoy. I didn't care for the Hill Tribe cuisine, however.

A TOUR OF PANAMA and the west coast of South America late 1999 was my last as a tour leader. First stop on the twenty-day cruise after sailing from Fort Lauderdale was Aruba, a small island in the Dutch West Indies near Venezuela. Particularly memorable were the divi-divi trees with trunks that permanently bent 90 degrees because of the wind.

Cartagena, Colombia, offered prime examples of beautiful Spanish colonial architecture. The Old City is surrounded by a twelve-foot wall. Outside is the mightiest of Cartagena's fortresses, the most outstanding feat of Spanish military engineering in South America. Bargaining in Spanish led to purchase of a handmade straw hat for $5 while I helped others shop there and in markets farther down the coast in Chile, where prices are fixed with no bargaining.

The Panama Canal transit from the Caribbean to the Pacific Ocean was fascinating. Canal pilots take over and "mules," now mechanical, nudged the ship through the locks. U.S. construction of the forty-eight-mile canal began in 1904 after the French began work on the project in 1881, but gave up due in part to engineering problems. In 2015, 14,702 vessels traversed the Panama Canal, which was turned over to Panama in 1999.

EXCEPT FOR CHILE, the west coast countries of South America are heavily influenced by local Indian cultures mixed with Spanish history and culture. This is much different than countries on the east coast which, except for Uruguay and Argentina, are heavily influenced by African culture. This was evident in the port of Manta, Ecuador, the smallest Hispanic nation in South American and on a tour of Quito, the oldest capital in South America. It was settled by Indians in the first century. In 1544, Spanish *conquistadores* defeated the Incas there.

A picturesque city of 800,000 Quito sits on the slopes of a narrow valley in the Andes, still retaining much of its colonial past.

After departing Ecuador, we observed a seafaring tradition, a "crossing the line" ceremony, when we passed over the equator.

Callao is the port city for Lima, capital of Peru with a population of 4 million. It was founded by Francisco Pizarro, the Spanish *conquistadore* who defeated the Inca Empire in 1535. Lima is the fastest-growing metropolis in South America. Like Ecuador and Bolivia, Peru is one of South America's true Indian countries. A flight over the Nasca Lines—mysterious gigantic figures carved on the desert hillsides representing fishes, spiders, and other geometric signs—was incredible. No one knows how the "world's oldest astronomical calendar" came to exist there.

After a tour of Pisco, Peru, the ship sailed south to the desert city of Arica in Chile, a country with a north-south length of 2,650 miles and an average width of 110 miles, and then continued to Valparaiso for transfer to Santiago. With an almost all-white population of 3.9 million, Santiago is the capital and dominant economic center of Chile, resembling a European city much like Buenos Aires.

Chile was the end of the line. Among the souvenirs of my cruise experience was an expanded waist line. It took several years to lose the excess pounds.

FAMILY-RELATED TRAVEL to several cities in the Lower 48 and Alaska, and vacations in Oahu and the Big Island in the 1980s provided memorial experiences. In the 1990s, we visited two other Hawaiian Islands. The smaller Kauai is our favorite. It is a beautiful island that had been the scene for filming of the movie *South Pacific*. It was less-frequently visited than the other islands.

Maui was a wonderful destination, too. Sunni, Michael, and I made the Maui trip alone because Richard and David could not get away from their business. We took a spectacular helicopter tour of the island, flying over Haleakala Mountain with its many sharp peaks and ridges and into dense fog over the twenty-mile-wide volcanic center. I was a scary feeling. I still shudder when I think about it.

OUR NATIONAL PARKS are favorite destinations for tourists from all over the world. In 1996, my Italian cousins—Gian Franco Fassio and his sons, Emanuele and Luca—asked me to join them for a road trip through the Southwest. The itinerary was ambitious. Starting in Las Vegas, we visited Hoover Dam and Lake Mead in Nevada; Bryce Canyon and Zion National Parks in Utah; Mesa Verde National Park in Colorado; Petrified Forest National Park, Meteor Crater, Monument Valley, and Montezuma's Castle in Arizona.

I probably would not have made this trip on my own were it not for my cousins' interest in coming all the way from Italy to see some of America's most spectacular natural beauty. We had a close encounter one night driving through the Navajo Tribal Reservation in Arizona. Three wild horses suddenly appeared out of nowhere and galloped across the road, missing the front of our rented car by a few feet. After we parted ways in Arizona, my cousins took a rafting trip down the Colorado River through the Grand Canyon.

BEGINNING IN 1994, I made the first of many week-long visits to River Ranch near Faywood, New Mexico, which Gene Simon bought in 1974 after selling the *Valley News-Dispatch*. These were wonderful vacations. But River Ranch was no dude ranch. I pitched in with Gene and his hired hand for all the ranch chores, dealing with cattle and every type of winged fowl from pigeons to peacocks. Wild turkeys knew where the grub was. Every night, they appeared out of the darkness to roost with the domestic turkeys and get their fill.

Gene was always building something. He found a use for any scrap of lumber. I loved riding Gene's horses. In the evenings, we had discussions about the newspaper business, international and national politics, current events, and diverse subjects Gene wrote about in his thought-provoking weekly column. I last visited the ranch in 2008.

I was saddened when my mentor and long-time good friend passed away in in 2012.

Chapter 38

■ ■ ■

A Good Look at the Old World

Most satisfying of the post-retirement travel were trips with my family, especially one-on-one travel with each of our sons to Italy and fifteen other countries in Europe.

David had been to Italy in 1988 with Richard to film the Luca Pacioli documentary for Seattle University, but had not seen much else beyond San Sepulcro in Tuscany. In fall, 1999, with David driving, we visited Asti. We were honored like visiting royalty at a Piedmontese dinner that brought together an aunt and several cousins, children of Mom's sisters and brother who got together for weddings, funerals, and special occasions such as our visit. Many of our relatives in the countryside tended to vineyards and bottled their own wines.

We also visited Cantina Bava, the winery whose wines I had introduced in the United States. The reception was the same in Torino.

No trip to Italy is complete without a tour of Venice, with its Grand Canal and St. Mark's Cathedral, and a drive south to Florence, where David was especially taken by Michelangelo's' statute of David. Then we drove through three Tuscany hill towns—Montalcino, Montepulciano, and San Gimignano—in the heart of another great wine region that, like Asti, produces some of Italy's finest wines, including the popular Chianti. The local history is fascinating. In ancient times, each town built its own castle and fortress as protection against attacks from neighboring towns.

The trip with David ended with the sights of Rome and Vatican City. I could have touched Pope John Paul II as he led the procession after the mass. It was the first of two unplanned visits to the mass in St. Peter's Cathedral within a year.

THE NEXT YEAR, MICHAEL and I visited Vatican City and took part in a huge outdoor mass attended by cardinals, prelates, and visitors from all over the world who had come to observe the eightieth birthday of Pope John Paul II. We had good seats. Our Rome stop came midway through a ten-week swing through Europe.

Michael had been in Italy with Sunni and me in 1987. He completed his undergraduate degree studies at the University of Washington in March, 2000. Like his Dad, he had the travel bug and wanted to explore Europe before settling into a job. None of his buddies were available, so he invited his Dad on an extended trip through sixteen countries. He knew exactly where he wanted to go and when to move on from one place to the next. I had visited many of these cities before, but traveling with my young son was a treasured experience. It was his trip. I was happy to share it with him.

It would take another book to describe our adventure. Our only luggage was a backpack with everything we needed, particularly wash-and-wear clothes. We didn't miss many cathedrals, museums, or bell towers, which Michael climbed. I didn't. We started and ended the trip in Paris, where the Eiffel Tower was emblazoned at night with the number 2000 marking the start of a new millennium.

Most American tourists that we saw were studying travel guides from internationally recognized travel-writer Rick Steves of Edmonds, Washington. His books were full of valuable information and insight on transportation, sightseeing, and small affordable places to stay. We used them extensively. We were never disappointed.

After touring the magnificent palace in Versailles, I rented a stick-shift car and drove west through France. Our destination was Mont St. Michel, the 1,200-year-old Benedictine abbey on a pinnacle of land on the Brittany coast where cars had to be out of the parking area before nightfall when the tide came in.

Then, by way of Bayeux with its famous tapestry, we drove to Omaha and Utah beaches in Normandy, where an Allied force of more than 156,000 American, British, Canadian soldiers had attacked on D Day—June 6, 1944. It was the largest amphibian invasion in history. More than 10,000 Allied troops died. Thousands of American are buried in a solemn, tranquil, and beautiful American cemetery not far from remnants of Nazi defense fortifications.

IN PARIS, WE ACTIVATED a sixty-day Eurail pass and headed for Brueges, Belgium, a fascinating medieval city. In Brussels, after seeing the famous bronze statue of Mannekin-Pis, we bought Leonidas chocolates and were appalled when we left them on the train on our way to Amsterdam, Netherlands, home of Rembrandt, Van Gogh and the Anne Frank House. From there, we went on to the tiny country of Luxemburg and then to Germany via Cologne to Koblenz at the juncture of the Moselle and Rhine rivers, where Sunni's mother was born and married her father.

In Koblenz, we were met by Angie Gloeckner, a cousin who had visited us in Seattle. Sunni had never met (and still hasn't met) Angie's parents. They didn't speak English, but we had a delightful dinner together. We took a riverboat trip down the Rhine with a stopover in Bacharach to Wurzburg and then booked a bus ride on the Romantic Road through medieval Bavaria's heartland to Rothenberg, Germany's best-preserved walled town. We walked on top of the wall. Our lodging was in a seventeenth-century building on the town square. The town had been spared from Allied bombing during WWII due to its history and uniqueness.

Michael understood the German at a candlelight Easter vigil in Munich, where Nazism had its start. At Englischer Garden the next day we saw several nude men and women sun-bathing. Nobody paid any attention. Nudism was legal in the park, even on Easter Sunday.

We made three side trips out of Munich. We visited Dachau, a concentration camp for Jews and others during the Nazi regime. The horror of it was difficult to comprehend, but a similar visit to another camp later was even more disturbing. In Neuschwanstein, the fairy-tale castle of "Mad King" Ludwig, we ran into Port of Seattle Director Mic Dinsmore and Patricia Davis, port commissioner, and their spouses. We also explored Innsbruck, Austria, a ski mecca that has hosted several Winter Olympics in a broad valley between high mountains in the Tyrol region of western Austria.

From Munich, we took a night train—our first—to Prague, Czech Republic, founded when Czechoslovakia was freed from Soviet domination in 1989. The historic capital of Bohemia, Prague is home to 1.26 million people and is Europe's fifth most-popular tourist destinations. We walked the banks of the Vitava River and crossed the famous Charles Bridge. We bought tickets from street vendors and enjoyed several concerts. Prague was much improved from my earlier visit. It is a delightful city worth several days.

BERLIN WAS ON OUR SCHEDULE at the same time as a visit by a Seattle Chamber of Commerce mission led by Mayor Paul Schell. Earlier, I had arranged to join the group, most of whom I knew, on a trip to Potsdam, a stop at an amusement park, and visit to a German beer garden. We joined the mission at its hotel in the evening where Michael entertained my friends with a piano concert in the lounge.

Krakow, Poland, turned out to be one of our favorite cities. The friendly people reminded me of the many Polish families I knew growing up in Pittsburgh and working on the *Valley Daily News*. The steel mills and coal mines of western Pennsylvania attracted many Polish immigrants, including the parents of my brother-in-law, Leonard Pulkowski.

Much of Poland had been severely damaged during the war, but Krakow was spared the bombing and devastation because it was near Auschwitz, the worst of the Nazi concentration camps. The camp was full of horrific sights—the original barracks, gas chambers, rooms piled high with suitcases, clothes, personal possessions, artificial limbs, even the hair of the victims. It was difficult to understand how this heartless inhumanity could have existed in a civilized society. Millions of Jews and hundreds of thousands of gypsies, political opponents, and Soviet prisoners were gassed at Auschwitz and in concentration camps in Germany, Poland, and other countries occupied by Hitler's Nazi regime.

In Budapest, Hungary, we heard that travelers took their chances selecting a place to stay from among those promoted at the train station, but we were pleased with our lodging. The city is comprised of two parts, old Buda and newer, more modern Pest, separated by the Danube River, which contrary to the popular song is not blue. Budapest was one of the most enchanting of medieval cities. We celebrated Michael's twenty-third birthday with a traditional goulash dinner.

Vienna, high on our must-visit list, didn't disappoint. We were tourists during the day and concert-goers in the evening, although I am tone deaf. Vienna is long famous as the musical center of Europe. We enjoyed an amazing classic performance of the Lippizzan horses, especially bred and trained at the Spanish Riding School. We also encountered one of Michael's university acquaintances and enjoyed a treat at the famous Sacher Torte Café. A day trip on a hydrofoil down the Danube to Bratislava, capitol of Slovakia, added another country to our growing list.

Salzburg, a train ride away, provided a glimpse of scenes featured in the movie *Sound of Music*. We could almost hear Julie Andrews' voice. We happened upon a chapel dedicated to Saint Virgil, an early Christian, in the ruins of an ancient church below the Salzburg train station. A local train took us south to picturesque Hallstatt, across a lake from the station. A building near the town church featured the skulls and limb bones of deceased residents, all labeled so one could visit long-departed relatives. We also visited an underground salt mine.

Venice, our gateway to Italy, was a city with which we were familiar. We had no problem communicating. English had become the international language, though locals appreciated a foreign visitor who could speak their language. My Italian was a big help.

Venice was unique with its many canals and small bridges. Grand *palazzos* stood at water's edge with their basements flooded, as they always had been. Because cars are not allowed, the transportation choices are bus-like passenger boats on the Grand Canal, water taxis, or the colorful and romantic gondolas.

We stayed in a comfortable *pensione* owned by Foundation Levi, evidence of Venice's once-thriving Jewish population and a reminder of Shakespeare's play, *Merchant of Venice.* Michael and I enjoyed what amounted to a pub crawl. A special treat was a boat ride to Murano, famous for its glass factories.

TRAINS IN EUROPE ARE EFFICIENT, comfortable, and on time—even in Italy, which once had a poor on-time record. From Venice, we went directly to Rome, the Eternal City, with ancient and modern sights, all of which I had seen many times but Michael had not visited since he was ten. We were moved by the wonders of Rome–the Colosseum, Pantheon, and the excavated ruins of the Forum. We threw Italian *lire* into *Fontana di Trevi*, featured in the film, *Three Coins in the Fountain*, hoping to continue our good luck.

We marveled at the excavated ancient ruins of Pompeii, a once beautiful city that had been buried for centuries after the eruption of Mount Vesuvius in 79 A.D. The city had been covered with mud, rather than destructive ash and lava, so everything was well-preserved. We saw casts of people in their last moments, rooms intact with paintings and mosaic-tile floors, and cobblestone streets rutted by the wheels of ancient wagons and chariots.

After visiting Florence, we rented a car for visits to Siena, Pisa, and the Tuscan hill towns Montalcino, Montepulciano, and San Gimigliano.

The Basilica of St. Francis in Assisi, with relics of the saint, was a worthwhile stop on the route north to the picturesque Republic of San Marino, population 25,000, a sixty-four-square-mile enclave within Italy and one of the world's smallest republics. Founded in 301 A.D. by an early Christian, its independence was recognized in 1291. Our hotel near the top of the three-peaked Mt. Tirano offered a spectacular view. San Marino has its own government and prints its own postage stamps—a big business—but speaks Italian and uses Italian currency. In many ways it is like any small Italian town.

We walked the beach at Rimini, a few miles east of San Marino on Italy's eastern coast, then drove across the country to walk the beach at La Spezia, on the west coast, all in one day. Cinque Terre—five villages hanging on cliffs between the mountains and the sea and once accessible only by water—are connected by a long walkway and accessible on narrow roads from each of the train stations above. We walked down the hills to Vernaccia and Monterosso, the two main villages. Portofino, a short distance north, was a well-known destination for wealthy folks. The harbor was filled with luxury yachts.

IN ASTI, WE RECEIVED warm family welcome that we always received as the lone American relatives, even though I had been to the region many times to visit relatives and had visited with David the year before. A glass of their best wine was poured immediately upon our arrival. This reminded me of my Dad, who always offered a glass of his wine to visitors as soon as they sat down.

A cousin, Paolo Giordano, who had visited us in Seattle, drove us to the Principality of Monaco, at 1.8 square miles the smallest country in Europe. Monte Carlo was filled with expensive cars for the Monte Carlo Grand Prix. Gambling is the lifeblood of Monaco.

However, we were not properly attired and were politely denied entry to the famous casino. Michael and Paolo swam at the beach. I watched.

Gian Franco Fassio, son of Dad's brother, Cesare, was twelve when I visited Torino in 1949. His mother implored me then not to encourage his interest in America, where many young Italians wanted to live. He was their only son.

Starting with one vending machine, he built a large company that served a major part of Torino, published a slick monthly magazine for the vending industry, and owned a villa overlooking the city. He was up to date on world affairs and, like many Europeans, knowledgeable about the United States. We always had stimulating discussions. I had accompanied him and his sons Emanuele and Luca a few years earlier on a national park tour of the American Southwest.

Lucerne, Switzerland was our destination after a stay in Lugano and Locarno in the only Italian-speaking canton of Switzerland, where German and French are also official languages. We enjoyed the sights along Lago Maggiore, which is mostly in Italy. Michael had been in Lucerne in 1987 with Sunni, whose father lived there briefly before coming to America. I had been in Lucerne in 1956. On a short side trip from Lucerne, we visited the small principality of Liechtenstein in the foothills of the Alps, German-speaking and independent since 1719.

Some of Europe's tallest mountains are south of Lucerne. We rode a train from Grindewald, across from Eiger Mountain, up to Jungfraujoch in the snow at 11,702 feet where we explored the Ice Palace, a glacial cave complete with ice sculptures of animals. Surprisingly, the cave was not really cold. The next day, a gondola from Murren took us up to Schilthorn, a building perched by itself at the top of a mountain that had been the location for a scene in a 1963 James Bond film. A train to Zermatt and then to Gornergrat for a tram ride up to view the cloud-covered Matterhorn completed our exciting Swiss mountain experiences.

MICHAEL HAD BEEN AN UNPAID volunteer for the Washington Council on International Trade for several months helping arrange details for an annual meeting in Seattle of the World Trade Organization in November, 1999. When we stopped In Geneva on the last leg of our trip, we were given a warm welcome and a tour of the WTO headquarters when Michael revealed that he had worked at the registration desk in Seattle. He had witnessed the ugly, disruptive protests, property damage, and confrontations by anarchists that gave WTO delegates a bad experience and Seattle a smear on its otherwise sterling reputation.

From Lausanne we went to Lyon, France, and on to Charles DeGaulle Airport in Paris for the flight home. Michael's planning had been nearly perfect. We went everywhere and saw everything that he had mapped out, and then some.

The ten weeks of traveling with my youngest son had been one of the most rewarding experiences of my life.

Chapter 39

■   ■   ■

Spain and Portugal

E ver since my first trip to Europe in 1949, I have looked forward to every trip since then as an opportunity to see new places and to observe the people and cultures of foreign countries. I'm sure I was influenced in my early years growing up with foreign-born parents in a melting-pot neighborhood full of good, hard-working people who had emigrated from many European countries. Even Italians, we knew, came from different regions of Italy, each with its own distinct dialects and customs.

By 2002, I had visited more than eighty countries on six continents, including almost every country in Europe. But there was more to be seen. With four years of high-school Spanish, I wanted to explore Spain where true Castilian is spoken. Spanish differed slightly in each new-world country.

That summer, Michael had a break between leaving a job and entering the Sullivan School of Law at Seattle University, so we took off for Spain and Portugal. Both countries were new to me except for Barcelona, where as a tour leader I had embarked on a Mediterranean cruise with a group of Americans in 1996.

A few experiences in Madrid stand out: His Majesty's Cavalry and the impressive changing of the guard at the Royal Palace and a bullfight featuring the leading matadors and picadors of Spain, which a visitor need witness only once to be convinced that bullfighting should be outlawed. After a day of sight-seeing, we sampled *tapas*, accompanied by some excellent Spanish wines, in several bars.

That evening, a few young men brushed by Michael on a crowded street. "Thieves!" I yelled. The men stopped. One of them handed Michael his wallet, claiming to have picked it up off the street. We had learned a long time ago never to keep anything important in your wallet and to carry only small amounts of cash in your pocket while guarding passports, credit cards, and larger amounts of cash in a money belt. Pickpockets are slick. Watch out for anyone, or a group, approaching too close. This is good advice for any traveler.

GEORGE ARGYROS, FORMER OWNER of the Seattle Mariners and a strong supporter of President George W. Bush, was the U.S. ambassador to Spain. We considered Argyros a good friend, although many in Seattle had not liked him as the M's owner. In an exchange of emails, he invited Michael and me to a dinner at the embassy with several leading Spanish government officials and possibly members of the royal family. Argyros, a Greek-American, had established good relations with King Juan Carlos I and Queen Sofia, daughter of the Greek king.

When he learned we were traveling only with backpacks, with no suits or ties, he invited us for an afternoon visit to the embassy since we would be unable to dress for dinner. We enjoyed a pleasant visit in his office. We were told by Seattle friends that Argyros had made substantial improvements to the embassy with his own funds.

Argyros inquired about the Mariners, whose play he followed daily. He told us of recent visits by several high-level U.S. officials, including Gen. Colin Powell. Our discussion was interesting and timely, though I regretted not being able to come for dinner.

We drove fifty miles north to Segovia, site of an ancient Roman aqueduct, cathedral, and medieval castle. Roast suckling pig is the culinary delight of Segovia. We like to try any area's specialty and will try almost anything, but this sampling was one too many.

Nearby was the Valley of the Fallen, where 50,000 Fascist and Loyalist soldiers died in the Spanish Civil War of the 1930s. The underground monument is a tribute to General Francisco Franco, the dictator who fought the leftist government and was supplied with military arms from Nazi Germany and fascist Italy. During the early years of World War II, Spain supported the Axis powers short of military involvement. General Franco moved to a policy of neutrality when the Allies took North Africa in 1943. A monarchy was re-established in 1947, but the general controlled the country as chief of state until his death in 1975.

GRANADA, A FIVE-HOUR TRAIN ride to the south, featured the magnificent Alhambra palace and fortress, the last stronghold of the Moorish Kingdom in Spain. The Moors (Muslims) were defeated in 1492 and the fortress became the royal court of Ferdinand and Isabella. Local cuisine still reflects the North African influence.

Alhambra is the most significant example of Islamic architecture. Rooms with their upper walls decorated in Arabic encryptions in geometric patterns and lower walls in mosaic tiles open onto the courtyards. I understood the local saying that "there is nothing worse in this life than to be blind in Granada."

In Granada, we rented a car for a fascinating drive through Spain. After more than fifty years of disuse, except for occasional visits to South America, my Spanish was fractured but slowly returning.

The sunny 150-mile southern coastline of Spain, the Costa del Sol, starts in the charming, old-world city of Nerja and ends in what is known as the "balcony of Europe," a terrace on a bluff overlooking Mediterranean beaches. The Caves of Nerja have Europe's most impressive stalactites and stalagmites in huge, well-lit caverns.

We took a ferry from Algeciras across the sea for a day in Tangier, Morocco, a busy Muslim city in North Africa. In the casbah I flinched, but Michael held steady, when a snake-charmer draped one of his snakes around Michael's neck. The contrast between European Spain and Arab Morocco was like night and day.

WE MADE A SIDE TRIP to Gibraltar, the British fortress on a promontory rising dramatically from the sea at the western entrance to the Mediterranean. To get to the Rock, we crossed a narrow, sandy isthmus in a neutral zone separating it from Spain. Britain claimed Gibraltar in 1704 during the War of Spanish Succession, creating friction between Britain and Spain that continues to this day. Spain wants the Rock back. Britain refuses to let it go. For many years, Spain would not allow direct travel from Spain to British Gibraltar.

We took an interesting tour inside the tunnels of the Rock, constructed with openings for cannons. A cable car took us to the top of the Rock where we saw the famous "apes" of Gibraltar, which actually are tailless Barbary macaque monkeys—the only wild monkeys in Europe. They are everywhere. We allowed an ape to sit on our shoulders. Winston Churchill is thought to have said, "If the apes of Gibraltar ever leave, Gibraltar will be lost." The apes are still there.

ANDALUCIA'S ROUTE OF the White Hill Towns—Arcos de la Frontera; Ronda, the largest; and Grazalema, all built by the Moors—are connected by narrow mountain roads and seemingly still part of the Medieval Moorish world. The streets are narrow and the white-washed houses with their tiled roofs face inner courtyards. These cities were on the front line of the centuries-long fight to re-capture Spain from the Muslims, who were slowly pushed back into Africa.

Nearby is Jerez, famous for its horses and sherry wine. Horses are my favorite animal. We got tickets at the Royal Andalusian School of Equestrian Art for the Horse Symphony, a daily horse ballet with choreography, Spanish music, and nineteenth-century costumes. The horsemanship is superb. We sampled several of Jerez's finest sherry wines and gave them all five stars.

The tomb of Christopher Columbus is in Seville's Cathedral, the third-largest church in Europe. Explorers Amerigo Vespucci, the Italian who gave his name to America, and Ferdinand Magellan sailed from Seville, then known as the gateway to the New World, in the sixteenth century.

Jews were expelled from Spain during the Inquisition in 1492 and resettled on several Mediterranean islands and in North Africa and the Middle East, but Seville still has a Jewish Quarter. Adding to the charm were thriving bars and a busy nighttime scene. We took in a flamenco show, something one must see to appreciate. When we think of Seville, we are reminded of the opera *The Barber of Seville*, Carmen, and Don Juan.

LAGOS WAS OUR ENTRY into Portugal and the Algarve, much like Spain's Costa del Sol with warm, sunny beach towns. We stayed in a *pensione* in Salema owned by an expatriate Englishman, walking the beaches, feasting on some of the best fish dinners I have ever had, and taking a scenic coastline boat tour. Salema, a quiet fishing village, was a welcome break from our travels. It is off the main road to Cape Sagres, a side trip that took us to the rugged southwestern tip of Europe where Prince Henry the Navigator's school sent explorers west when many believed the earth was flat.

Lisbon, Portugal's capital, was rebuilt after a devastating earthquake in 1755, and now has a main boulevard similar to Paris' Champs Elysees. Its vintage trolleys wind through the old parts of town, climbing steep hills and providing good views of the city. The Belem district recalls Portugal's golden age, when it became Europe's richest power after Vasco da Gama's voyage to India more than 500 years ago.

We left Lisbon in the dark hours of the morning to begin our trip home. We hurriedly jumped out of the cab. The cab sped off. Michael discovered that a rolled-up rug purchased in Tangier had been left in the trunk. I learned the major differences in Spanish and Portuguese. It was impossible to communicate our problem. Some taxi driver in Lisbon had a new rug and Michael was out $200.

Chapter 40

■　■　■

On the Road Again

As many times as I had traveled around Europe, especially Italy, I never had seen the southern half of Italy or crossed the Adriatic Sea. In October, 2009, Michael and I did that on a vacation break from his job as an assistant state attorney general in Washington.

On all trips since my retirement, we have carried our belongings in backpacks. We stayed in *pensiones* or *albergos* recommended by Rick Steves, usually within walking distance of train stations. When we rented a car, we looked for easy access and parking.

On this trip, I spent a few days relaxing in Fiumicino, Rome's airport town, where I met Michael. Our walkie-talkie radio communications were excellent. It is easy to get lost if separated in foreign cities. We bused south to Sorrento and took a scenic ride down the Amalfi Coast, an adventure itself along the high road above the cliffs and towns, with stops along the way. This is a must tour for anyone who has lived in the flat Midwest all their lives.

On our return to Sorrento, we took a ferry to the Isle of Capri. Once an idyllic place idolized in songs, it was filled with tourists, but still managed to retain a good deal of its charm. After another ferry to Naples, we were ready for an overnight trip on a Tirrenia Lines ferry to Palermo, with comfortable sleeping accommodations and an early-morning arrival.

PALERMO, CAPITAL OF SICILY and the largest seaport on the island, is full of art treasures and beautiful buildings with a colorful history dating to 800 B.C. It is a creation of nearly every people and culture that ever touched its Mediterranean shores: Phoenicians, Greeks, Romans, Byzantine, Arabs, and the Normans, plus the French, Spanish, and others. All made Sicily different in many ways than the rest of Italy. Sicilians can be blond and blue-eyed as well as swarthy. It did not become a part of the unified nation of Italy until 1865.

We visited all the major sites. One, the Capuchin Monastery Catacombs, is a unique and macabre tourist attraction with about 8,000 corpses and 1,250 mummies of prelates and famous people in their everyday clothes posed in cabinets or propped against the walls. The first mummy was placed here in 1599 and the last, a small child, in 1920. It was a status symbol to be preserved and put on view so your relatives could visit you forever.

From Palermo, we took a train across mostly flat, agricultural Sicily to Messina, a city I visited in 1993 on a Mediterranean cruise. From there it was a short ferry ride across the narrow Strait of Messina to Reggio Calabria, at the extreme tip of the toe of the Italian boot, famous for its Greco-Roman museum. Sicily and the region of Calabria—both agricultural areas—were the homeland of a great percentage of the Italian immigrants to the United States in the late 1800s and early 1900s. Immigrants from the more prosperous central and northern Italy came later, including my parents in 1920 and 1921.

WE RENTED A CAR with an automatic transmission (rare and expensive to rent in Italy) for the drive east to the Adriatic Sea port city of Brindisi, the main naval port of the Roman Empire and the end of the ancient Appian Way. We stopped for two days in Mesagne, a small city eight miles west of Brindisi, where Sunni's father, Richard DeVirgilis, was born. The area's phone book confirmed many variations of the name "Virgil," apparently descendants of the ancient Roman poet, Virgil, who visited Brindisi often and is believed to be buried there. It was nice to know I had married a descendant of Virgil.

Our major objective was Bari, a larger Adriatic port that was a major commercial center for trade with eastern Mediterranean and served as the principal Italian naval base. It was heavily damaged during WWII. Enroute we stopped in Alberobello in the Trulli District, known for its picturesque stone buildings, *trulli*, which are shaped into cones, often whitewashed, and adorned with stone peaks bearing crosses. They originated centuries ago as farmhouses, townhouses, and barns.

Other fascinating stops on the way included Sibari, an ancient Greek colony, with preserved ruins; Ostia Antica, an ancient port city once home to 60,000 people from all corners of the Roman Empire; and Locatondo, burial place of Giuseppe Garibaldi, the general who liberated the Italian peninsula to help create the nation of Italy in the 1860s.

DUBROVNICK ON THE DALMATIAN coast of Croatia was our destination on an overnight Jadrolinija ferry boat from Bari across the Adriatic Sea. Sleeping accommodations were comfortable. We had no idea where we were going to stay. But as we were leaving the ferry port, we were approached by a retired, English-speaking civil servant with pictures of his place just outside the Old City. He drove us there. It was one of the nicest rooms of the entire trip. The bus stop was a few minutes away, making it easy to spend the next few days touring the Old City. Dubrovnik was besieged for seven months by Serb and Montenegro soldiers when Croatia declared its independence in 1991 after the breakup of communist Yugoslavia.

When we walked the perimeter atop the medieval wall we observed some of the destruction from heavy shelling. The city has been rebuilt as one of the top tourist attractions on the Mediterranean Sea. We rated Dubrovnik, founded in the seventh century, as one of the best cities we had visited.

A bus ride north to the Croatian city of Split took us through a sliver of seashore territory in the country of Bosnia-Herzegovina, where the Bosnia War of 1991-94 took 100,000 lives in ethnic killing by the Serbs. Appropriate frontier formalities were observed. Other than adding another country to our list of places visited, we had no other experience there.

Our major reason for going to Split was to take an overnight Blue Line Ferry to Ancona, Italy, where we were met by Gian Carlo Berzano, young son of Cousin Giuseppe, who drove us the few hundred miles to Asti in time for lunch. That night Giuseppe invited all my cousins and their families to a restaurant for a festive dinner, at which I gave my obligatory speech in Italian. Michael had to leave for home before I finished my trip in Torino, where I spent a few days with Cousin Gian Franco Fassio and his family and Cousin Renata Fossati. As always, it was a warm visit.

IN SPRING, 2013, I RETURNED to Italy with Richard to visit places not included on a Rick Steves tour he was taking with his family a few months later. I had visited most of these places. Richard had not been to Italy since 1989. He did not have a chance to visit family then so he was meeting many relatives for the first time.

We arrived in Milan, where we were picked up by Gian Franco for a few days in Torino. He gave us a good tour and an introduction to his Nuova Cigat business. Rich and I wasted a few hours in line at Torino's Egyptian Museum, the best outside of Cairo, before giving up and heading for Asti where Giuseppe did what he always did by gathering all the relatives for dinner so they could meet Richard. He also took us on a tour of the surrounding countryside, a vast vineyard of Piedmont grapes. In Repergo, the farmhouse where my aunt's family lived in 1949 as sharecroppers was in shambles.

As small farmers left for the city, a young cousin had bought several farms. He owned a substantial number of cattle. Lacking pasture land, my cousin opted to slaughter the calves for veal. We also visited Agliano Terme, a small town where my father was born, and the Bava winery in Cocconato. Another first cousin, Annamaria Pia Giordano, lived in the small town of Portacomaro, near Asti, where parents of Pope Francis I lived before immigrating to Argentina. I was surprised to meet so many people in Asti who had relatives in Argentina. Many Piedmonteses, like my Uncle Virgilio, went there when they could not come to the United States after a restrictive immigration law passed in 1924.

BOLZANO IN THE TRENTINO, Alto-Adige, near the Dolomites, was a place I had always wanted to visit ever since hearing my father talk about Bolzano, an objective of the Italian Army in WW I. It was then part of Austria called Bolzen. Dad had spent the war on the Austrian front, mostly on Monte Bianco in the nearby Dolomites. A scenic half-hour ride to Castelrotto in the heart of the Dolomites provided a scenic view of the high mountains surrounding Bolzano. Ceded to Italy after the war, the Tyrol still retains much of its German-Austrian-Tyrolean character. Bolzano-Bolzen is a rarity, a bilingual city with street signs in both German and Italian and many family names that definitely are not Italian-sounding. The hotel owners had German names. Richard had studied German in high school. I spoke Italian, but English was understood by most people.

In Bologna, we rented a stick-shift car for the next several days with Richard as the driver. Rain and fog prevented us from seeing the small Republic of San Marino so we journeyed southward through Tuscany, with must stops to sample the fine wines. We dropped the car off in Florence, where we had the pleasure of staying in the Bellevue Hotel before taking the bullet train to Naples. Rich walked through all the ruins in Pompeii while I rested, having been there before.

It was a short trip to Sorrento, where we had planned to stay while taking a bus tour of the Amalfi Coast. Our timing was off, however. We did not know that a major bicycle race down the Amalfi Coast was organizing in Sorrento. The road was closed to other traffic for two days. We made the most of the situation. Rich rented a Renault Twizy, a tiny two-person vehicle, one in front and one in back. We had never seen a car like this before. We went up into the hills, observing lemon trees everywhere, to an area noted for producing delicious *limoncello* liquor.

Back in Rome and a night's stay in Fiumicino, my thirteenth trip to Italy came to an end. We flew home the next day. Rich had received a good sampling of the Piedmont and many small, historic towns of Italy.

I had much enjoyed the one-on-one trips to Italy with each of my sons. They got to know their Italian relatives and could stay in touch with them in the years ahead.

Chapter 41

■   ■   ■

End of the Printed *P-I*

O n January 9, 2009, Steven Swartz, then president of the Hearst's Newspaper Division, announced to a stunned *Seattle Post-intelligencer* staff that the newspaper was for sale. If no buyer came forward, Hearst would discontinue publishing the paper in printed form, he said, but that an online edition might be continued. Hearst had no interest in acquiring the *Seattle Times.*

The announcement came thirty-three years after Hearst hired me in August, 1976. When I arrived at the *P-I*, Hearst had just broken off negotiations with *Times* for a Joint Operating Agreement. The *P-I* was in "probable danger of financial failure," but it was hoped that I might be able to turn the newspaper around. It was not to be. The paper's downward spiral, which experts believe started before 1965, was stopped but not reversed. Eventually negotiations with the *Times* resumed and in May, 1983, a JOA was implemented after twenty-eight months of litigation.

The agreement provided that the two newspapers would jointly operate all business functions, including printing, circulation and distribution, marketing, and advertising sales. All of those functions were to be taken over by the *Times*. Some *P-I* employees in those departments became *Times* employees; others lost their jobs. At the *P-I*, only the newsroom remained essentially intact. The purpose of the JOA, which had to have federal approval to avoid running afoul of antitrust laws, was to preserve two independent editorial voices in an environment in which at least one of the newspapers was demonstrably failing financially.

A handful of *P-I* executives and administrative positions, including mine, were preserved to protect Hearst's interests and support the newsroom.

In 1983, the *Seattle Times* was an afternoon newspaper and the *P-I* was delivered in the morning. But reader preferences were shifting dramatically away from afternoon papers almost everywhere, and it became increasingly clear to *Times* management that it could not continue publishing an afternoon paper successfully in the long term. And so, after still further negotiations, Hearst and the Seattle Times Co. agreed as of the beginning of 2000 to begin publishing and delivering both the *Times* and the *P-I* as morning papers. Before the end of the first year of this operating arrangement, however, the Seattle Times Co. began reporting financial losses.

The Joint Operating Agreement included a clause that gave either party the option to terminate the agreement upon experiencing three consecutive years of losses. When the Seattle Times Co. threatened to terminate the JOA, Hearst filed a lawsuit seeking to prevent it from doing so. Among other things, Hearst claimed that a thirty-eight-day strike in 2000 had contributed to the operating losses being claimed by the *Times* and should not be considered in determining lack of profitability under the termination clause.

I TESTIFIED IN A SWORN deposition in the Hearst lawsuit on July 24, 2004. I had retired in 1993, so I could address only those events in my ten years (1983-'93) as the publisher of the *P-I* under the JOA. I cited many steps taken by the *Times*, the costs of which the *P-I* had to share and many of which *P-I* Business Manager Bill Cobb and I viewed as unfair or unnecessary. Current and recent *P-I* executives were also deposed. Roger Oglesby, who had taken over as publisher from J.D. Alexander in 2000, had done his best under the very contentious arrangement, made more difficult by the *Times* move to morning publication. It had become difficult enough for two daily newspapers to survive in a metropolitan market and even more so when both published in the morning.

After eighteen months of litigation and binding arbitration, a settlement was reached stipulating that the *Times* could not revisit dissolving the JOA under the termination clause until 2016 at the earliest. Hearst received $24 million under the settlement. But just as the future began to look a little brighter for the *P-I*, the 2008 Recession hit with destructive force and newspaper advertising revenue collapsed in Seattle and all across the country. That led to the announcement in January of 2009 that the *P-I* would cease publication if no buyer stepped forward.

None did.

THE *POST-INTELLIGENCER* rolled off the presses at the *Seattle Times* plant for the last time on Tuesday, March 17, 2009, with a commemorative edition reviewing its illustrious 146-year history. "The Voice of the Northwest Since 1863" became a smaller, online-only edition, available at seattlepi.com. In recognition of the growing prominence of online journalism, Roger Oglesby had announced in

2007 that the web would be the *P-I*'s primary publishing platform. Now it is its only platform.

After retiring, I made a decision not to visit the *P-I* unless invited. I never wanted any of my predecessors to come around when I was on the job. I knew this was the right decision. Few invitations came. Contacts were minimal. I had an occasional lunch with J.D. Alexander and served as a table host at the annual *P-I* Sports Star of the Year Awards banquet. When possible, I attended memorial services for current and former employees who passed away.

Roger was the last publisher of the *P-I*. He had joined the paper and Hearst in 2000 from the *Los Angeles Times*, where he had been president of the Orange County edition. I made it a point to welcome him to Seattle, offered to provide any information about the *P-I* and the market that I could, and sponsored his membership in Seattle Rotary. We got together almost weekly at Rotary lunches.

My only regular contacts with former associates at the *Seattle Post-Intelligencer* as of this writing are lunches every two months with John Joly, an associate from the *Detroit Free Press* and retired *P-I* public-affairs director; John Currie, retired business manager, who joined the paper from Hearst's *San Francisco Examiner* after the late Bill Cobb's retirement in 1995; and Roger, who moved back to the state after a few years living elsewhere in retirement. We reminisce and keep up to date on people we knew at Hearst and the newspaper industry in general as well as engage in interesting discussions of politics and current events. I also keep in touch with Lee Guittar, retired Hearst executive, now living in Florida.

THE NEWSPAPER INDUSTRY has changed drastically since I started in the daily field in 1950. At first the changes evolved slowly, but since the mid-1980s the pace of change accelerated. Many of the optimistic forecasts made in my speech at the University of Pittsburgh in 1989 have been overtaken by the electronic age.

The newspaper industry was traditionally labor intensive, involving printing presses, several mechanical operations, and physical distribution of a printed paper to readers' doorsteps and to retail outlets. But readership has declined dramatically. Losses in newspaper circulation worsened and have been most pronounced on metropolitan papers. Internet competition for classified advertising virtually killed newspapers' most profitable source of revenue. Younger generations increasingly rely on other sources of information. And it may not have helped that many newspapers offered their product on the internet at no cost. The systems get more sophisticated each year. Today's innovation is tomorrow's obsolescence.

There are many ways to explain the decline of the newspaper industry as I knew it, but perhaps the simplest and most straightforward way to understand it is to think of it as, in fact, an issue of advancing technology. When Johannes Gutenberg invented the movable-type printing press, it revolutionized communication. For the first time in human history, ideas, accounts of historical events, and man's most treasured beliefs could be shared widely on a scale that was previously unthinkable. And even into the latter half of the twentieth century, the printing press had few rivals for communicating information quickly and accurately to a mass audience.

Newspaper publishers had been able to build empires around their ability to transmit the latest news and information available directly to households all across the country every day, and often multiple times daily through successive editions requiring huge, expensive printing presses no one else in town could afford. Then came the internet, and suddenly all that old technology – the type-setting equipment, the presses, the trucks, all of it – became a mountain of expense weighing down media companies delivering information that was being outdated quickly and continually by online competitors.

Without the ability to deliver information first and exclusively, the newspaper business model began to crumble.

IN ADDITION TO THE *P-I,* many other major newspapers have bitten the dust, or curtailed home delivery, in recent years.

The *Detroit Free Press* and *Detroit News* entered into a joint operating agreement in the 1980s and reduced home delivery to three days a week in 2008. The *Free Press'* owner, Knight-Ridder Newspapers, was sold to the McClatchy chain. Several other chains with long histories of quality journalism were sold, too, including the Chicago Tribune Co., which owned several newspapers, broadcast stations, the Chicago Cubs, and newsprint mills and timberlands in Canada. The Chicago Tribune Co. was sold to local investors, as were several major papers and chains that were bought by individuals or groups with no previous newspaper affiliation, such as Jeff Bezos, the Seattle billionaire creator of Amazon, who bought the *Washington Post,* long considered one of America's great newspapers.

My first two daily papers wound up with different owners. The *Valley Daily News* (now the *Valley News-Dispatch*) first was sold to the Gannett chain and later to Richard Mellon Scaife, Pittsburgh billionaire who also owned papers in Pittsburgh and Greensburg. The *Wilmington News-Journal* papers were sold to Gannett as well.

The newspaper map has been transformed dramatically since I entered the field in 1950. With the transformation came cataclysmic changes.

Today, sadly, anybody or any organization can post on the internet information of all kinds—including outlandish, slanted, inaccurate, or distorted facts—that many people will believe. Fake news is posted on social media to damage the reputation of political candidates. Talking heads on television and radio talk shows with biased, sometimes even hateful opinions, are widely quoted and their views are passed on to others as facts.

Information on almost any subject is available, accurate or inaccurate, on a handheld device that fits in your pocket. No need to leaf through the pages of a bulky, printed newspaper. Digital delivery is easier. You can choose to read only what interests you, without having to peruse the smorgasbord of stories that appear on the printed pages, which may or may not interest you.

Too many people are uninformed, badly informed, or don't care to be informed on crucial issues, and don't bother to vote. The probing for facts, the checks and balances with government and business that newspaper have traditionally provided, have been diminished. Newspapers publish corrections as soon as possible to avoid libel suits. Most other information- spreaders do not. Email and other social media are hacked. Privacy is endangered.

The journalism profession has lost its appeal. Democracy is the worse for it.

There has never been a time in recent decades when investigative reporting of government and politics has been more vitally important than during the elections of 2016 and in light of events in 2017. Two great American newspapers, the *New York Times* and the *Washington Post*, have taken the lead in reporting the facts and proving again why newspapers are still the most reliable watchdog of government.

Epilogue

It has been, and continues to be, a good life. I have enjoyed the twenty-three years that have gone by with increasing speed since retiring in 1993. Fortunately, it has been filled with activity—lots of travel and plenty to do in the Seattle area, which included some things on my "bucket list."

Yet, the best benefit of all in retirement has been the enjoyment of my family on a relaxed schedule. Sunni has had a great influence on my life and on the lives of Richard, David, and Michael. She could have had a career outside the home, but chose early on to be a full-time mother while utilizing her skills to manage a family-owned commercial building from home. She understood my absences for business. She rarely traveled with me unless one of our sons could come, too. The idea of an ocean cruise did not appeal to Sunni, but she did not object to my trips as a tour leader in the 1990s. She is in charge of managing the affairs of our home.

Without Sunni's ability to be independent and to take action when needed, I could not have done nearly as much outside the home.

Richard and David had graduated from universities and launched their careers, but Michael was still in high school when I retired. Each has developed into successful men. Because of my job, I missed the opportunity to participate in sports and other extra-curricular activities with Rich and Dave that I was able to do with Michael.

When my sons were growing up, I introduced each as "my son." As they matured and made their own mark it changed to my sons introducing me as "my Dad." That was to be expected. Life goes on.

Richard and David operated a successful business in Seattle, Modern Digital, for more than twenty-five years. Michael has almost ten years' experience as an assistant attorney general for the State of Washington, handling utilities and transportation cases. Each has been actively involved in volunteer work. Richard has served two terms as president of the Seattle International Film Festival (SIFF), the largest festival of its kind in North America, which shows more than 400 independent films from ninety countries shown over a four-week period. They each have chosen to live in the greater Seattle area.

Like all grandparents, we believe our five grandchildren are outstanding young people and we are immensely proud of them. We enjoy watching them grow and become their own person.

Since childhood, baseball has been my favorite sport, first as a player in the Pittsburgh area into my mid-twenties and as a fan in each big-league city since. Although Rich and Dave never had much interest in baseball, Michael played in Little League and was a bat-boy for the Seattle Mariners in 1993 at the age of sixteen when Ken Griffey Jr. hit his eighth home run in as many games to tie a Major League Baseball record.

During my *P-I* years, we used the newspaper's Mariners season tickets for several games a year. In retirement, I have had two season tickets for each of the eighty-one home games. Several friends take most of them, but I go to twenty-five or more games each season. Michael and I saw Randy Johnson's no-hitter in 1990 and another no-hitter shared by six pitchers in 2012. I also witnessed Felix Hernandez's perfect game with a friend, Ted Van Dyk, a veteran of the Washington, D.C. political scene. Each of our sons has gone with me to Mariners spring training in Peoria, Arizona. Michael still goes regularly and is a member of the RBI Club. We look forward to a World Series in Seattle someday.

Our sons have close relationships with one another and they include their "old man," a term we used as a kid. Particularly enjoyable has been an annual retreat with my sons for a weekend or longer. We traveled with Richard's camper trailer to state campgrounds east of the Columbia River for four years. For the past five years, we have rented cottages on Whidbey Island or along the Pacific Ocean in western Washington. We barbeque lamb and salmon, crack Dungeness crab, roast marshmallows, enjoy relaxing libations, play cards and *bocce*, try fishing, and watch movies—but above all, we talk.

The question-and-answer sessions that Richard videotaped during two retreats to save for our grandchildren and future Fassio generations became the motivation to compile these lifetime experiences in a memoir.

I recalled my teenage years when the biggest "big shot" I ever met was an Italian-American who was an unsuccessful candidate for the Pittsburgh City Council. He was highly regarded in the community. Since then, I have met and come to know a great many famous and influential people in government, business, and in all walks of life who were true "big shots." I found that that most of them were just regular people. Here and there were a few who were overly impressed with their own importance and a few who lost interest in being friends when I no longer bought ink by the barrel. But that, too, was to be expected. That's part of the experience of living life.

I have not been overseas since the trip to Italy with Richard in 2013. David and I visited my sisters and their families in Pittsburgh that same year. We were able to spend some time with my oldest sister, Christina, in a nursing home before she passed away in April, 2014. Richard and I visited Ida and her family in 2016.

I still have a certain amount of pride in being a native of Pittsburgh. The city has about half the population of its boom years when steel mills lined the banks of the three rivers in the "Steel City" and nearby towns. On the plus side, the city has become more attractive. I didn't realize that most western Pennsylvanians have a distinct, identifiable accent until I left the Pittsburgh area at the age of thirty-one. I never lost certain phrases and pronunciations that are the lingering products of my youth in a blue-collar environment that was a true melting pot of many European migrants.

But the Seattle area is home now. Like all the Seattle natives I know, I wouldn't think of living anywhere else. Other than the few trips, my activity in the past few years has been all local—not terribly exciting, but always busy and fulfilling. For many years, I have enjoyed working out. For relaxation, I have a few hobbies and read.

The "bucket list" I made in 1993 has been frequently added to, prioritized, or subtracted from as a "mission" was accomplished. Not all have been addressed. Some of what remains on the list will be tackled . . . someday.

There will always be something to do

About the Author

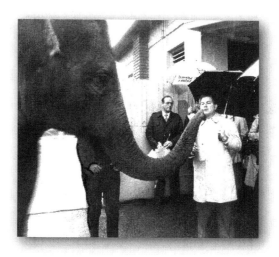

"Bamboo" the elephant reaches out to the author, who chaired the "Save
Our Elephants" campaign for Seattle's Woodland park Zoo in 1985.

Virgil Fassio was born in Pittsburgh, the son of parents who immigrated to the United States from Italy after World War I. The author graduated from the University of Pittsburgh; served in the U.S. Navy and Naval Reserve, retiring with the rank of commander; and earned national recognition for his work on six newspapers, most recently the *Seattle Post-Intelligencer*, from which he retired in 1993. Fassio and his wife, Sunni, live in Bellevue, Washington.

Index

52031469R00227

Made in the USA
San Bernardino, CA
09 August 2017